DANCE OF THE DIALECTIC

Dance of the Dialectic

Steps in Marx's Method

BERTELL OLLMAN

UNIVERSITY OF ILLINOIS PRESS
URBANA, CHICAGO, AND SPRINGFIELD

⊛ This book is printed on acid-free paper.

Library of Congress Cataloging-in-Publication Data
Ollman, Bertell.
Dance of the dialectic : steps in Marx's method / Bertell Ollman.
p. cm.
Includes bibliographical references and index.
ISBN 978-0-252-02832-8 (cloth : alk. paper)
ISBN 978-0-252-07118-8 (pbk. : alk. paper)
1. Marx, Karl, 1818–1883. 2. Communism. 3. Dialectical materialism.
4. Philosophy, Marxist. I. Title.
HX39.5.O55   2003
335.4'11—dc21   2002151570

We must force the "frozen circumstances to dance by singing to them their own melody."

—Karl Marx, "Toward the Critique of Hegel's Philosophy of Law"

CONTENTS

Acknowledgments *ix*

Introduction: Marxism, This Tale of Two Cities *1*

STEP 1

1. The Meaning of Dialectics *11*

STEP 2

2. Social Relations as Subject Matter *23*

3. The Philosophy of Internal Relations *36*

4. In Defense of the Philosophy of Internal Relations *51*

STEP 3

5. Putting Dialectics to Work: The Process of Abstraction in Marx's Method *59*

    The Problem: How to Think Adequately about Change and Interaction *59*
    The Solution Lies in the Process of Abstraction *60*
    How Marx's Abstractions Differ *63*
    The Philosophy of Internal Relations *69*
    Three Modes of Abstraction: Extension *73*
    Level of Generality *86*
    And Vantage Point *99*
    The Role of Abstractions in the Debates over Marxism *110*

STEP 4

6. Studying History Backward: A Neglected Feature of Marx's Materialist Conception of History   *115*

7. Dialectic as Inquiry and Exposition   *127*

8. Marxism and Political Science: Prolegomenon to a Debate on Marx's Method   *135*

9. Why Dialectics? Why Now? or, How to Study the Communist Future Inside the Capitalist Present   *155*

STEP 5

10. Critical Realism in Light of Marx's Process of Abstraction   *173*

11. Marx's Dialectical Method Is More Than a Mode of Exposition: A Critique of Systematic Dialectics   *182*

12. Why Does the Emperor Need the Yakuza? Prolegomenon to a Marxist Theory of the Japanese State   *193*

Bibliography   *217*

Index of Names and Ideas   *223*

ACKNOWLEDGMENTS

In the movie *Bizarre, Bizarre,* Claude Simon plays a famous Parisian mystery writer who gets all his best ideas for stories from his milkman, who tells them to his maid, who passes them on to Simon. While Simon never confesses, I feel the need to confess that I, too, have a milkman. And in this volume, which brings together the best of my life's work on dialectics, I should like to acknowledge the enormous contribution that Paule Ollman, my wife... and milkman, has made to all my thinking and writing as a scholar and political actor for over forty years. Her insights, enthusiasms, and careful critical judgments are to be found in everything I've done. It delights me no end to publicly recognize her influence and her role as my full intellectual partner and to dedicate my book, which is really our book, to her. Of the many scholars who have contributed to my thinking on dialectics over the years, I also want to single out Bill Livant and thank him for *all* his questions and even some of his answers. Finally, I wish to thank Hani Zubida for all the flexibility and good cheer he showed in helping me prepare this manuscript for publication.

* * *

The chapters that comprise *Dance of the Dialectic* first appeared in the following publications and have been at least partly revised for inclusion in this volume:

Chapters 1, 5, and 6—from my book *Dialectical Investigations* (New York: Routledge, 1993).

Chapters 2, 3, 4, and 7—from my book *Alienation: Marx's Conception of Man in Capitalist Society,* 2d ed. (New York: Cambridge University Press, 1976); reprinted with the permission of Cambridge University Press.

Chapter 8—from my book *Social and Sexual Revolution: Essays on Marx and Reich* (Boston: South End Press, 1979); reprinted with the permission of South End Press.

Chapter 9—from *Science and Society* 62 (Fall 1998): 338–57; reprinted with the permission of S&S Quarterly, Inc.

Chapter 10—from *After Postmodernism: An Introduction to Critical Realism,* ed. Jose Lopez and Garry Potter (London: Athlone Press, 2001), 285–98; reprinted with the permission of Continuum International Publishing Group, Ltd.

Chapter 11—from *New Dialectics and Political Economy,* ed. Robert Albritton (Houndmills, England: Palgrave Publishers, 2002), 177–84; reprinted with the permission of Palgrave Publishers, Ltd.

Chapter 12—from *New Left Review* 8 (Mar.–Apr. 2001): 73–98; reprinted with the permission of New Left Review, Ltd.

DANCE OF THE DIALECTIC

INTRODUCTION

Marxism, This Tale of Two Cities

1

Marxism, understood as the ideas of Karl Marx and Friedrich Engels, offers us a tale of two cities: one that claims to have freedom but doesn't, and another that possesses bountiful freedom for all, but few know where it is or how to get there. The first city is called "capitalism." In this city, whose institutions are widely viewed as the very embodiments of freedom, nothing is free. Everything costs, and most things cost more than those who need them can afford. For most of its citizens, what is called "freedom" is having the right to compete for things that remain just outside their grasp. But no one keeps them from competing or from thinking that one day they (or their children) may succeed.

The other city is called "communism." Here, people enjoy the freedom to develop their potential as human beings in peace and friendship with each other. Their's is not the freedom to want what cannot be had but to do and be and become what they want. This city can't be found on a map, because until now it only exists in the shadows of the first city. It is, in effect, what capitalism could be, what it has all the means and conditions for becoming once the inhabitants of capitalism overthrow their rulers along with the rules that organize life in their city. The rulers are the capitalist class, or those who own and control the means of production, distribution, and exchange, and the principal rule by which they operate is profit maximization. The capitalists have managed to keep communism a well-guarded secret by using their power over the mike—for in this society you need a microphone to be heard—to ensure that no one learns that communism is really about freedom, while endlessly repeating the cannard that something called "communism" was already tried in a few underdeveloped countries and that it didn't work.

There is a lot in Marxism, of course, that cannot be captured by this tale of two cities, but it does help to bring out the singular nature of Marx's subject matter: it is not capitalism, it is not communism, it is not history. Rather, it is the internal relations between all of these. It is how communism evolves as a still unrealized potential within capitalism and the history of *this* evolution stretching from earliest times to a future that is still far in front of us. Unaware of what exactly Marx has set out to study, most writers on Marxism, friendly and unfriendly, have great difficulty characterizing what he finds. For example, in so far as Marx describes and explains how capitalism functions, some writers consider Marxism a science. In so far as he presents capitalism as wanting, others insist that Marxism is essentially a critique of capitalism. In so far as he discovers a potential in capitalism for communism and outlines what that might look like, still others view Marx as mainly a visionary. And in so far as Marx advocates a political strategy for moving from here to there—and Lenin's question, "What is to be done?" is always lurking somewhere in his consciousness—Marxism gets treated as a doctrine on how to make the revolution.

Science, critique, vision, and strategy for revolution are ordinarily understood apart from one another—some would even maintain that they are logically incompatible—and most interpreters of Marxism have emphasized only one or a couple of these themes while dismissing or trivializing the others (or, in some cases, using them as occasions to berate Marx for inconsistency). Yet the evidence for the importance of all four currents in Marx's writings is overwhelming. Moreover, they are usually so intertwined and so mutually dependent that it is very difficult to separate them completely from each other. Hence, I am inclined to view Marxism as an unusual, perhaps unique, combination of all four—science, critique, vision, and recipe for revolution—and Marx himself therefore as a scientist, critic, visionary, and revolutionary, with each of these qualities contributing to and feeding off the others.

The problem this raises, of course, is—how is this possible? How does one mix things that don't appear to mix? What allows Marx to construct theories—for this is what I am claiming—that are at the same time scientific, critical, visionary, and revolutionary? For the tale of two cities presented above, this translates as—what allows Marx to discover communism inside capitalism, and how does what he finds constitute both a criticism of capitalism and the basis of a strategy to overturn it? At the core of every science is a search for relations, especially relations that are not immediately obvious, and in studying capitalism Marx uncovers relations between what is, what could be, what shouldn't be, and what can be done about it all. He finds all this, first of all, because it is there, but what *permits* him to find it—while most students of capitalism only come up with the appearances (mislabeled as "facts")—is his dialectical method. It is dialectics, and Marx's dialectics in particular, that not only allows but requires him to knit together what most others consign to separate mental compartments.

2

Dialectics, in one form or another, has existed for as long as there have been human beings on this planet. This is because our lives have always involved important elements of change and interaction; our environment, taken as a whole, has always had a decisive limiting and determining effect on whatever went on inside it; and "today," whenever it occurs, always emerges out of what existed yesterday, including the possibilities contained therein, and always leads (and will lead), in the very same ways that it has, to what can and will take place tomorrow. In order to maximize the positive effects of these developments on their lives (and to reduce their negative effects), people have always tried to construct concepts and ways of thinking that capture—to the extent that they can understand it (and to the extent that the ruling elites have allowed it)—what is actually going on in their world, especially as regards the pervasiveness of change and interaction, the effect of any system on its component parts (including each of us as both a system with parts and as a part of other systems), and the interlocking nature of past, present, and future. The many ways our species has performed this task has given rise to a rich and varied tradition of dialectical thought, the full measure of which has yet to be taken.

Marx's version of dialectics was derived from his encounters on the philosophical plane with such giants as Epicurus, Aristotle, Spinoza, Leibniz, and especially Hegel, and through his lived experience with a capitalism that had only recently come to maturity. Capitalism, it is important to note, stands out from earlier class societies in the degree to which it has integrated all major (and, increasingly, most minor) life functions into a single organic system dominated by the law of value and the accompanying power of money but also in the degree to which it hides and seeks to deny this singular achievement. The fragmentation of existence together with the partial and one-sided character of socialization under capitalism have inclined people to focus on the particulars that enter their lives—an individual, a job, a place—but to ignore the ways they are related, and thus to miss the patterns—class, class struggle, alienation, and others—that emerge from these relations. More recently, the social sciences have reinforced this tendency by breaking up the whole of human knowledge into the specialized learning of competing disciplines, each with its own distinctive language, and then by studying almost exclusively those bits that permit statistical manipulation. In the process, capitalism, the biggest pattern of all and one whose effect on people's lives is constantly growing, has become virtually invisible.

I am painfully aware that many of those who reject Marx's analysis of capitalism don't simply disagree with it. That would make political discussions relatively easy. Instead, the typical reaction is to treat the capitalism Marx speaks about as if it isn't there. I'm reminded of the movie *Harvey*, in which Jimmy Stewart often converses with his friend Harvey, a six-foot, two-inch invisible white rabbit. Except he is the only one who sees Harvey; those around him see only an empty chair. Similarly, when Marx and Marxists refer to capitalism, the eyes of most of their readers glaze over. Well, capitalism is not an invisible rabbit, but neither is it something that is immediately apparent. For it to be noticed, let alone understood, people's attention has to be drawn to certain relations, the elements of which are not always obvious. But if most of its inhabitants don't even see capitalism, the system, any effort to explain how it works must be accompanied by an equally strenuous effort to display it, to simply show that it exists and what kind of entity it is. Widely ignored in the literature on Marx, revelation, therefore, is as crucial to Marxism as explanation, and indeed the latter is impossible without the former.

By allowing Marx to focus on the interconnections that constitute the key patterns in capitalism, the dialectic brings the capitalist system itself, as a pattern of patterns, into "sight" and makes it something real that requires its own explanation. In a world made up of mutually dependent processes, however, the interconnections between things include their ties to their own preconditions and future possibilities as well as to whatever is affecting them (and whatever they are affecting) right now. Consequently, the patterns that emerge and require explanation include material that will extend Marx's explanation, when it comes, into the hitherto separate realms of criticism, vision, and revolution. Consider once again the spread of relations unearthed in Marx's tale of two cities. The whole panoply of otherwise confusing dialectical categories such as "contradiction," "abstraction," "totality," and "metamorphosis" serve to avoid static, partial, one-sided, and one-dimensional (temporally speaking) understandings by making some part of these interconnections easier to think about and to deal with. All of Marx's theories have been shaped by his dialectical outlook and its accompanying categories, and it is only by grasping dialectics that these theories can be properly understood, evaluated, and put to use.

3

My own encounter with dialectics began when I was doing research for my doctoral dissertation, later published as *Alienation: Marx's Conception of Man in Capitalist Society* (1971; 2d ed. 1976). Marx's writings were decidedly not one-sided; nor did he seem to have much trouble presenting a world in constant motion, where mutual interaction and interpenetration of temporal dimensions were the rule and even large scale transformations a frequent occurrence. That much was clear. What was less clear, especially to a young student steeped in linguistic philosophy, were the concepts he used to present such a picture. Despite the absence of definitions—Marx never offered any—it was not hard to know, in a general way at least, what he was talking about, but whenever I pressed a point the precision and clarity I had been trained to look for eluded me. And when I sought to construct my own definitions from the way Marx used his key concepts in his writings, I was shocked to discover that their apparent meanings varied with the context, often considerably. I was not the first, of course, to note or to be bothered by the elastic quality of Marx's meanings. Vilfredo Pareto, the Italian sociologist, provided the classic statement of this problem long ago when he said, "Marx's words are like bats. One can see in them both birds and mice" (1902, 332).

But once we recognize this problem, what are our choices? (1) We could ignore it. (2) We could treat what Marx means (or seems to) on most occasions, or on what we take to be the most important occasion, as what Marx really means by a particular concept. (3) We could use this inconsistency as a club with which to beat Marx for being hopelessly confused, or sloppy, or even dishonest. Or (4) we could seek an explanation of Marx's usage in his view of the world and the place that language and meaning have in that view. I had spent too much time puzzling over Marx's linguistic practice to ignore what I had found, and while it is possible to single out one main meaning for some of his concepts, this left too many other meanings unaccounted for. Even with this difficulty, however, I was already learning too much from Marx to dismiss him as irredeemingly confused or careless. That left an investigation into his view of the world that may have allowed and even required just such a use of language.

Taking the latter path, I soon arrived at the philosophy of internal relations, a carryover from Marx's apprenticeship with Hegel, which treats the relations in which anything stands as essential parts of what it is, so that a significant change in any of these relations registers as a qualitative change in the system of which it is a part. With relations rather than things as the fundamental building blocks of reality, a concept may vary somewhat in its meaning depending on how much of a particular relation it is intended to convey. Could this be the answer to the paradox stated so eloquently by Pareto? As it turned out, the philosophy of internal relations had received relatively little attention in the already extensive literature on Marx's dialectic. And while several major interpreters of Marx, such as Georg Lukács, Jean-Paul Sartre, Henri Lefebvre, Karel Kosik, Lucien Goldmann, and Herbert Marcuse, appeared to recognize that Marx's rejection of Hegel's idealism did not include his philosophy of internal relations, none saw fit to build their interpretation of dialectics around it nor to use it as a basis for explaining Marx's unusual use of language.[1] I did.

However, in what became *Alienation* my chief aim in reconstructing Marx's dialectic was to understand what he said about human nature and alienation. What served to explain a particular theory, though, was not enough to account for how he arrived at this theory nor to help people study other aspects of society in the manner of Marx. The philosophy of internal relations, after all, is only a philosophy. It underlies and makes possible a certain method for inquiring into the world and organizing and expounding what one finds, but an adequate grasp of this method requires that equal attention be paid to other elements of the dialectic, and especially to the "process of abstraction."

The philosophy of internal relations bans finite parts from Marx's ontology. The world, it would have us believe, is not like that. Then, through the mental process of abstraction, Marx draws a set of provisional boundaries in this relational world to arrive at parts that are better suited—chiefly through the inclusion of significant elements of change and interaction—to the particular investigation he has in mind. The resulting findings, encapsulated in the theories of

Marxism, all bear the imprint of these initial abstractions. Consequently, in my next major work on Marxism, *Dialectical Investigations* (1993), the philosophy of internal relations cedes its position at the center of my account to Marx's process of abstraction. Together—and, despite the evidence of my earliest writings, they must be used together—the philosophy of internal relations and the process of abstraction offer the greater part of what is distinctive about my approach to dialectics, an approach meant to advance current efforts to study capitalism (or any part thereof) as well as to help us grasp and make better use of Marx's own achievements.

Recent years have witnessed a modest renaissance of interest in dialectics, as a growing number of Marxist writers have adopted it as a priviledged vantage point from which to examine Marx's other theories. The latest stage of capitalism, what some have dubbed "globalization," and the collapse of the Soviet Union have also sent many of these same scholars back to the moment of method for help in explaining these phenomena. The result is that dialectical method is one of the liveliest areas of Marxist research and debate today, particularly in the Anglo-Saxon world.[2] Word of this development is only beginning to reach the broader academy. Is it too much to hope that a serious exchange of views with at least some mainstream scholars may yet replace the benign (and not so benign) neglect and worse to which Marxist dialectics has traditionally been subjected by non-Marxist thinkers? My work on dialectics has also always been shaped, in part, by my strong desire to help make such an exchange possible.[3]

In the pages that follow, my fullest treatment of the philosophy of internal relations can be found in chapters 2, 3, and 4. Chapter 1 gives an introductory overview of our entire subject. Chapter 5, which is the longest and probably most important chapter in the book, details Marx's process of abstraction and shows its organic tie to the philosophy of internal relations. Chapter 6 explains how Marx used his method to study the past in its internal relation to the present. Chapter 7 presents the kind of inquiry and exposition that follows from Marx's adherence to a philosophy of internal relations. Chapter 8 expands on the work of the previous chapter to include all the different moments of Marx's method and shows how it helped him arrive at his understanding of the capitalist state. Chapter 9 explains how dialectical method is used to study the communist future in its internal relation to the present and provides the best summary of the earlier chapters. Here, one will also find most of the scaffolding with which Marx constructed his tale of two cities. In chapters 10 and 11, my interpretation of Marx's method is contrasted with that of two increasingly popular schools of dialectical thinking, Critical Realism and Systematic Dialectics. Finally, chapter 12 offers a case study in the use of some elements in Marx's dialectical method to analyze the more peculiar features of the Japanese state.

The essays and chapters (many considerably revised) from earlier books brought together in this volume span thirty years and represent the best of my life's work on dialectics.[4] If they often seem as if they were written as consecutive chapters for this book, it is because the project of which they are all a part was formulated at the time of *Alienation,* and my fundamental views on dialectics have changed relatively little since then. This also accounts for the modest amount of repetition in some of the middle and later chapters as I try once again to link whatever is new to the philosophy of internal relations. Given most readers' lack of familiarity with this philosophy and the difficulty they are likely to have in applying it, the frequent return to internal relations and the practice of abstracting that it makes possible (and requires) also serves an important pedagogical function. Learning how to use Marx's dialectical method, especially becoming good at it, also requires a radical transformation in the way one *thinks* about anything, and the philosophy of internal relations—as we shall see—is the crucial enabling step in this process.

A final word on the role of Friedrich Engels. The extraordinary and even unique intellectual partnership that Marx enjoyed with Engels led practically everyone for a century and more to treat Engels as coequal spokesman along with Marx for the doctrines of Marxism. In recent decades, however, there is a growing body of scholarship that argues for important differences in the thinking of these two men, particularly in the area of dialectics. I do not share this position for reasons that were already given in some detail in *Alienation,* but that does not mean that I devote as much attention to Engels's writings on dialectics as I do to Marx's (Ollman 1976, 52–53). For the elements of dialectics with which I have been most concerned, chiefly the philosophy of internal relations and the process of abstraction, it is Marx who has provided the bulk of my raw materials. Yet I have not hesitated to use Engels's comments in arriving at my own interpretation of Marxism, including Marxist dialectics, whenever they seemed particularly helpful, and I have no problem encouraging readers to do the same.

Notes

1. The main works by these authors on dialectics can be found in the bibliography.

2. Among the more important contributors to this debate are David Harvey, Richard Lewin, Richard Lewontin, Fredric Jameson, István Mészáros, Enrique Dussell, Ruy Fausto, Michael Löwi, Lucien Sève, Jindrich Zelený, Tom Sekine, Derek Sayer, Antonio Negri, Andrew Sayers, Erwin Marquit, Sean Sayers, Martin Jay, Scott Warren, Kosmas Psychopedis, Joachim Israel, Christopher Arthur, Tony Smith, Joseph O'Malley, Roy Bhaskar, Milton Fisk, Joseph Fracchia, John Allen, Terrell Carver, Rob Beamish, Roslyn Bologh, George E. McCarthy, Robert Albritton, John Rees, Carol Gould, David-Hillel Rubin, Joseph McCarney, Ira Gollobin, Howard Sherman, Nancy Hartsock, Paul Diesing, Guglielmo Carchedi, Patrick Murray, Fred Moseley, Paul Mattick Jr., Kevin Anderson, Michael A. Lebowitz, Stephen A. Resnick, Richard D. Wolff, Susan Buck-Morss, Ronald J. Horvath, Kenneth D. Gibson, N. Patrick Peritore, Graham Priest, J. W. Frieberg, Paul Paolucci, Bill Livant, Peter Skillman, Martin Nicolaus, Simeon Scott, and Paul Sweezy. And there are others. The main works by these authors on dialectics can be found in the bibliography.

3. An admirable example of what is possible in the way of a useful exchange on dialectics with non-Marxist thinkers is provided by the libertarian philosopher Chris Scibarra in *Total Freedom* (2000).

4. For readers interested in my other writings on and uses of dialectical method, see especially *Alienation* (1976), chaps. 1, 4, 5, and 33 and appendix 2; *Social and Sexual Revolution* (1979), chaps. 2, 5, and 6; *Dialectical Investigations* (1993), chaps. 3, 5, and 9; *Market Socialism: The Debate among Socialists* (1998), chap. 4; and "What Is Political Science? What Should It Be?" (2000).

STEP 1

CHAPTER 1

The Meaning of Dialectics

1

Have you ever tried to hop on a car while it was still moving? How different was it from entering a car that was stationary? Would you have been able to get into the moving car if you were blindfolded? Would you have been able to do it if you were not only blindfolded but didn't know in which direction it was moving or even how fast it was going?

Why all these silly questions? Obviously, we all agree on the answers, and anyone in his or her right mind would make sure to know how fast and in which direction a car is moving before trying to climb aboard. Well, what about society? Society is like a vehicle that every one of us tries to climb aboard to find a job, a home, various social relationships, goods to satisfy our needs and fancies— in short, a whole way of life. And who can doubt that society is changing. In fact, no century has experienced as much social change as ours, and no period has experienced faster change than the period since World War II. But just how fast is it changing and, more important, in what direction?

Will American, or British, or Japanese society as it is coming to be in the next few years be able to give you the things you want from it, that you are expecting, that you are preparing for? Being an optimist, you may answer "yes," but if so, you are looking—and none too closely—at things as they are now. But society, as you admit, is changing, and very fast. Have you studied what our democratic capitalist society is changing into, or are you like the blindfolded person trying to get onto a moving vehicle, not knowing either the speed or direction in which it is traveling?

How, then, does one study the infinitely complex organism that is modern society as it evolves and changes over time? Marxism enters the picture as the most systematic (though, obviously, still incomplete) effort yet undertaken to provide such an analysis. Focusing on how goods are produced, exchanged, and distributed in the capitalist era, it tries to account for the structure as well as the dynamics of the entire social system, including both its origins and likely future. We also learn how the few who benefit most from capitalism use a mixture of force and guile to order the lives and thinking of the great majority who would benefit most from a radical change. Finally, Marxism also lays out a method (dialectics) and a practice (class struggle) for updating this study and helping to bring about the most desirable outcome. No one who is about to climb aboard the moving vehicle that is our rapidly changing society can afford to proceed without it.

2

What we understand about the world is determined by what the world is, who we are, and how we conduct our study. As regards this last, in our day the problems involved in grasping reality have been compounded by an approach that privileges whatever makes things appear static and independent of one another over their more dynamic and systemic qualities. Copernicus could have been speaking about the modern academy instead of the astronomers of his day when he said, "'With them it is as though an artist were to gather the hands, feet, head, and other members for his images from diverse models, each part excellently drawn, but not related to a single body, and since they in no way match each other, the result would be a monster rather than man'" (qtd. in Kuhn 1962, 83). The existing breakdown of knowledge into mutually indifferent and often hostile academic disciplines, each with its own range of problematics and methods, has replaced the harmonious enlightenment we had been promised with a raucous cacophony of discordant sounds. In the confusion, the age-old link between knowledge and action has been severed, so that scholars can deny all responsibility for their wares while taking pride in knowing more and more about less and less. It is as a way of criticizing this state of affairs and developing an integrated body of knowledge that a growing number of researchers are turning to Marxian dialectics.

With all the misinformation conveyed about dialectics, it may be useful to start by saying what it is not. Dialectics is not a rock-ribbed triad of thesis-antithesis-synthesis that serves as an all-purpose explanation; nor does it provide a formula that enables us to prove or predict anything; nor is it the motor force of history. The dialectic, as such, explains nothing, proves nothing, predicts nothing, and causes nothing to happen. Rather, dialectics is a way of thinking that brings into focus the full range of changes and interactions that occur in the world. As part of this, it includes how to organize a reality viewed in this manner for purposes of study and how to present the results of what one finds to others, most of whom do not think dialectically.

The main problem to which dialectics is addressed is set out clearly in Marx's retelling of the Roman myth of Cacus (1971, 536–37). Half man, half demon, Cacus lived in a cave and came out only at night to steal oxen. Wishing to mislead his pursuers, Cacus forced the oxen to walk backward into his den so that their footprints made it appear that they had gone out from there. The next morning, when people came looking for their oxen, all they found were footprints. Based on the evidence of these footprints, they concluded that, starting from the cave, their oxen had gone into the middle of a field and disappeared.

If the owners of the oxen had taken a methodology course at an American university, they might have counted the footprints, measured the depth of each step, and run the results through a computer—but they would have arrived at the same wrong conclusion. The problem here arises from the fact that reality is more than appearances and that focusing exclusively on appearances, on the evidence that strikes us immediately and directly, can be extremely misleading. How typical is the error found in this example? According to Marx, rather than the exception, this is how most people in our society understand the world. Basing themselves on what they see, hear, and bump into in their immediate surroundings—on footprints of various kinds—they arrive at conclusions that are in many cases the exact opposite of the truth. Most of the distortions associated with bourgeois ideology are of this kind.

To understand the real meaning of the footprints, the owners of the oxen had to find out what happened the night before and what was going on in the cave that lay just over their horizon. In a similar way, understanding anything in our everyday experience requires that we know something about how it arose and developed and how it fits into the larger context or system of which it is a part. Just recognizing this, however, is not enough, for nothing is easier than slipping back into a narrow focus on appearances. After all, few would deny that everything in the world is changing and interacting at some pace and in one way or another, that history and systemic connections belong to the real world. The difficulty has always been how to think adequately about them, how not to distort them, and how to give them the attention and weight that they deserve. Dialectics is an attempt to resolve this difficulty by expanding our notion of anything to include, as aspects of what it is, both the process by which it has become that and the broader interactive context in which it is found. Only then does the study of anything involve one immediately with the study of its history and encompassing system.

Dialectics restructures our thinking about reality by replacing the commonsense notion of "thing" (as something that has a history and has external connections with other things) with notions of "process" (which contains its history and possible futures) and "relation" (which contains as part of what it is its ties with other relations). Nothing that didn't already exist has been added here. Rather, it is a matter of where and how one draws boundaries and establishes units (the dialectical term is "abstracts") in which to think about the world. The assumption is that while the qualities we perceive with our five senses actually exist as parts of nature, the conceptual distinctions that tell us where one thing ends and the next one begins both in space and across time are social and mental constructs. However great the influence of what the world is on how we draw these boundaries, it is ultimately we who draw the boundaries, and people coming from different cultures and from different philosophical traditions can and do draw them differently.

In abstracting capital, for example, as a process, Marx is simply including primitive accumulation, accumulation, and the concentration of capital—in sum, its real history—as part of what capital is. Abstracting it as a relation brings its actual ties with labor, commodity, value, capitalists, and workers—or whatever contributes to its appearance and functioning—under the same rubric as its constituting aspects. All the units in which Marx thinks about and studies capitalism are abstracted as both processes and relations. Based on this dialectical conception, Marx's quest—unlike that of his commonsense opponents—is never for why something starts to change (as if it were not already changing) but for the various forms this change assumes and why it may *appear* to have stopped. Likewise, it is never for how a relation gets established (as if there were no relation there before), but again for the different forms it takes and why aspects of an already existing relation may *appear* to be independent. Marx's critique of the ideology that results from an exclusive focus on appearances, on the footprints of events separated from their real history and the larger system in which they are found, is also of this order.

3

Besides a way of viewing the world, Marx's dialectical method includes how he studied it, how he organized what he found, and how he presented these findings to his chosen audience. But how does one inquire into a world that has been abstracted into mutually dependent processes? Where does one start, and what does one look for? Unlike nondialectical research, where one starts with some small part and through establishing its connections to other such parts tries to reconstruct the larger whole, dialectical research begins with the whole, the system, or as much of it as one understands, and then proceeds to an examination of the part to see where it fits and how it functions, leading eventually to a fuller understanding of the whole from which one has begun. Capitalism serves Marx as his jumping-off point for an examination of anything that takes place within it. As a beginning, capitalism is already contained, in principle, within the interacting processes he sets out to investigate as the sum total of their necessary conditions and results. Conversely, to begin with a supposedly independent part or parts is to assume a separation with its corresponding distortion of meaning that no amount of later relating can overcome. Something will be missing, something will be out of place, and, without any standard by which to judge, neither will be recognized. What are called "interdisciplinary studies" simply treat the sum of such defects coming from different fields. As with Humpty Dumpty, who after the fall could never be put together again, a system whose functioning parts have been treated as independent of one another at the start can never be reestablished in its integrity.

The investigation itself seeks to concretize what is going on in capitalism, to trace the means and forms through which it works and has developed, and to project where it seems to be tending. As a general rule, the interactions that constitute any problem in its present state are examined before studying their progress over time. The order of inquiry, in other words, is system before history, so that history is never the development of one or two isolated elements with its suggestion, explicit or implicit, that change results from causes located inside that particular sphere (histories of religion or of culture or even of economics alone are decidedly undialectical). In Marx's study of any specific event or institutional form, these two types of inquiry are always interwoven. The fuller understanding of capitalism that is the major result of such a study is now ready to serve as a richer and therefore more useful starting point for the next series of investigations.

4

Given an approach that proceeds from the whole to the part, from the system inward, dialectical research is primarily directed to finding and tracing four kinds of relations: identity/difference, interpenetration of opposites, quantity/quality, and contradiction. Rooted in his dialectical conception of reality, these relations enable Marx to attain his double aim of discovering how something works or happened while simultaneously developing his understanding of the system in which such things could work or happen in just this way.

In what Marx calls the commonsense approach, also found in formal logic, things are either the same/identical or different, not both. On this model, comparisons generally stop after taking note of the way(s) any two entities are either identical or different, but for Marx this is only the first step. Unlike the political economists, for example, who stop after describing the obvious differences between profit, rent, and interest, Marx goes on to bring out their identity as forms of surplus-value (that is, wealth created by workers that is not returned to them in the form of wages). As relations, they all have this quality, this aspect that touches upon their origins, in common. The interest Marx takes in delineating the special features of production or of the working class, without neglecting all they have in common with other economic processes and other classes, are good examples of his approaching identity and difference from the side of identity. The relations that stand in for things in Marx's dialectical conception of reality are sufficiently large and complex to possess qualities that—when compared to the qualities of other similarly constituted relations—appear to be identical and others that appear to be different. In investigating what these are and, especially, in paying extra attention to whichever half of this pairing is currently most neglected, Marx can arrive at detailed descriptions of specific phenomena without getting lost in one-sidedness.

While the relation of identity/difference treats the various qualities that are

examined with its help as given, the interpenetration of opposites is based on
the recognition that to a very large degree how anything appears and functions
is due to its surrounding conditions. These conditioning factors apply to both
objects and the persons perceiving them. As regards the former, for example, it
is only because a machine is owned by capitalists that it is used to exploit workers. In the hands of a consumer or of a self-employed operator, that is, conditioned by another set of factors, operating under different imperatives, it would
not function in this way. As regards the latter, when people conditioned as capitalists look at a machine, they see a commodity they have bought on the market, perhaps even the price they paid for it, and something that is going to make
them a profit. When people conditioned as workers, however, look at the same
machine, they only see an instrument that will determine their movements in
the production process.

The perspectival element—recognizing that things appear very different depending on who is looking at them—plays a very important role in dialectical
thought. This doesn't mean that the truths that emerge from viewing reality
from different vantage points are of equal value. Involved as they are in the work
of transforming nature, workers enjoy a privileged position from which to view
and make sense out of the developmental character of the system, and with his
interest in the evolution of capitalism this is the vantage point that Marx most
often adopts for himself.

The notion of the interpenetration of opposites helps Marx to understand
that nothing—no event, institution, person, or process—is simply and solely
what it seems to be at a particular place and time, that is, situated within a certain set of conditions. Viewing it in another way, or by other people, or under
drastically changed conditions may produce not only a different but the exact
opposite conclusion or effect. Hence, the interpenetration of opposites. A losing strike in one context may serve as the start of a revolution in another; an
election that is a farce because one party, the Republicans, has all the money
and the workers' parties have none could, with an equalization of the conditions of struggle, offer a democratic choice; workers who believe that capitalism is an ideal system when they have a good job may begin to question this
when they become unemployed. Looking for where and how such changes have
already occurred and under what set of still-developing conditions new effects
are likely to occur helps Marx gauge both the complexity of the part under examination and its dependence on the evolution of the system overall.

What is called quantity/quality is a relation between two temporally differentiated moments within the same process. Every process contains moments of
before and after, encompassing both buildup (and builddown) and what that
leads to. Initially, movement within any process takes the form of quantitative
change. One or more of its aspects—each process being also a relation composed
of aspects—increases or decreases in size or number. Then, at a certain point—
which is different for each process studied—a qualitative transformation takes

place, indicated by a change in its appearance and/or function. It has become something else while, in terms of its main constituting relationships, remaining essentially the same. This qualitative change is often, though not always, marked by the introduction of a new concept to designate what the process has become.

Only when money reaches a certain amount, Marx says, does it become capital, that is, can it function to buy labor-power and produce value (1958, 307–8). Likewise, the cooperation of many people becomes a new productive power that is not only more but qualitatively different than the sum of individual powers that compose it (Engels 1934, 142). Looking for quantity/quality change is Marx's way of bringing into single focus the before and after aspects in a development that most nondialectical approaches treat separately and even causally. It is a way of uniting in thought the past and probable future of any ongoing process at the expense (temporary expense) of its relations in the broader system. And it is a way of sensitizing oneself to the inevitability of change, both quantitative and qualitative, even before research has helped us to discover what it is. While the notion of quantity/quality is in no sense a formula for predicting the future, it does encourage research into patterns and trends of a kind that enables one to project the likely future, and it does offer a framework for integrating such projections into one's understanding of the present and the past.

Of the four major relations Marx investigates in his effort to make dialectical sense out of capitalist reality, contradiction is undoubtedly the most important. According to Marx, "in capitalism everything seems and in fact is contradictory" (1963, 218). He also believes it is the "contradictory socially determined features of its elements" that is "the predominant characteristic of the capitalist mode of production" (1973, 491).

Contradiction is understood here as the incompatible development of different elements within the same relation, which is to say between elements that are also dependent on one another. What is remarked as differences are based, as we saw, on certain conditions, and these conditions are constantly changing. Hence, differences are changing; and given how each difference serves as part of the appearance and/or functioning of others, grasped as relations, how one changes affects all. Consequently, their paths of development do not only intersect in mutually supportive ways but are constantly blocking, undermining, otherwise interfering with, and in due course transforming one another. Contradiction offers the optimal means for bringing such change and interaction as regards both present and future into a single focus. The future finds its way into this focus as the likely and possible outcomes of the interaction of these opposing tendencies in the present, as their real potential. It is contradiction more than any other notion that enables Marx to avoid stasis and one-sidedness in thinking about the organic and historical movements of the capitalist mode of production, about how they affect each other and develop together from their origins in feudalism to whatever lies just over our horizon.

The commonsense notion of contradiction is that it applies to ideas about things and not to things themselves, that it is a logical relation between propositions (if I claim "X," I can't at the same time claim "not X") and not a real relation existing in the world. This commonsense view, as we saw, is based on a conception of reality as divided into separate and independent parts—a body moves when another body bumps into it. Whereas nondialectical thinkers in every discipline are involved in a nonstop search for the "outside agitator," for something or someone that comes from outside the problem under examination and is the cause for whatever occurs, dialectical thinkers attribute the main responsibility for all change to the inner contradictions of the system or systems in which it occurs. Capitalism's fate, in other words, is sealed by its own problems, problems that are internal manifestations of what it is and how it works and are often parts of the very achievements of capitalism, worsening as these achievements grow and spread. Capitalism's extraordinary success in increasing production, for example, stands in contradiction to the decreasing ability of the workers to consume these goods. Given capitalist relations of distribution, they can buy ever smaller portions of what they themselves produce (it is the proportion of such goods and not the actual amount that determines the character of the contradiction), leading to periodic crises of overproduction/ underconsumption. For Marx, contradiction belongs to things in their quality as processes within an organic and developing system. It arises from within, from the very character of these processes (it is "innate in their subject matter"), and is an expression of the state of the system (1973, 137).

Without a conception of things as relations, nondialectical thinkers have great difficulty focusing on the different sides of a contradiction at the same time. The result is that these sides are examined, if at all, in sequence, with one invariably receiving more attention than the other, their mutual interaction often mistaken for causality. A frequent criticism Marx makes of political economists is that they try to "exorcise contradictions" (1968, 519). By viewing capitalist forces of production and capitalist relations of distribution separately they miss the contradiction. A lot of effort of bourgeois ideology goes into denying, hiding, or otherwise distorting contradictions. Bad faith and class-interest politics, however, account for only a small part of these practices. For nondialectical thinkers, operating out of a commonsense view, real contradictions can only be understood as differences, paradox, opposition, strain, tension, disequilibrium, dislocation, imbalance, or, if accompanied by open strife, conflict. But without the dialectical notion of contradiction, they seldom see and can never adequately grasp the way processes actually interpenetrate and can never gauge the forces unleashed as their mutual dependence evolves from its distant origins to the present and beyond. For Marx, on the other hand, tracing how capitalist contradictions unfold is also a way of discovering the main causes of *coming* disruptions and *coming* conflict.

On the basis of what he uncovers in his study of identity/difference, the interpenetration of opposites, quantity/quality, and contradiction—a study that starts with the whole and proceeds inward to the part, and which conceives of all parts as processes in relations of mutual dependence—Marx reconstructs the working of capitalist society. Organizing reality in this way, he is able to capture both the organic and historical movements of capitalism in their specific interconnections. The still unfinished results of this reconstruction are the particular laws and theories we know as Marxism.

5

It is clear that Marx could not have arrived at his understanding of capitalism without dialectics, nor will we be able to develop this understanding further without a firm grasp of this same method. No treatment of dialectics, therefore, however brief, can be considered complete without a warning against some of the common errors and distortions associated with this way of thinking. For example, if nondialectical thinkers often miss the forest for the trees, dialectical thinkers just as often do the opposite, that is, play down or even ignore the parts, the details, in deference to making generalizations about the whole. But the capitalist system can only be grasped through an investigation of its specific parts in their interconnection. Dialectical thinkers also have a tendency to move too quickly to the bottom line, to push the germ of a development to its finished form. In general, this error results from not giving enough attention to the complex mediations, both in space and over time, that make up the joints of any social problem.

There is also a related tendency to overestimate the speed of change, along with a corresponding tendency to underestimate all that is holding it back. Thus, relatively minor cracks on the surface of capitalist reality are too easily mistaken for gaping chasms on the verge of becoming earthquakes. If nondialectical thinking leads people to be surprised whenever a major change occurs, because they aren't looking for it and don't expect it, because it isn't an internal part of how they conceive of the world at this moment, dialectical thinking—for just the opposite reasons—can lead people to be surprised when the expected upheaval takes so long in coming. In organizing reality for purposes of grasping change, relative stability does not always get the attention that it deserves. These are all weaknesses inherent in the very strengths of dialectical method. Ever present as temptations, they offer an easier way, a quick fix, and have to be carefully guarded against.

Nothing that we have said in our account so far should be taken to deny the empirical character of Marx's method. Marx does not deduce the workings of capitalism from the meanings of words or from the requirements of his theories, but like any good social scientist he does research to discover what is the case. And in his research he makes use of the entire range of materials and resources that were available in his time. Nor do we wish to claim that Marx was the only dialectical thinker. As is well known, most of his dialectic was taken over from Hegel, who merely(?) filled in and systematized a way of thinking and an approach to studying reality that goes all the way back to the Greeks. And in our time there are non-Marxist thinkers, such as Alfred North Whitehead and F. H.

Bradley, who have developed their own versions of this approach. Despite its heavy ideological content, common sense, too, is not without its dialectical moments, as is evidenced by such insights as "every cloud has its silver lining" and "that was the straw that broke the camel's back." Elements of dialectics can also be found in other social science methods, such as structural functionalism, systems theory, and ethnomethodology, where it constitutes most of what is of value in these approaches.

What stands out about Marx's dialectical method is the systematic manner in which he works it out and uses it for the study of capitalist society (including—because the dialectic requires it—its origins and probable future), the united theory of knowledge (set out in the still incomplete theories of Marxism) to which it leads, the sustained critique of nondialectical approaches (suggested in our remarks on ideology throughout) that it makes possible, and—perhaps most striking of all—its emphasis on the necessary connection posed by dialectics itself between knowledge and action.

As regards this last, Marx claims, the dialectic "is in its essence critical and revolutionary" (1958, 20). It is revolutionary because it helps us to see the present as a moment through which our society is passing, because it forces us to examine where it has come from and where it is heading as part of learning what it is, and because it enables us to grasp that as agents as well as victims in this process, in which everyone and everything are connected, we have the power to affect it. In keeping in front of us the simple truth that everything is changing, the future is posed as a choice in which the only thing that cannot be chosen is what we already have. Efforts to retain the status quo in any area of life never achieve quite that. Fruit kept in the refrigerator too long goes rotten; so do emotions and people; so do whole societies (where the proper word is "disintegration"). With dialectics we are made to question what kind of changes are already occurring and what kind of changes are possible. The dialectic is revolutionary, as Bertolt Brecht points out, because it helps us to pose such questions in a manner that makes effective action possible (1968, 60).

The dialectic is critical because it helps us to become critical of what our role has been up to now. In Marxist terms, one doesn't advocate class struggle or choose to participate in it (common bourgeois misconceptions). The class struggle, representing the sum of the contradictions between workers, broadly defined, and capitalists, simply is, and in one way or another we are all already involved, often—as we come to discover—on the wrong side. On learning about it and where we fit into it, we can now decide to stop acting as we have been (the first decision to make) and what more or else we can do to better serve *our own* interests. What can be chosen is what side to take in this struggle and how to conduct it. A dialectical grasp of our socially conditioned roles and the equally necessary limits and possibilities that constitute our present provides us with the opportunity for making a conscious and intelligent choice. In this manner does knowledge of necessity usher in the beginnings of real freedom.

STEP 2

CHAPTER 2

Social Relations as Subject Matter

1

The only extensive discussion of Marx's concepts (or categories) and the conception of social reality that finds expression in them appears in his unfinished introduction to the *Critique of Political Economy*. This seminal work, which was first published by Karl Kautsky in 1903, has been unjustly ignored by most Anglo-Saxon writers on Marxism.[1] Here we learn that "in the study of economic categories, as in the case of every historical and social science, it must be borne in mind that as in reality so in our mind the subject, in this case modern bourgeois society, is given and that the categories are therefore but forms of expression, manifestations of existence, and frequently but one-sided aspects of this subject, this definite society" (Marx 1904, 302). This distinction between subject and categories is a simple recognition of the fact that our knowledge of the real world is mediated through the construction of concepts in which to think about it; our contact with reality, in so far as we become aware of it, is contact with a conceptualized reality.

What is unusual in Marx's statement is the special relation he posits between categories and society. Instead of being simply a means for describing capitalism (neutral vehicles to carry a partial story), these categories are declared to be "forms," "manifestations," and "aspects" of their own subject matter. Or, as he says elsewhere in this introduction, the categories of bourgeois society "serve as the expression of its conditions and the comprehension of its own organization" (1904, 300). That is to say, they express the real conditions necessary for their application, but as meaningful, systematized, and understood conditions. This is not merely a matter of categories being limited in what they can be used to describe; the story itself is thought to be somehow part of the very concepts with which it is told. This is evident from Marx's claim that "the simplest economic category, say, exchange-value, implies the existence of population, population that is engaged in production within determined relations; it also implies the existence of certain types of family, class, or state, etc. It can have no other existence except as an abstract one-sided relation of an already *given concrete and living aggregate*" (1904, 294 [emphasis added]).

One of the more striking results of this approach to language is that not only the content but also the categories are evaluated by Marx in terms of "true" and "false." Thus, in criticizing Proudhon, Marx claims that "political-economic categories" are "abstract expressions of the real, transitory, historic, social relations" (Marx and Engels 1941, 12) and that they "*only remain true* while these relations exist" (Marx 1904, 301 [emphasis added]; also Marx n.d., 117–22). By deciding to work with capitalist categories, Proudhon, according to Marx, cannot completely disassociate himself from the "truths" these categories contain. According to the commonsense view, only statements can be true or false, and to use this same measure for evaluating concepts seems unwarranted and confused.

Three conclusions stand out from this discussion: that Marx grasped each political-economic concept as a component of society itself, in his words, as an "abstract one-sided relation of an already given concrete and living aggregate"; that it is intimately linked with other social components to form a particular structure; and that this whole, or at least its more significant parts, is expressed in the concept itself, in what it is intended to convey, in its very meaning. If these conclusions are unclear, it is because the kind of structure they take for granted is still vague and imprecise. To properly understand concepts that convey a particular union, we must be at ease with the quality of this unity, that is, with the way its components combine, the properties of such combinations, and the nature of the whole that they constitute. Only by learning how Marx structures the units of his subject matter, only by becoming aware of the quality and range of what is known when he considers he knows anything, will the relations between concepts and reality that have been set out in these conclusions become clear.

2

What is distinctive in Marx's conception of social reality is best approached through the cluster of qualities he ascribes to particular social factors. Taking capital as the example, we find Marx depicting it as "that kind of property which exploits wage-labor, and which cannot increase except on condition of getting a new supply of wage-labor for fresh exploitation" (Marx and Engels 1945, 33). What requires emphasis is that the relation between capital and labor is treated here as a function of capital itself and part of the meaning of the word "capital." This tie is extended to cover the worker as well, whom Marx refers to as "variable capital" (1958, 209). The capitalist is incorporated into the same whole: "capital is necessarily at the same time the capitalist . . . the capitalist is contained in the concept of capital" (1973, 512). Elsewhere, Marx asserts that "the means of production monopolized by a certain section of society" (1959a, 794–95), "the products of laborers turned into independent powers" (1958, 153), and "money," "commodities," and even "value that sucks up the value creating powers" are also capital (Marx 1958, 571). What emerges from these diverse characterizations is a conception of many tied facets whose sense depends upon the relations Marx believes to exist between its components: property, wage-labor, worker, work, product, commodities, means of production, capitalist, money, and value (the list can be made longer still).[2]

It is insufficient to accuse Marx of loose and misleading presentation for, as we shall see, all social factors are treated in the same manner. But if it is not incompetent writing, then Marx is offering us a conception of capital in which the factors we generally think of as externally related to it are viewed as co-elements in a single structure.

It is this system-owning quality of capital that he has in mind when he refers to it as a "definite social relationship." This conception is contrasted with Ricardo's, where capital "is only distinguishable as 'accumulated labor' from 'immediate labor.'" In the latter case, where capital "is something purely material, a mere element in the labor process," Marx claims, "the relation between labor and capital, wages and profit, can never be developed" (1968, 400). Marx believes he is only able to trace out these connections because they are already contained in his broad conception of capital. If they were not, he would, like Ricardo, draw a blank. *Every factor that enters into Marx's study of capitalism is a "definite social relationship."*

3

The relation is the irreducible minimum for all units in Marx's conception of social reality. This is really the nub of our difficulty in understanding Marxism, whose subject matter is not simply society but society conceived of "relationally." Capital, labor, value, and commodity are all grasped as relations, containing in themselves, as integral elements of what they are, those parts with which we tend to see them externally tied. Essentially, a change of focus has occurred from viewing independent factors that are related to viewing the particular way in which they are related in each factor, to grasping this tie as part of the meaning conveyed by its concept. This view does not rule out the existence of a core notion for each factor but treats this core notion itself as a cluster of relations.

According to the commonsense view, a social factor is taken to be logically independent of other social factors to which it is related. The ties between them are contingent rather than necessary; they could be something very different without affecting the vital character of the factors involved, a character that adheres to a part that is thought to be independent of the rest. One can logically conceive, so the argument goes, of any social factor existing without its relations to others. In Marx's view, such relations are internal to each factor (they are ontological relations), so that when an important one alters, the factor itself alters; it becomes something else. Its appearance and/or function has changed sufficiently for it to require a new concept. Thus, for example, if wage-labor disappeared, that is, if the workers' connection to capital radically changed, capital would no longer exist. The opposite, naturally, is also true: Marx declares it a "tautology" that "there can no longer be wage-labor when there is no longer any capital" (Marx and Engels 1945, 36). Max Hirsch is clearly right, therefore, when he points out that if "capital" is defined as a "means of exploitation and subjection of the laborer," a machine used by a farmer who owned it would not be capital, but it would be capital if he hired a man to operate it (1901, 80–81). Rather than an obvious criticism, which is how Hirsch intends it, this paradox merely illustrates the character of capital as a social relation.

In this study, I shall use the term "relation" in two different senses: first, to refer to a factor itself, as when I call capital a relation, and also as a synonym of "connection," as in speaking of the relation between different factors. Marx and Engels do the same. Besides calling capital a "social production relation [*Verhält-nis*]" (1959a, 794), Marx refers to money as a "relation of production," the mode of production itself as the "relation in which the productive forces are developed" (1973, 120), and the list of such remarks is far from complete (n.d., 137). His use of "relation" as a synonym of "connection" is more extensive still, with the result that *Verhältnis* probably occurs more frequently than any other expression in Marx's writing, confounding critics and translators alike.[3] It is not entirely satisfying to use "relation" to convey both meanings, but, rather than introduce a new term, I accede to Marx's practice, with this single change: for the remainder of this book, I shall capitalize "relation" (henceforth "Relation") when it refers to a factor, as opposed to the connection between factors, to aid readers in making this important distinction. Besides, such obvious alternatives to "Relation" as "structure," "unit," and "system" suggest a closed, finished character, which is belied by Marx's treatment of real social factors. "Relation" appeals to me, as it must have to him, as the concept that is better adapted to take account of the changes and open-endedness that constitute so large a part of social life.

4

The outlook presented here must not be confused with the view that has found great favor among sociologists and others, which holds that social factors are *unintelligible* except in terms of relations. It is important to realize that Marx took the additional step indicated in his claim that society is "man himself in his social relations" (1973, 712). On one occasion, Marx specifically berates apparent allies who accuse economists of not paying enough attention to the connections between production and distribution. His complaint is that "this accusation is itself based on the economic conception that distribution exists side by side with production as a self-contained sphere" (1904, 276). Marx's own version of this relationship is presented in such claims as, "Production is . . . at the same time consumption, and consumption is at the same time production" (1904, 278).[4]

For the average social scientist—starting with a conception of factors as logically independent of one another—the conjunction of parts in Marx's analysis is mechanical, an intrusion; it exists only where found and disappears once the investigator's back is turned, having to be explained and justified anew. One result is the endless attempts to account for causality and the accompanying need to distinguish between cause and condition. In such studies, one side of the interaction invariably wins out over the other (comes first) leading to "economic determinism" or "existentialism" or other partial positions.

In Marx's case, all conjunction is organic, intrinsic to the social units with which he is concerned and part of the nature of each; that it exists may be taken for granted. On this view, interaction is, properly speaking, *inneraction* (it is "inner connections" that he claims to study [1958, 19]). Of production, distribution, consumption, and exchange, Marx declares, "mutual interaction takes place between the various elements. Such is the case with every organic body" (1904, 292). What Marx calls "mutual interaction" (or "reciprocal effect" or "reciprocal action") is only possible because it occurs within an organic body. This is the case with everything in Marxism, which treats its entire subject matter as "different sides of one unit" (1904, 291).[5]

It is in this context that we must place Marx's otherwise confusing and confused use of "cause" and "determine." There are not some elements that are related to the factor or event in question as "causes" (meaning, among other things, that which does not condition) and others as "conditions" (meaning, among other things, that which does not cause). Instead, we find as internally related parts of whatever is said to be the cause or determining agent everything that is said to be a condition, and vice-versa. It is this conception that permits Engels to say that the whole of nature has "caused" life (1954, 267–68).

In practice, however, "cause" and "determine" are generally used to point to the effect produced by any entity in changing one or more of the relations that make up other entities. But as each one develops with the direct and indirect aid of everything else, operating on various levels, to single out any aspect as determining can only be a way of emphasizing a particular link in the problem under consideration. Marx is saying that for this factor, in this context, *this* is the influence most worth noting, the relation that will most aid our comprehension of the relevant characteristics.[6]

5

The whole at rest that I have been examining is but a limiting case of the whole in movement, for, in Paul Lafargue's words, Marx's "highly complicated world" is "in continual motion" (*Reminiscences*, n.d., 78).[7] Change and development are constantly occurring; structure is but a stage in process.

To introduce the temporal dimension into the foregoing analysis, we need only view each social factor as internally related to its own past and future forms, as well as to the past and future forms of surrounding factors. Capital, for Marx, is what capital is, was, and will be. He says of money and commodities, "before the production process they were capital only in intention, in themselves, in their destiny" (1971, 399–400).[8] It is in this manner, too, that labor is seen in the product it will soon become and the product in the labor it once was. In short, development—no matter how much facelifting occurs—is taken as an attribute of whatever undergoes development.

The present, according to this relational model, becomes part of a continuum stretching from a definable past to a knowable (if not always predictable) future. Tomorrow is today extended. To speak of such a relation between the present and the future within the context of formal logic would indicate belief in a vitalistic principle, divine will, or some other metaphysical device. But, here, all social change is conceived of as a coming-to-be of what potentially is, as the further unfolding of an already existing process, and hence discoverable by a study of this process taken as a spatial-temporal Relation. The "destiny" of money is rooted in its existing structure. So is the "destiny" of any society. What will become of it (or, more accurately, what is likely to become of it) is pieced together by an examination of the forces, patterns, and trends that constitute the major existing Relations. It is the result of such research into any particular factor or set of factors that is conveyed by Marx's concept of "law."[9]

The commonsense view recognizes two types of laws: inductive laws, which are generalizations based on the results of empirical research, and deductive laws, which are a priori statements about the nature of the world. For the first, evidence is relevant, and the predictions it occasions are never more than probable. For the second, evidence is irrelevant, and the predictions occasioned are necessary. Marx's laws possess characteristics that we associate with both of these types. Like inductive laws, Marx's laws are based on empirical research. Unlike them, however, his laws are not concerned with independent events whose ties with each other and with surrounding circumstances are contingent. Marx says that in political economy "law is chance"; the elements related have no ties other than those actually uncovered by research (Rubel 1959, 52). Whereas, for Marx, the relations he discovers are considered already present as real possibilities in the relations that preceded them (they exist there as temporally internal relations).

As regards deductive laws, Marx's laws also deal with the nature of the world, but they do so on the basis of evidence and are forever being modified by evidence. As a result, they cannot be encapsulated in simple formulae that hold true for all time. Still, strictly speaking, all Marx's laws are tautologies: given these are "A's" relations, this is what "A" must become, and in the becoming, "A" may be said to obey the law of its own development. Such laws express no more necessity than that contained in the particular group of relations for which they are standing in. The very uncertainties in the situation are their uncertainties. Yet, by including within the law all possible developments prefigured by the relevant relations, the law itself may be said to be necessary. All that happens to a factor is the necessary working out of its law. Consequently, rather than coloring Marx's findings in any way, it is his findings that lend these laws their entire character.

The relations bound up in any factor generally make one kind of development more probable than others, and Marx often uses "law" to refer to this development alone. "Law" in this sense is the same as "tendency," and on one occasion, he goes as far as to say that all economic laws are tendencies (1958, 8).[10]

6

Until this point, the discussion has been limited to social factors that are generally recognized as such—capital, labor, class, etc.—though Marx's interpretation of them was shown to be highly unusual. However, in seeking favorable vantage points from which to analyze capitalism, a system contained relationally in each of its parts, Marx sometimes felt obliged to create new parts. This was simply a matter of mentally carving up the whole in a different manner for a particular purpose. The result is, in effect, a new social factor, a new unit in which to think about and refer to society. Perhaps the most important new social unit created in this way is the "relations of production," the core of which lies in the complex interaction of production, distribution, exchange, and consumption. Another is "surplus-value." These two Relations occupy a central position in Marx's work.

The novelty of having the relations of production as a subject matter becomes evident when we consider the limited concern of most capitalist economists. The latter are interested in studying (more particularly, in measuring) what goes on in the "economy," a sector of life artificially separated from other sectors, whose necessary links with human beings as regards both preconditions and results are seldom investigated.

What *kind* of productive activity goes on in a society where people obtain what they want through the exchange of value equivalents? What *kind* of political, cultural, religious, and social life fosters such exchange and is, in turn, fostered by it? These questions are beyond the bounds of relevance established by capitalist economics, but they are well within the boundaries set by Marx. He tells us in *Capital* I, for example, that he wants to examine "*Why* is labor represented by the value of its product and labor-time by the magnitude of that value?" (1958, 80 [emphasis added]). This is really a question about how the particular "economy" that capitalist economists are content to describe came into existence and how it manages to maintain itself. By conceptualizing his subject matter as "relations of production," as a union of the main processes involved (as a factor centering upon this union), Marx facilitates his efforts to deal with this wide-ranging problem. The result, *Capital*, is not properly speaking an economic treatise but—as many readers have noted—a work on social praxis.

7

Returning to Marx's discourse, the problem of misinterpretation arises from what might be called his practice of making definitions of all his descriptions. Whatever Marx discovers about any factor, particularly if he considers it important, is incorporated into the meaning of its denoting term and becomes a part of its concept. Marx's concepts, then, are meant to convey to us the already structured information they express for him; it is in this way that they acquire a "truth value" distinct from that of the statements in which they are found (Marx and Engels 1941, 12).

Therefore, whatever Marx understands about his society, including its processes of change and the projections he has made from them, is already contained in each of the major concepts used to explain what it is he understands. Such meaning lies heavy on Marx's terms. It is this that allows Marx to equate "economic categories" with "historic laws" and makes "logic" a synonym for "law" in Marxism (Marx and Engels 1941, 12). "Law" refers to relations in the real world, while "logic," as Marx ordinarily uses it, refers to these same relations as reflected in the meanings of their covering concepts.

Marcuse offers the same insight when he claims that Marx's categories are negative and at the same time positive: "they present a negative state of affairs in the light of its positive solution, revealing the true situation in existing society as the prelude to its passing into a new form. All the Marxian concepts extend, as it were, in these two dimensions, the first of which is the complex of given social relations, and the second, the complex of elements inherent in the social reality that make for its transformation into a free social order" (Marcuse 1964, 295–96).[11] That readers make any sense of Marx's terminology at all suggests that many of the relations he sees in reality correspond, more or less, to our commonsense view of the world (which is not much to assume) and that it is these relations that constitute the core meanings of most of his concepts.[12]

Though each of Marx's major concepts has the theoretical capacity to convey the entire analysis made with its help, in practice Marx's current interest governs the degree to which the relations bound together in any social factor (and hence the meaning of its covering concept) are extended. As he moves from one problem to the next, whole new areas inside each social Relation become relevant, and some areas that were relevant in the previous context cease being so. In this way, what was formerly assumed is expressed directly, and what was expressed is now assumed. Class, for instance, has a vital role in explaining the state but only a small part in accounting for exchange, and the size of the Relation, class, in Marx's thought (and the meaning of "class" in Marx's writing) varies accordingly.

It is this practice that is responsible for the "manipulation" of classificational boundaries (both those that were generally accepted and those he himself seemed to lay down earlier) that so many of Marx's readers have found in his work (see my introduction). Yet, each such restriction of the social whole is merely practical, a means of allowing Marx to get on with his current task. Should he ever want to extend the size of any factor, and hence the meaning of its concept, to its relational limits, he can do so. Thus, we learn, "Man, much as he may therefore be a particular individual . . . is just as much the totality—the ideal totality—the subjective existence of thought and experienced society present for itself" (Marx 1959b, 105).

8

If each of Marx's concepts has such breadth (actual or potential) and includes much of what is also expressed by other concepts, how does Marx decide on any given occasion which one to use? Why, for example, call interest (which, for him, is also capital) "interest" and not "capital"? This is really the same problem approached from the other side. Whereas before I accepted Marx's nomenclature and tried to find out what he meant, I am now asking—given his broad meanings—why does he offer the names that he does? The unorthodox answer given to the first question has made this second one of special importance.

It may appear that I have only left Marx a nominalist way out, but this is not so. The opposition between the view that the world gives rise to our conceptions and the view that naming is an arbitrary process is, in any case, a false one. The real problem is to discover the various precise ways in which what actually exists, in nature as well as in society, affects the ways we conceive of and label it; and how the latter, in turn, reacts upon what exists, particularly upon what we take to be "natural" structures. In short, this is a two-way street, and to be content to travel in only one direction is to distort. Marx's own practice in naming takes account of both the real world as it is and his conceptualization of it, which decides (as distinct from determines) what it can be. The former is seen in Marx's acceptance of the core notion of each factor, which is simply what the factor, being what it is, strikes everyone that it is (the idea is of necessity quite vague); and the latter stands out in the decisive importance he attributes to the function of each factor (grasped as any part of its core notion) in the particular subsystem of society he is examining.

In setting out what can and cannot be called "fixed capital," Marx says, "it is not a question here of a definition, which things must be made to fit. We are dealing here with definite functions which must be expressed in definite categories" (1957, 226). Thus, capital in a situation where it functions as interest would be called "interest," and vice-versa. However, a change in function only results in a new name (as opposed to a descriptive metaphor) if the original factor is actually conceived to be what it is now functioning as. That is, capital can only *act as* or *appear to be* interest and, hence, can never really deserve its name unless we are able to conceive of the two as somehow one. This, of course, is just what Marx's relational conception allows him to do. Through its internal ties to everything else, each factor is everything else viewed from this particular angle, and what applies to them necessarily applies to it, taken in this broad sense. Thus, each factor has—in theory—the potential to take the names of others (of whatever applies to them) when it functions as they do, that is, in ways associated with their core notions.

When Marx calls theory a "material force" (1970, 137), or when Engels refers to the state as an "economic factor" (Marx and Engels 1941, 484), they are misusing words only on our standard.[13] On the relational view, theory and state are being given the names of their own facets, whose core functions they are performing. Thus, Marx says, in the instance quoted, that theory becomes a material force "once it gets a hold of men," that is, once it becomes a driving factor in their lives, strongly influencing character and actions. This role is generally performed by a material force, such as the mode of production, but theory can also perform it, and when it does it is said to become a "material force."

To understand Marx's nomenclature, however, it is not enough to know that naming attaches to function, which in turn is conceived of within a relational whole. The question arises whether the particular function observed is objective (actually present in society) or subjective (there because Marx sees it to be). The answer is that it is both: the functions, according to which Marx ascribes names, exist, but it is also true that they are conceptualized in a manner that allows Marx to take note of them. Other people viewing the same "raw facts" with another conceptual scheme may not even observe the relation he has chosen to emphasize.

For example, when Marx calls the worker's productive activity "variable capital," he is labeling a function that only he sees; in this case, because this is how such activity appears "from the point of view of the process of creating surplus-value," a unit that Marx himself introduced (1958, 209). It is only after we finish reading *Capital* and accept the new concept of "surplus-value" that "variable capital" ceases to be an arbitrary name for labor-power. Generally speaking, we understand why Marx has used a particular name to the extent that we are able to grasp the function referred to, which in turn depends on how similar his conception of the relevant factors is to our own.

Marx's concepts, it is clear, have been tailored to fit both his unique vision of capitalism and his unusual conception of social reality. The great lesson to be drawn from all this is that Marx's concepts are not our own, no matter how much they may appear so. In short, the fact that Marx uses the same words as we do should not mislead us into believing that he has the same concepts. Words are the property of language and are common to all who use this language. Concepts, or ideas about the world that find expression in words (or words in so far as they contain such ideas), are best grasped as the property of individuals or of schools of thought. Expressing what he knows as well as how he knows it, Marx's concepts tell us much more (often), much less (sometimes), and much different (always) than we think they do. In his preface to the English edition of *Capital* I, Engels says it is "self-evident that a theory which views modern capitalist production as a mere passing stage in the economic history of mankind, must make use of terms different from those habitual to writers who look upon the form of production as imperishable and final" (Marx 1958, 5). Whether the need for new terms (concepts) here is "self-evident" is debatable; that Marx felt such a need is not.

Moreover, as if this were not enough, the very sense conveyed by Marx's concepts is unstable. What he understands at any given time of the interrelations that make up social reality is reflected in the meanings of the words he uses. But these interrelations are constantly changing, and, further, Marx is forever learning more about them through his research. Hence, eight years later, in his introduction to *Capital* III (after a considerable volume of misinterpretation had passed under the bridge), Engels also warns that we should not expect to find any "fixed, cut-to-measure, once and for all applicable definitions in Marx's works" (Marx 1959a, 13–14).[14]

The lack of definitions (that is, of statements obviously meant as definitions) in Marx's writings has often been belabored, but it should now be clear what difficulty he had in providing them. Viewing the world as undergoing constant change and as devoid of the clear-cut classificational boundaries that distinguish the commonsense approach, Marx could not keep a definition of one factor from spilling over into everything. For him, any isolating definition is necessarily "one-sided" and probably misleading. There are critics, such as Sartre, who have accepted Engels's dictum.[15] More typical is the reaction of R. N. Carew-Hunt, who is so convinced of the impossibility of such an approach to meaning that he claims (against the evidence) that Marx does not manipulate language in this way, though his dialectic, according to Carew-Hunt, requires that he do so (1963, 50). Basically unaware of Marx's relational conception, most critics simply cannot take the concepts that are entailed by this conception for what they are.[16]

9

What emerges from this interpretation is that the problem Marx faces in his analysis is not how to link separate parts but how to individuate instrumental units in a social whole that finds expression everywhere. If I am right, the usual approach to understanding what Marx is getting at must be completely reversed: from trying to see the way in which labor produces value, we must accept at the outset a kind of equation between the two (the two social Relations express the same whole—as Marx says, "Value is labor" [1959a, 795])—and try instead to see the ways in which they differ. Marx's law of value is concerned with the "metamorphosis of value," with the various forms it takes in the economy, and not with its production by labor. This, and not what Smith and Ricardo had said before, is the economic theory illustrated in the massive volumes of *Capital*.

So, too, instead of seeking a strict causal tie between the mode of production and other institutions and practices of society that precludes complex social interaction, we must begin by accepting the existence of this interaction and then seek out the ways in which Marx believes that the effects proceeding from the mode of production and other economic factors (narrowly understood) are more important. Such interaction, as we have seen, is a necessary part of each social Relation. This, and not technological determinism, is the conception of history illustrated in all Marx's detailed discussions of political and social phenomena. If Marx is at ease with a foot on each side of the fence, it is because for him the fence does not exist. In light of this analysis, most of Marx's opponents are guilty of criticizing him for answers to questions he not only did not ask but—given his relational conception of reality—could not ask. Marx's real questions have been lost in the process. They must be rehabilitated.

Notes

1. Quite the reverse is the case in France, where Maximilien Rubel, Henri Lefebvre, and Louis Althusser—to mention only a few of the better-known writers—have all made heavy use of this work.

2. Marx also says, "Capital . . . is nothing without wage-labor, value, money, price, etc." (1904, 292).

3. Though generally translated as "relation," Verhältnis is sometimes rendered as "condition," "proportion," or "reaction," which should indicate something of its special sense. Maximilien Rubel has mentioned to the author that Verhältnis, coming incessantly into the discussion, was perhaps the most difficult term he had to deal with in his many translations of Marx's writings into French. As well as using the French equivalents of the words already listed, Rubel also rendered Verhältnis on occasion as système, structure, and problème. Another complication arises from the fact that Beziehung, another standard term in Marx's vocabulary, can also be translated into English as "relation," though it is generally translated as "connection." I intend the concept "relation" to contain the same complexities that I take to exist in Marx's concept Verhältnis.

4. Alfred G. Meyer has ventured close to this formulation by presenting Marxism as among other things a system of "reciprocally interdependent variables" (1963, 24ff.). But this still begs all the old questions regarding the quality of their interdependence: if the variables are logically independent, how can they reciprocally affect one another? If they are not, what does this mean? It is my impression that in this manner what is called "functionalism" is generally either inconsistent or incomprehensible. For too many writers on Marxism, friends and foes alike, talk of "interdependence" and "interaction" is simply a matter of papering over the cracks. But once these cracks appear (once we ascribe a logical independence to factors), they cannot be gotten rid of so easily; and if we take the further step and dismiss the notion of logical independence, the entire terrain of what is taken for granted has been radically altered.

5. The "totality" of social life that Marx seeks to explain is, as he tells us on another occasion, "the reciprocal action of these various sides on one another" (Marx and Engels 1964, 50).

6. It is highly significant, too, that in his political and historical works, as opposed to his more theoretical writings in economics and philosophy, Marx seldom uses bestimmen ("determine"), preferring to characterize relations in these areas with more flexible-sounding expressions. English translators have tended to reinforce whatever "determinist" bias is present in Marx's work by generally translating bedingen (which can mean "condition" or "determine") as "determine." Compare, for example, the opening chapter of The German Ideology with the German original.

7. Lafargue was Marx's son-in-law and the only person to whom Marx ever dictated any work. Consequently, Lafargue was in an excellent position to observe the older man's thinking. Of his subject matter, Lafargue says, Marx "did not see a thing singly, in itself and for itself, separate from its surroundings: he saw a highly complicated world in continual motion." Then, quoting Vico ("'Thing is a body only for God, who knows everything; for man, who knows only the exterior, it is only the surface'"), Lafargue claims that Marx grasped things in the manner of Vico's God (*Reminiscences* n.d., 78).

8. Elsewhere, Marx refers to the "destiny" of man being to develop his powers (Marx and Engels 1964, 315).

9. Of economic laws and the political economy of his day, Marx says, "it does not comprehend these laws—that is, it does not demonstrate how they arise from the very nature of private property" (1959b, 67–68). The changes occurring in private property (which he inflates here to the size of the economy) are said to be discoverable in its component relations.

10. Marx also speaks of "a general rate of surplus-value—viewed as a tendency, like all other laws" (1959a, 172).

11. Unfortunately, Marcuse does not attempt to explain how such a use of terms is possible, what it presupposes in the way of a conceptual scheme, and the problems of communication it necessarily poses. Without the foundations that I try to supply in chapters 2 and 3 of this work, such correct insights—of which there are many in the writings of Marcuse, Korsch, Lukács, Lefebvre, Goldmann, Dunayevskaya, Sartre, Sweezy, Kosik, the early Hook, and a few others—are left to hang unsupported, and are in the final analysis unconvincing.

12. Common sense is all that strikes us as being obviously true, such that to deny any part of it appears, at first hearing, to involve us in speaking nonsense. In this work, I also use "common sense" to refer to that body of generally unquestioned knowledge and the equally unquestioned approach to knowledge that is common to the vast majority of scholars and layman in Western capitalist societies.

13. Other striking examples of what most readers must consider a misuse of words are Engels's reference to race as an "economic factor" and Marx's reference to the community as a "force of production" (Marx and Engels 1941, 517; Marx 1973, 495).

14. Because the appearance of things is constantly changing, Engels declares, "the unity of concept and appearance manifests itself as essentially an infinite process" (Marx and Engels 1941, 529).

15. Sartre offers an enlightening comparison between Marx, whose concepts evolve with history and his research into it, and modern Marxists, whose concepts remain unaffected by social change: "The open concepts of Marxism have closed in" (1963, 26–34). On this subject, see also Lefebvre 1947, 204–11.

16. The conception of meaning presented here can also be found in Hegel. Hook is one of the few commentators who recognizes their common and unusual approach to meaning when, referring to the views of Marx and Hegel, he says, "Meanings must develop with the objects of which they are the meanings. Otherwise, they cannot be adequate to their subject matter" (1963, 65–66).

It is interesting to note that one of the major reasons that has led current linguistic philosophy to make a radical distinction between what a term means and what it refers to (between definitions and descriptions) is the alleged instability of the latter. To equate what a term means with what it refers to is, first, to have meanings that change with time and place (sometimes drastically) and, second, to get involved with those conditions in the real world that help make what is being referred to what it is. In short, this conception of meaning inclines one toward a conception of internal relations. It is from this exposed position that the question currently in vogue, "Don't ask for the meaning, ask for the use," marks a total retreat.

CHAPTER 3

The Philosophy of
Internal Relations

1

Marx's scholarly concern was with capitalism, and in studying this society he naturally operated with *social* Relations, his vocabulary reflecting the real *social* ties that he uncovered in his research. What remains to be explained, however, is how Marx could conceive of social factors as Relations where physical objects are involved. For in his discussions, machines, the real articles produced, the worker's person, et cetera, are all components of one social Relation or another. We learn, for example, that "capital is, among other things, also an instrument of production, also past personal labor" (1904, 270). According to the definition given earlier, every such component is itself a Relation. It follows from this that Marx also conceives of *things* as Relations. Unless this conclusion can be defended, the interpretation I have offered of social Relations will have to be drastically altered. By drawing together the relevant evidence and tracing the history of the broad philosophical position that underlies Marx's practice, I shall try in this chapter to provide such a defense.

Most modern thinkers would maintain that there cannot be relations without things just as there cannot be things without relations. Things, according to this commonsense view, constitute the basic terms of each relation and cannot themselves be reduced to relations. However, this objection only applies to Marx if what he is doing is caricatured as trying to reduce the terms of a relation to that which is said to stand between them. But his is not an attempt to reify "between" or "together." Instead, as we saw in the previous chapter, the sense of "relation" itself has been extended to cover what is related, so that either term may be taken to express both in their peculiar connection.

No one would deny that things appear and function as they do because of their spatial-temporal ties with other things, including man as a creature with both physical and social characteristics. To conceive of things as Relations is simply to interiorize this interdependence—as we have seen Marx do with social factors—in the thing itself. Thus, the book before me expresses and therefore, on this model, relationally contains everything from the fact that there is a light on in my room to the social practices and institutions of my society that made this particular work possible. The conditions of its existence are taken to be part of what it is and are indicated by the fact that it is just this and nothing else. In the history of ideas, where every new thought is invariably an old one warmed over, this view is generally referred to as the philosophy of internal relations.[1]

There are four kinds of evidence for attributing a philosophy of internal relations to Marx. First, he makes statements that place him on the side of those who view things as Relations. He declares, for example, that "the thing itself is an objective human relation to itself and to man" (1959b, 103). Marx also calls man (who, after all, has a body as well as a social significance) the "ensemble [aggregate] of social relations" (Marx and Engels 1964, 646). Elsewhere, this same creature is said to be "a natural object, a thing, although a living conscious thing" (1958, 202). Marx can refer to man as a thing as well as an ensemble of social relations because he conceives of each thing as a Relation, in this instance, as the ensemble of social relations. Engels's comments are often more explicit still, as when he maintains that "the atom itself is nothing more than a Relation" (Marx and Engels 1941, 221).

To be sure, Marx also speaks—particularly when treating the fetishism of commodities—of social relations that are taken for things. However, it is not difficult to interpret these instances as attempts to make a distinction between two kinds of Relations, one of which (in conformity with ordinary usage) he calls "things." The view I am proposing does not require that Marx cease speaking of "things," only that they also be grasped as Relations. While statements indicating the existence of things can be interpreted relationally, his statements that present things as Relations cannot be interpreted as easily in a way that accords the former their customary independence.

Second, even if Marx's direct comments on the subject of things as Relations are ambiguous, his treatment of man and nature (or its material components) as Relations with internal ties to one another is not: "That man's physical and spiritual life is linked to nature means simply that nature is linked to itself" (1959b, 74). Likewise, when he declares that man "is nature" or that his objects "reside in the nature of his being," the ties to which our attention is drawn are clearly *not* external ones (1959b, 156). Rather, the individual is held to be in some kind of union with his or her object; they are in fact relationally contained in one another, which requires that each be conceived of as a Relation.

The same inner tie is presented from the other side when Marx declares that he views "the evolution of the economic foundations of society" as a "process of natural history" (1958, 10) or includes among the forces of nature "those of man's own nature" along with "those of so-called nature" (1973, 488). Unless we accord Marx a conception of things as Relations, those comments (of which I have quoted but a few) that reveal man as somehow an extension of nature, and nature as somehow an extension of man, can only be understood meta-phorically or as poetic utterances.[2]

Third, if we take the position that Marx drew an indelible line between things and social Relations we are left with the task of explaining what kind of inter-action he saw in the physical world and how the two worlds of nature and soci-ety are related. Does Marx view natural development on the model of cause and effect? He specifically states his opposition to seeking for first causes in econom-ics and religion, where it is the relations in which the so-called first causes stand that still require explanation (1959b, 68–69). In a rare instance where he records the connection he sees between two physical objects, his adherence to a philoso-phy of internal relations is evident. "The sun," he says, "is the object of the plant—an indispensable object to it confirming its life—just as the plant is an object of the sun, being an expression of the life awakening power of the sun, of the sun's objective essential power" (1959b, 157). The sun's effect on the plant, which most of us are inclined to treat causally, is considered by Marx to be an "expression" of the sun itself, a means by which it manifests what it is and, in this way, part of it.

To clarify this, Marx adds, "A being which does not have its nature outside itself is not a natural being, and plays no part in the system of nature" (1959b, 157). Each physical object, by virtue of being a natural object, is more than whatever part of it is apparent or easy to isolate. As natural objects, the sun and the plant have their natures—as Marx puts it—outside themselves, such that the relation between them is conceived as appertaining to each and is part of the full meaning conveyed by their respective concepts.[3]

It is not only the difficulty of attributing to Marx a causal explanation of physical phenomena but also—as I have indicated—the problems raised by combining a commonsense view of nature with his conception of social rela-tions that argues for his having a philosophy of internal relations. Sidney Hook offers the arresting case of a critic who makes a clean break between Marx's social relations, of which he gives one of the better accounts, and the objects of nature. Hook claims that "the Marxian totality is social and limited by other totalities" and that "for Marx there are wholes not the whole" (1962, 62). This raises the practical problem of how to explain the effect of the physical world on social phenomena. For example, how are we to interpret Marx's claim that the mode of production determines what occurs in other social sectors when the mode of production includes machines and factories (physical objects) as well as the way people use these objects and cooperate among themselves (so-cial relations)? The former suggests a causal interpretation of this claim, for this is the kind of explanation into which physical objects generally enter, while the latter suggests one that emphasizes reciprocal action between the parts, for this is the kind of explanation into which social relations generally enter.[4]

In *From Hegel to Marx* and *Towards the Understanding of Karl Marx*, Hook wavers between these two incompatible explanatory models. Under pressure to choose, in *Marx and the Marxists* he finally settles on a causal account, and Marx's conception of history is declared a "monistic theory" with the mode of production held solely responsible for all major social developments (1955, 37, 36). In the last analysis, the division of Marxism into separate wholes simply does not allow Hook to use his own considerable insights into Marx's social relations to explain the complex interaction he knows is there. This is not to dismiss the fact that for a variety of reasons Hook's views on Marxism have changed over the years. I have simply indicated the position taken in his early works, which allowed for and even rendered likely this later development.

Fourth and last, I believe I am justified in ascribing a philosophy of internal relations to Marx because it would have required a total break with the philosophical tradition in which he was nourished for this not to be so. Hegel, Leibniz, and Spinoza had all sought for the meanings of things and/or of the terms that characterize them in their relations inside the whole (variously referred to as "substance," "nature," "God," etc.); and, judging by his voluminous notebooks, these are thinkers the young Marx studied with the greatest care (Marx and Engels 1932, 99–112).

It is chiefly because the philosophy of internal relations is currently held in such disrepute that it is assumed that Marx could not have accepted it and, consequently, that the burden of proof rests upon me to show that he did. In presenting evidence from Marx's writings that places him in this tradition I have agreed to play the role of prosecutor. I should now like to suggest, however, that if Marx inherited this conception from his immediate predecessors, the burden of proof rests with those who believe he discarded it, in which case we are also entitled to know the conception of things and social factors with which he replaced it—an atomist outlook, such as is implied in the interpretation of Marxism as "economic determinism," or something completely different for which no name exists, as Althusser claims, or what? In the remainder of this chapter and in the one that follows I shall briefly sketch the history of the philosophy of internal relations and respond to some of the "devastating" criticisms that have kept writers of all persuasions from even taking seriously the possibility that Marx might have shared this view.

2

The philosophy of internal relations, which can be traced as far back as the early Greek philosopher Parmenides, first came into prominence in the modern period in the work of Spinoza. Spinoza's own version of this philosophy is constructed upon Aristotle's definition of "substance" as that which is capable of independent existence. Since only nature taken as a whole is capable of independent existence, it is, according to this view, the sole substance. It is such a unified nature that Spinoza labels "God." All components of this single substance, whether material things or thoughts, are conceived of as its transient forms, as its "modes" of being, and, hence, expressive of the sum of interrelations that determines their individual characters. For Spinoza, who accents the totality, the parts are strictly adjectival (1925, pts. 1 and 2).

Leibniz, on the other hand, puts his emphasis on the parts and devotes little attention to the whole he sees reflected in each. Not one but an infinite number of substances exists for him. By asserting that these substances, which he calls "monads," have individual qualities but no extension, Leibniz is refusing to treat what we ordinarily take to be things as the basic units of reality. However we understand the queer mental construct that is Leibniz's monad, what stands out clearly from his account is the relational tie that exists between each one and the universe. Hence, he can claim, "there is no term so absolute or so detached that it doesn't enclose relations and the perfect analysis of which doesn't lead to other things and even to everything else, so that one could say that relative terms mark expressly the configuration which they contain" (1966, 195).[5]

Coming a century later, Hegel was perhaps the first to work through the main implications of the philosophy of internal relations and to construct in some detail the total system that it implied. In this he was aided—as is often the case in philosophy—by the character of the impasse bequeathed to him by his immediate predecessor, Kant. The latter had convincingly demonstrated that things are no more than the qualities by which we know them but found such a conclusion unacceptable. Determined to believe that what appears is something more than (really, for him, something behind) what actually strikes our senses, Kant invented the nebulous "thing-in-itself," which remains the same through all changes in the entity.

Hegel exhibited less timidity before Kant's first conclusion, that things dissolve upon inspection into their qualities, but considered that the decisive task is to show how this conclusion must be understood. Setting aside for the moment the idealistic content of Hegel's philosophy, his main contribution consists of providing the context of the whole, or "Absolute," in which to place both Kant's problem and answer. Thus, for Hegel, the thing under examination is not just the sum of its qualities but, through the links these qualities (individually or together in the thing) have with the rest of nature, it is also a particular expression of the whole. To a great extent, the distinctiveness of Hegel's system lies in the various means used to maintain our awareness of the whole while he sets about distinguishing between its parts. His formidable vocabulary receives most of its character from this task. For example, when Hegel refers to things as "determinations," "moments," or "phenomena," he means to suggest something partial and unfinished, something whose full analysis requires that it be conceived of as including far more (both in space and through time) than is immediately apparent.

In establishing the identity of each thing in its relation to the whole, as a mode of expression of the Absolute, Hegel alters the notion of identity used by Kant and of truth itself. Mathematical equality ($1 = 1$) is replaced as the model for comprehending identity by what may be called "relational equality," where the entity in question is considered identical with the whole that it relationally expresses. For Hegel, "Self-relation in essence is the form of identity," where "essence" refers to just such extended relations (1965, 211). However, identity in this sense is clearly a matter of degree; small, simple things possess less identity with the whole than large, complex ones. For most modern philosophers, this proposition is manifestly absurd, but Hegel not only embraces it but uses it as a central thesis on which to construct other notions.

Thus, he maintains that truth "is the whole" (1964, 81). If things are more or less identical with the whole that they express, then what can be said about them is more or less true, depending on how much of what can be truly said of the whole is said about them. Each thing being relationally identical with the whole, all that is true of the latter is its entire truth; and everything short of that—which means all that we say about particular things (determinations, moments, etc.)—is partial truth. Hegel himself registers the practical effect of this interpretation for his phenomenological undertaking when he declares that knowledge "can only be set forth fully . . . in the form of system" (1964, 85).[6] To state what is known about any one thing is to describe the system in which it exists; it is to present, as Hegel invariably did, each part as a facet of the whole. Returning to Kant's dilemma, Hegel, while denying the existence of a "thing-in-itself" behind observed reality, affirms that through their interrelations things are much more than they appear.

Is this the aspect of Hegel's philosophy that Marx disparaged as idealist? I think not. Hegel constructed the framework described here in order to treat ideas, characterizing what I have called the "whole" as "Absolute Idea" or "Reason." Marx's criticism is always directed against how Hegel chose to apply this framework and his preferred subject matter and *never* against the relational quality of his units or the fact of system that this entails.[7] Essentially, his complaint is that having produced the category of "Absolute Idea" from the real world by generalizing from the thinking of living men, Hegel produces the real world, the actual thoughts of men, out of this category. Individual ideas are given a mystical significance by representing them as moments in the life of a generalization that they themselves have given rise to.

After reversing the real relation between ideas and their concept, Hegel is led to reverse the real relation between ideas and nature—it is impossible for nature to effect the immanent unfolding of what is absolute. There is nothing left for the material world to be but an externalization and profanation of what people think about it. Without ever stating explicitly that ideas create matter (there has been considerable confusion over this point), by presenting real developments as following upon and reflecting what occurs in the realm of ideas, this is the general impression that Hegel conveys. Marx pinpoints his error as that of "considering the real as the result of self-coordinating, self-absorbed, and spontaneously operating thought" (1904, 293). There is, in short, no contradiction between opposing the role Hegel gives to ideas and their concept and accepting the relational framework that houses these views. Feuerbach—from whom Marx derived much of his criticism of Hegel—did just this.[8] And, indeed, Marx's silence on Hegel's relational conception, while criticizing so much of what he wrote, speaks eloquently in favor of this interpretation.[9]

Marx's philosophical rebellion began with his refusal to accept the independent development of ideas, a refusal in which he was by no means unique. In his case, this led to study that showed that social change generally preceded Hegel's vaunted history of ideas. He concluded that it was just these "material" relations, relegated by Hegel to the backside facets of an all-pervasive thesis, that required the closest investigation in order to comprehend both ideas and the real world. What has been insufficiently recognized, however, is that in stressing social factors Marx does not dispense with the broad philosophy of internal relations in which he was initially introduced to them. Naturally, a new focus of interest as well as the real ties he uncovers in research required the adoption of some fresh concepts, but they too were incorporated into this relational scheme.

It is hardly remarkable (though seldom remarked upon) that whenever any system-owning attribute of a factor is at question, Marx generally relies on Hegel's vocabulary. "Identity," "abstract," "essence," and "concrete," for example, are all used by Marx, as they were by Hegel, to mark some aspect of the whole in the part. These terms, which appear in rich profusion throughout Marx's writings—late as well as early—cannot be consistently interpreted in any other way. Likewise, it is clear that the unusual approach to meaning that was attributed earlier to both these thinkers is a necessary result of the relational conception they shared.

One of the more significant effects of Marx's refusal to countenance the independent development of ideas is that the concept of the whole, which in the form of Absolute Idea served Hegel as the source of its particular expressions, no longer has the central role to play in the system it represents. It remains the sum of all relations and that which is expressed in each but offers little help, as a distinct concept, in elucidating any one of them. The real world is too complex, diffuse, and unclear in its detail to serve as an adequate explanation for any of the events that go on inside it. One result is that whereas Hegel offers a large assortment of terms in which he attempts to capture the whole—"Absolute Idea," "Spirit," "God," "Universal," "Truth"—Marx does not offer any (unless we choose to consider "capitalist mode of production" or "history," meaning class history, in this light). It is likely that this difference is at least partly responsible for the belief that Marx did not hold a philosophy of internal relations. However, what essentially characterizes this view is the internal nature of the tie between the parts (whatever parts) and not the function of the whole qua whole in clarifying these ties. In this same tradition, some thinkers, such as Spinoza and Hegel, devote considerable attention to what they take to be the totality, and others, such as Leibniz and Marx, do not.

Naturally, the conception of change and development embedded in Marx's "materialistic" philosophy of internal relations differs significantly from its counterpart in Hegel's philosophy. The reconciliation that Hegel foresaw as the eventual outcome of history was the World Spirit becoming conscious of itself. In this context, development could only be the self-discovery of the greater ideational form of whatever is developing. The individual is reduced to passivity, except in so far as he or she partakes in his or her thoughts of the understanding that properly belongs to the World Spirit.

Even before Marx, the school of Young Hegelians led by Bruno Bauer replaced Hegel's World Spirit as subject with man. In the early works of this group, reconciliation was understood, however imprecisely, in terms of revolutionary activity. Disappointed by the failure of the radical movement of their day, they adopted by 1843 the pose of "Critical Criticism" for which they are better known, holding that reconciliation occurs through "right interpretation," through people coming to understand the world.[10] Marx, who was a close friend of Bauer's during his student days in Berlin, developed the Young Hegelians' early perspective: if man is the subject, the way to reconcile himself with the world, now understood as his object (actual or potential), is actively to change it. Change becomes a matter of man transforming his existence. From being a passive observer of development, as in Hegel, the individual has become the actor whose daily life brings it about.

Even from this brief outline, it is apparent that Marx's Hegelian heritage is too complex to allow simple characterization. Hegel never ceased being important for Marx, as Lenin, for example, perceived when he wrote in his notebook in 1914, "It is impossible completely to understand Marx's *Capital*, and especially its first chapters, without having thoroughly studied and understood the whole of Hegel's *Logic*. Consequently, half a century later none of the Marxists understood Marx" (1961, 180).[11] To those who argue that Marx made his break with Hegel in 1842, 1844, or 1848, my reply is that there was no such break. This does not mean that I would like to join the ranks of critics who maintain that Marx was a Hegelian, with its connotations of idealist bias, foreshadowed behavior, and metaphysical posturing. In my opinion, the choice offered by these two positions is not the real one. If by "theory" we mean—as I think we should—an explanation in general terms of particular events or conditions, it is doubtful whether Marx in any period of his life, going back to university days, ever agreed with any of Hegel's theories, which gave to the World Spirit and ideas generally a role that he found unacceptable.[12] However, as regards the epistemological decision concerning the form in which any and all subject matter is considered, Marx never wavered from the relational conception bequeathed to him by Hegel.

Of what then does Marx's movement away from Hegel, which practically all writers on this subject have noted, consist? If we rule out Hegel's concrete theories (which Marx always rejected) and the philosophy of internal relations (which he always accepted), this development could only involve the meaning of the concepts Marx borrowed as well as those new ones he introduced. By transferring his attention to the real world, Marx instills the concepts taken from Hegel with fresh meaning while removing their idealistic content. This upheaval was not accomplished in a moment; it had to be worked out, and this took time.

Likewise, by progressively shifting his main area of concern from philosophy to politics and then to economics, the information and ties Marx uncovered became parts—and sometimes the major part—of the sense conveyed by these same concepts. I have already noted that the meanings of Marx's concepts were extended through his research and that their particular denotations were determined by what was relevant to the problem under consideration. But Marx's research never ceased, and new problems were constantly arising out of actual events and his study of them. It is in the developing meanings of Marx's concepts, which reacted upon his system but left its relational features intact, that we can best observe his growing estrangement from Hegel. The character of this *evolution*, which began when Marx the student read Hegel and registered his first uncertainties, is seriously distorted by any talk of "breaks" and even of "stages" and "periods."

3

Marx never dealt with the special problems raised by the materialist content he gave to the philosophy of internal relations. No doubt this would have been part of the work he wanted to do on Hegel, but the pressing claims of his social and economic studies and of political activity never allowed him to begin. Provided that he could successfully operate with his relational view, he gave low priority to its elaboration and defense. This task was undertaken to some degree by Engels, particularly in his writings on the physical sciences, but more directly by the German tanner Joseph Dietzgen. "Here is our philosopher," Marx said on introducing Dietzgen to the Hague Congress of the First International (Dietzgen 1928, 15).[13] Yet, despite further eulogies by Engels, Dietzgen's work remains relatively little known.[14] However, Dietzgen's views provide a necessary supplement to Marx's own. The relationship between these two thinkers is clearly set out by Anton Pannekoek, who claims that Marx demonstrated how ideas "are produced by the surrounding world," while Dietzgen showed "how the impressions of the surrounding world are transformed into ideas" (1948, 24).[15]

Mindful of the dangers of using what one thinker says to support an interpretation of another, I shall limit my comments to features that Marx could not have missed in praising Dietzgen's work. Like Hegel, Dietzgen affirms that the existence of any thing is manifested through qualities that are its relations to other things. Hence, "Any thing that is torn out of its contextual relations ceases to exist" (1928, 96). So, too, Dietzgen declares—in almost the same words as Hegel—"The universal is the truth," meaning that the full truth about any one thing includes (because of its internal relations) the truth about everything (1928, 110).[16]

But unlike Hegel—and Marx, too—who proceeds from these foundations to an investigation of the whole in each part, Dietzgen's inquiry is directed toward how such parts get established in the first place. For Hegel and Marx's approach suggests that the preliminary problem of deciding which units of the whole to treat as parts has already been solved. Yet, it may legitimately be asked whether the unity posited by this conception does not preclude the very existence of those separate structures in which they claim to have caught sight of this unity. This is essentially the problem of individuation, or "abstraction," and it constitutes a major stumbling block for any philosophy of internal relations.

Dietzgen's contribution to the solution of this problem is his account of what can occur in individuation and what does occur. He asks, "Where do we find any practical unit outside of our abstract conceptions? Two halves, four fourths, eight eighths, or an infinite number of separate parts form the material out of which the mind fashions the mathematical unit. This book, its leaves, its letters, or their parts—are they units? Where do I begin and where do I stop?" (1928, 103). His answer is that the real world is composed of an infinite number of sense-perceptible qualities whose interdependence makes them a single whole. If we began by applying the relational conception to social factors and then to things, we see now that it can also apply to qualities. Because the process of linking up qualities may be stopped at any point between the individual quality and the whole, the ways of dividing up the latter into distinct parts called "things" is endless. One result is that what appears as a thing here may be taken as an attribute of some other thing there. Every quality can be conceived of as a thing, and every thing as a quality; it all depends where the line is drawn. So much for what is possible.[17]

What actually occurs, that is, the construction of units of a particular size and kind out of the "formless multiplicity" presented to our senses, is the work of the human mind. In Dietzgen's words, "the absolutely relative and transient forms of the sensual world serve as raw material for our brain activity, in order through abstraction of the general or like characteristics, to become systematized, classified or ordered for our consciousness" (1928, 103). The forms in which the world appears to our senses are "relative" and "transient," but they are also said to possess the "like characteristics" that allow us to generalize from them. "The world of the mind," we learn, finds "its material, its premise, its proof, its beginning, and its boundary, in sensual reality" (1928, 119). In this reality, like qualities give rise to a single conception because they are, in fact, alike. This is responsible, too, for the wide agreement in the use of concepts, particularly those that refer to physical objects. Yet it is only when we supply these similar qualities with a concept that they become a distinct entity and can be considered separately from the vast interconnection in which they reside.

According to Dietzgen, therefore, the whole is revealed in certain standard parts (in which some thinkers have sought to reestablish the relations of the whole), because these are the parts in which human beings through individuation or abstraction have actually fragmented the whole. The theoretical problem of individuation is successfully resolved by people in their daily practice. The fact that they do not see what they are doing as individuating parts from an interconnected whole is, of course, another question, and one with which Dietzgen does not concern himself. He is content to make the point that, operating with real sense material, it is the abstracting activity of people that gives the world the particular "things" that these same people see in it. Even mind, we learn, results from abstracting certain common qualities out of real experiences of thinking; they become something apart when we consider them as "mind" (1928, 120).[18]

Dietzgen's practical answer to the problem of individuation suggests how structures can exist within a philosophy of internal relations, something Althusser for one has declared impossible.[19] Yet, if individuation is not an arbitrary act but one governed by broad similarities existing in nature itself, there is a necessary, if vague, correlation between such natural similarities and the structures conveyed by our concepts. This is how the study of any conceptual scheme, whether based on a philosophy of internal relations or not, teaches us something about the real world (unfortunately, this cannot be pressed—as many insist on doing—beyond what is common to all conceptual schemes). That Marx, through his study of capitalism, came to stress certain social relations as more important does not in any way conflict with his conception of each part as relationally containing its ties of dependence to everything else. The fact that some ties are preferred and may, for certain purposes, be viewed as forming a structure is no more surprising than any other act of individuation (conceptualization) based on real similarities.

The significant service Dietzgen renders Marx is to show how a proper balance can be reached on a relational view between accepting the reality of the external world (including, too, the general trustworthiness of sense perception) and holding that the conceptual activity of human thought is responsible for the precise forms in which we grasp the world. Marx's support for Dietzgen and, more so, his own practice in abstracting new social units show clearly that he accepted such a balance. Yet by stressing the first part (in criticism of his idealist opponents) and neglecting to develop the second, he left his epistemology open to misinterpretation as a kind of "naive realism"; and it is this belief that lies behind the widespread, mistaken use of ordinary-language criteria to understand Marx's concepts.[20]

4

The line of reasoning I have followed so far in this work may be summarized as follows: either Marx means what he seems to (what common sense and ordinary language strongly suggest he means), or he does not. If he does, many of his claims appear one-sided and are easy to falsify. Furthermore, he frequently wrote sentences that are utter nonsense and he was wise enough to avoid his own theories when describing any concrete situation. The attempt by some "vulgar" Marxists to defend the master while accepting the widespread interpretation of Marxism popularly referred to as "economic determinism" is vulnerable at every point.

If Marx did not mean what we ordinarily mean in using the same terms, however, it is incumbent upon those who take this view to offer not only an alternative interpretation but also another basis for their interpretation than common sense. It is not enough to claim that words in Marxism have unusual meanings (no matter what we take them to be) without making clear how Marx could use words in this way. In undertaking the latter task, I followed a thread leading from Marx's *actual* use of concepts to the way in which he referred to concepts, his view of them as social components, his treatment of social components as Relations, his use of Relations as meanings, and, finally, to his belief in a philosophy of internal relations that served as the necessary framework for these practices.

Besides placing Marx in this tradition, I have also tried to make the point that the relational conception shared by such thinkers as Spinoza, Leibniz, Hegel, and Marx cannot be rejected out of hand. Yet, holding that it can be defended is not quite the same as defending it. This is an important distinction, and it is one readers should bear in mind. Only after examining the main criticisms directed against this relational conception (chapters 4 and 5), seeing how it is connected to other aspects of Marx's method, in particular to the process of abstraction (chapters 5–9), and then seeing how Marx applies this philosophy to problems in the real world (chapters 6, 8, 9, and 12) will it be possible to make a fair evaluation of its worth.

Notes

1. Outside Marx's peculiar conception of things as Relations, there is nothing so unusual in viewing the whole as bound up in some sense in each of its parts. Writing in 1880, William James says, "it is a common platitude that a complete acquaintance with any one thing, however small, would require a knowledge of the entire universe. Not a sparrow falls to the ground but some of the remote conditions of his fall are to be found in the milky way, in our federal constitution or in the early history of Europe" (1956, 216). I remain unconvinced, however, that what James calls a "platitude" ever really was so common, or that if it was it is now, or that if it was and is now that it has ever been more than an unintegrated hypothesis for most of the thinkers concerned. Marx's philosophy of internal relations goes further by conceptualizing these ties in each part and is—as I hope to show—thoroughly integrated in his work.

2. Eugene Kamenka has noted that Marx sometimes incorporates nature in man, but he treats this as an unfortunate metaphysical departure and an occasion for criticism (1962, 97–99).

3. Engels, whose extensive studies in the physical sciences were well known to Marx, never offers what we ordinarily take to be a causal explanation. Instead, his position is that "natural science confirms what Hegel has said . . . that reciprocal action is the true *causa finalis* of things. We cannot go back further than to knowledge of this reciprocal action, for the very reason that there is nothing behind to know" (1954, 307). And this mutual effect does not occur between conceptu-

ally distinct parts, for as Engels tells us, "What Hegel calls reciprocal action is the organic body" (1954, 406). To explain change in the physical world by referring to the reciprocal action of its parts is said to be the same thing as presenting the world as an organic body.

4. We come across a similar problem within the mode of production itself in trying to grasp, for example, the tie Marx posits between the distribution of the means of production and the distribution of the working population that corresponds to it. Unless the physical means of production are conceived of as internally related to the people who work on them, the distribution of the two cannot be part of an organic union, allowing for full reciprocal effect. In this case, there will be a strong temptation to interpret this relation causally, to find that the distribution of the means of production brings about the distribution of population, whereas Marx himself refers to the latter's tie to the former as a "further determination of the same Relation [*eine weitere Bestimmung desselben Verhältnisses*]" (1953, 17). This has been mistranslated in the English version as "what is practically another wording of the same fact" (1904, 286). It is in this manner that the interpretation I am offering is often hidden by translators who do not know quite what sense to make of *Verhältnis*.

5. For the clearest statement of Leibniz's views on this subject, see his *Monadologie* (1952).

6. Truth that can only be presented in the form of a system can only be evaluated by the criterion of coherence. On one occasion, Hegel goes so far as to equate truth with consistency (1965, 52). Such an approach to truth leaves as the number-one problem of logic to "examine the forms of thought touching their ability to hold truth" (1965, 52), that is, roughly, how much of the system that is the whole truth is actually set out (brought to the fore and made an object of consciousness) in each of our concepts.

7. Typical of statements that indicate this distinction is Marx's claim that "*The Phenomenology* is, therefore, an occult critique . . . but inasmuch as it keeps steadily in view man's estrangement, even though man appears only in the shape of mind, there lie concealed in it *all* the elements of criticism, already *prepared* and *elaborated* in a manner often rising far above the Hegelian standpoint" (1959b, 150).

8. Of Hegel's philosophy, Feuerbach had said, "We only have to make of the predicate a subject, and of this subject the object and principle, we only have therefore to invert speculative philosophy in order to have the revealed truth, pure and naked truth" (1959, 224). In the inversion performed by Feuerbach, the philosophy of internal relations remains unaltered.

9. Marx's critique of Hegel (which includes as well, it must be noted, his favorable remarks) is to be found throughout his writings. The most important discussions of Hegel occur in the *Economic and Philosophical Manuscripts of 1844* (1959b, 142–71), "Critique of Hegel's 'Philosophy of Right'" (1970, 1–127), and "A Contribution to the Critique of Hegel's 'Philosophy of Right' Introduction" (1970, 128–42). I would also add, since it is perhaps the clearest treatment of Hegel's central philosophical fault, Marx's attack on the "Mystery of Speculative Construction" in *The Holy Family* (Marx and Engels 1965, 78–83). Despite all the pages devoted to Hegel, however, Marx's position is nowhere fully worked out. On the whole, because most of what he wrote on this subject came early in life and was more often than not directed against thinkers who had accepted the worst of Hegel, Marx's attitude appears more negative than it really is. Later on, he often mentioned in letters to friends (Engels, Kugelmann, Dietzgen) that he would like to write something on the positive value of Hegel's method, but he never had the opportunity to do so. My own sketchy and one-sided treatment of the Marx-Hegel link can be supplemented by reading Marcuse's *Reason and Revolution* (1964) and Shlomo Avineri's *The Social and Political Thought of Karl Marx* (1968).

10. The widespread impression that the Young Hegelians were always Critical Critics, an impression due mainly to Marx's attack on them in *The Holy Family* (Marx and Engels 1965) and to Hook's popular study *From Hegel to Marx* (1963), has been corrected in David McLellan's *The Young Hegelians and Karl Marx* (1969).

11. It is interesting to speculate what revisions this late enthusiasm for Hegel would have caused in Lenin's major philosophical effort, *Materialism and Empirio-Criticism* (1909), written at a time when—according to Lenin—"none of the Marxists understood Marx" (1961, 180).

12. In a poem written in 1837, when Marx was only nineteen years old, Kant's and Fichte's pre-occupation with the world of thought is contrasted with his own concern for the everyday life of man (Marx and Engels 1932, 42). It is in this context that Marx's oft quoted letter to his father, written in the same year, in which he speaks of moving "closer" to the Hegelian view of the world, must be understood (1962, 15).

13. Marx's enthusiasm for Dietzgen was not unqualified. To Kugelmann, he writes of a "certain confusion and . . . too frequent repetition" in a manuscript that Dietzgen had sent him, but he makes it clear that despite this the work "contains much that is excellent" (1941, 80). Since these comments were directed to the manuscript of Dietzgen's work and forwarded to him, it is not unlikely that they affected the published version.

14. Engels writes, "And this materialist dialectic, which for years has been our best working tool and our sharpest weapon, was, remarkably enough, discovered not only by us, but also, independently of us and even of Hegel, by Joseph Dietzgen" (Marx and Engels 1951, 350–51). Engels too was not altogether unambiguous in his estimation of Dietzgen, whose work he, like Marx, first saw in manuscript form. Writing to Marx, Engels complains that Dietzgen's use of the dialectic appears "more in flashes than as a connected whole." "The account of the thing-in-itself as a thing made of thought," however, is scored as "brilliant" (Marx and Engels 1941, 252).

15. This is the nature of their relationship; whether one accepts the claims made by Pannekoek is something else again.

16. This approach to truth is accompanied, as in the case of Hegel, by a use of "identity" to express what I have called "relational equality" (Dietzgen 1928, 111).

17. Dietzgen asks further, "Is not every *thing* a part, is not *every* part a thing? Is the color of a leaf less of a thing than that leaf itself? . . . Color is only the sum of reactions of the leaf, light, and eye, and so is all the rest of the matter of a leaf an aggregate of different interactions. In the same way in which our faculty of thought deprives a leaf of its color attribute and sets it apart as a 'thing itself,' may we continue to deprive that leaf of all its other attributes, and so doing we finally take away everything that makes the leaf. Color is according to its quality no less a substance than the leaf, and the leaf is no less an attribute than its color. As the color is an attribute of the leaf, so the leaf is an attribute of the tree, the tree an attribute of the earth, the earth an attribute of the universe. The universe is the substance, substance in general, and all other substances are in relation to it only particular substances or attributes. But by this world-substance is revealed the fact that the *essence of the thing-in-itself, as distinguished from its manifestations, is only a concept of the mind or mental thing*" (1928, 103–4). It should be recalled that it is Dietzgen's account of the "thing-in-itself as a thing made of thought" that Engels said was "brilliant."

18. Though Dietzgen makes a determined assault on the empiricist dogma that perception is passive and that our mind merely registers the effect produced upon it by external reality, his account of the process of individuation or abstraction remains partial. The link with language is underdeveloped, and the effect of physical needs and of various social and economic structures on the process of abstraction requires elucidation. Much of the relevant work on these subjects, of course, was unavailable in Dietzgen's time, but what was available—such as Marx's own writings—was not always put to the best use.

19. It is because of the supposed inability of this relational view to house structures that Althusser rejects the conclusion to which so much of his work points. Instead, after clearly demonstrating the impossibility of isolating social factors in Marxism, he argues that Marx instigates a revolution in philosophy by making the "structure of the whole" (a previously untried concept) ultimately responsible for the character and development of any part (1965, 166). On my view, in attempting to reconstruct the whole from each major vantage point, Marx is erecting—if we insist on this expression—as many structures of the whole as there are major units in his analysis. The whole grasped as the interrelated conditions necessary for the existence of capital, for example, has a somewhat different structure from this same whole grasped as the interrelated conditions necessary for the alienation of workers, et cetera. The difference in where we begin leads to a dif-

ference in perspective, in the size and importance of other factors, and in the relevance of the various ties between them. Althusser's fundamental error lies in misusing the concept of structure in much the same way that Hegel misuses the concept of idea; that is, a generalization based on examining many particular instances (in this case, various particular structures of the whole) is treated as an independent entity, which is then said to determine the very instances that gave rise to it. Althusser has in fact confused structure with complexity, so that when Marx speaks of the social whole as an "already given concrete and living aggregate [*schon gegebnen konkreten, lebendigen Ganzen*]" (1953, 22), Althusser paraphrases this as a "complex, structured, already given whole [*un tout complexe structure déjà donnée*]" (1966, 198). The transition, apparently slight but possessing serious ramifications, from the idea of complexity to that of structure has no basis in Marx's text.

20. After Dietzgen, the philosophy of internal relations has been largely ignored by Marx's followers and critics alike. Though a number of writers have alluded to relational elements in Marx's thought, I am not aware of a single full-scale study of the philosophy in which they are embedded, with the possible exception of Hyman A. Levy's *A Philosophy for a Modern Man* (1938). As a result, it was left to thinkers as far removed from the Marxist tradition as F. H. Bradley and Alfred North Whitehead (to mention only the major figures) to continue wrestling with the problems posed by this relational conception. See, for example, Bradley's *Appearance and Reality* (1920, 25–34 and 572–85), where there is a particularly good discussion of the concept "relation." Though burdened with a cumbersome jargon, Whitehead's is (along with Levy's book) the most noteworthy attempt to work out a relational view of physical nature. See, especially, *The Concept of Nature* (1957) and *Process and Reality* (1929).

CHAPTER 4

In Defense of the Philosophy
of Internal Relations

1

In my interpretation, Marx's dialectical method—to borrow a Maoism—"stands on two legs": internal relations and the process of abstraction. Before probing further into Marx's use of the latter, a brief survey of some of the major criticisms that have been leveled against the philosophy of internal relations should prove very useful. Perhaps the most frequent objection concerns the difficulty (some would claim the impossibility) of identifying particulars on this view. How, in other words, do we distinguish—which includes pointing out to others and getting them to accept—that these relations, no more and no other, constitute a chair, a man, or any other particular thing? This is really a version of the problem of individuation mentioned in chapter 3.

Stuart Hampshire, who makes this criticism, admits that there are many possible ways to break up reality, but he says that the requirements of communicability necessitate that we always conceive of it as broken up into more or less distinct pieces. According to him, "we must unavoidably think of reality as consisting of persisting things of different types and kinds," since there must be a "type of term which enters into utterances having the function 'This is a so-and-so'" (1959, 17). For him, there must be a possibility of making an absolute distinction between a thing and its properties. What is taken as the thing serves as a point of reference that remains the same throughout all changes occurring in its properties and in the point of view of the perceiver. The penalty for transgressing this rule, for taking each thing as the sum of its qualities and each quality as potentially a thing, is simply that people will not be able to understand what one is saying.[1]

This argument receives indirect support from Peter Strawson, who declares that we only succeed in identifying particular things because these are the forms in which they actually exist. If Hampshire's refusal to countenance the possibility of identifying particulars on the relational view is based on what is required to communicate, Strawson—who does not discount this approach—makes his stand against the same opponent on the basis of a commonsense conception of reality. His book *Individuals* begins and ends with the assertion that people believe that the world is composed of particular things ("objective particulars") and that he conceives it as his task to find reasons to support this view (1965, 15 and 247). It is indicative of the degree to which Strawson is willing to abide by the judgment of common sense regarding the existence of particular things that his work does not contain a single chapter on perception. Essentially, he limits himself to explaining why basic particulars must be material bodies.

If material bodies have, as Strawson believes, a preconceptual existence as things, how do we identify them? For Strawson, the formal conditions for identifying any thing are satisfied if but a single individuating fact is known of it, something that is true of it and of nothing else (1965, 23 and 25). He then admits, however, that every possible individuating fact relates "the particular concerned . . . to other items in that unified framework of knowledge of particulars of which each of us has a part in his possession" (1965, 26–28). It is not too much to say that the term that functions for Hampshire as "this is a so-and-so" is represented here as performing its function by situating the entity in question among other entities, by operating, in short, as a disguised Relation. And how could it be otherwise? How could anything be grasped on its own? What would it even mean to say that it was? Shape, color, function, et cetera—all the qualities by which we know any thing—can only be grasped in their real relations to other similar and contrasting qualities (1965, 44–45).[2]

The objections raised by Hampshire and Strawson are really of two sorts and require different answers. The latter maintains that identification on the relational view cannot occur because, in actual practice, identification involves the use of particulars. But he then ascribes to these particulars an "identifiability dependence." Once it is admitted, however, that what really individuates such a particular is its unique relations with others, there is no longer any "factual" barrier to viewing its relations as being within the thing itself. It might even be argued that an analysis of the process of abstraction that satisfactorily accounts for individuation, in the manner of Dietzgen, inclines one to adopt this relational view. In any case, the fact that Strawson (with little or no real empirical study) finds that the people in his culture conceive of reality as divided into basic material bodies is no evidence that this is the only way it can be conceived. Their Oxford colleague, A. J. Ayer, makes a similar complaint when he accuses both Strawson and Hampshire of an "*a priori* anthropology, in assuming that certain fundamental features of our own conceptual system are necessities of language, which is the modern equivalent of thought" (1964, 33).[3]

Once again, what must be stressed is that the philosophy of internal relations is a matter of conception and not of fact. To strike at its factual basis one would have to show that the apparent interdependence of qualities or of what are taken as things is false, and this, of course, no one has attempted to do. The question, then, is—as between the commonsense and relational conceptions—which one do we adopt? If the analogy helps—do we view the bottle as half empty or half full? Neither answer is wrong; yet each carries its own implications. The main criterion that counts, or should count, in making this choice is the utility of each approach in solving and/or avoiding problems. This is the only fair standard by which to judge Marx's relational conception, but as a standard it can't be used until this conception has been "put to work."

2

For the moment, I am concerned with the serious problems raised by the philosophy of internal relations such that some modern thinkers have refused to admit that others could even hold such a view (while often attacking them at the same time for holding it). Here, Hampshire's objection occupies a central place, for if it is true that the relational view makes it impossible for a person to communicate the information he or she has in mind to someone else, then indeed we need go no further. Yet, what is the status of Hampshire's criticism— where does its certainty lie? If it is possible to conceive of things in terms of their relations, the question whether what is conceived in this manner can be communicated or not is an empirical one. And since one could only deny this possibility at the outset on the basis of an "*a priori* anthropology," Hampshire's judgment requires testing by experience. Thus, whether Marx's relational conceptions can be communicated is not for me to say at this time; my purpose is to communicate them. Later, others will tell me if I have succeeded and—only then—if it is possible to succeed.[4]

What has been said requires qualification in one important respect: any attempt to test the viability of the relational view using measures that have come out of another conceptual framework must be satisfied with general results. Once it is granted, for example, that Marx's conceptual scheme is not our own, the criticism that it does not succeed perfectly in conveying facts we have fashioned becomes, as Ayer rightly points out, "trivial." According to Ayer, "the work a language does depends upon its categorical structure, so that no language which differs radically from our own in this respect can be capable of doing exactly the same work" (1964, 34). Thus the very accusation that Marx is unable to communicate particulars cannot even be expressed on the relational view, where "particulars," as Hampshire understands them, do not exist and where "identity" is often used to register a relation between what many would consider disparate entities (see chapter 3).

Can Marx communicate what he wants to say despite this difference in conception? Ayer claims that a language that is structurally different from our own—and incapable of doing exactly the same work—may still convey "substantially the same information" (1964, 34). If this is so, it is on such generous criteria that we must judge Marx's success in communication. It is worth noting in this regard that Spinoza, Leibniz, and Hegel, who are roundly denounced for their adherence to the philosophy of internal relations, have all managed more or less to communicate their views. How else—taking only the most obvious example—are some modern thinkers able to criticize them for holding just these views?

What qualifies, in Marx's case, as "substantially the same information" can be divided into two areas: first, do we know when he is speaking about people, work, factories, government, et cetera? And second, do we know all that he means in such cases, that is, do we grasp all that he wants his concepts to convey? If despite Marx's relational view we generally know what he is talking about, it is because—as Dietzgen says—people, being what they are, conceptualize the same kinds of things from their shared world of sense impressions. Whether those things are then viewed as particulars or Relations, the basic information (the essential sense impressions) that each individual has an interest in communicating is the same. Thus the central features, or core relations, of any of Marx's conceptions will correspond more or less to what others who use the same term take as the thing proper.

The real problem, as we have seen, is whether Marx succeeds in communicating those additional features that his relational view permits him to append to these core notions. If there is any difficulty in understanding Marx, it is not a matter of knowing when he is talking about capital but grasping all that he makes a part of it on each occasion. Thus we can say that "capital" conveys "substantially the same information" as Hampshire's and, most likely, the reader's own concept of the same name in virtue of the core notion that all share, but that Marx intends his concept to convey something more than this. And again, whether Marx succeeds in making this additional meaning understood can only be judged in the last analysis by whether we succeed in understanding him.

3

Still another major objection that has been leveled against the philosophy of internal relations concerns what is considered the practical impossibility of conceiving of the whole in each of its parts. Ayer—appearing now for the opposition—simply ridicules Leibniz's notion that a true statement about any particular individual implies the whole of human history (1964, 32). As regards Marx's work, some critics, such as Heinrich Popitz, who have caught a glimpse of Marx's ability to view the whole in a part, treat their revelation as ipso facto a criticism (Popitz 1953, 113). Yet, on the other side, thinkers of the stature of Lukács and Sartre have recognized this aspect of Marx's thought and consider it one of his strengths (Lukács 1971, 170; Sartre 1963, 27–28). Are both sides in this debate speaking of the same thing?

Our commonsense conceptions of "whole" and "part" are derived from a view of the world in which the whole (any whole) is the sum of its parts, themselves separate and distinct units that have simply been added together (an external relation). The model and often the actual analogy in which we understand the whole is the spatial one of the closed circle. But the claim that the whole is involved in each of its parts does not make use of these ordinary-language conceptions; it could not at the risk of speaking nonsense. This is really the same problem dealt with above, when Hampshire dares those who subscribe to the philosophy of internal relations to identify particulars, where neither "identity" nor "particular" means the same thing to them as it does to Hampshire.

In this instance, what is referred to as a "part" is a relational construct, a unit abstracted from reality for some particular end whose interdependence with other similarly constituted units is kept clearly in view; and "whole" is just this interdependence, which, again for a special purpose, may be conceptualized within any of its parts. No exacting knowledge of particulars is required. No conceptual boundaries are violated. The world is not being forced into a gopher hole. It is simply that, on the basis of this philosophy, concepts of "part" and "whole" are acquired that allow one to speak of what is going on in this manner. Clearly, to grasp what is being said, one must first understand the relational view that fashions the concepts for saying it.

The difficulty, it may be argued, still remains; for how is it possible to conceive of even such a whole in one of its parts when the part is known and the whole, which by definition includes the future as well as the past, is not? But once it is conceded that we are dealing here with different conceptions of whole and part, one should be prepared to concede that the sense in which the former is viewed in the latter may also be unique. Only with a whole that is conceptualized as a sum of separate parts (as a closed circle), that is to say, on the commonsense view, are we dealing with something whose character appears finished and ultimately knowable in its entirety. However, as the expression of universal interdependence throughout time, the whole on the relational view is—as odd as this may sound—never completed, and no thinker in the tradition I outlined has pretended to know all the details.

This qualification does not restrict Hegel, Marx, Dietzgen, and others from viewing what they do know of the whole as relationally contained in whatever parts are treated for the moment as distinct units. What they do know includes not only the particular interactions they have observed but the patterns of change and development to which such phenomena give rise. When projected into the future as possibility, potential, probability, or certainty (depending on the writer and the "facts"), these patterns become elements of the unexperienced whole that are conceived of in the part under examination. It is in this manner, as Marcuse indicated earlier in our text, that the main concepts with which Marx treats capitalism already contain something of his views on communism. Some thinkers who subscribe to a philosophy of internal relations, such as Hegel, give this whole, which necessarily contains elements of which they are ignorant, a central role to play in their system. Others, like Marx, do not. For all of them, however, the whole is incomplete, and to that extent the part (any part) is also unknown.

In closing, I would like to stress that I am under no illusion that these brief remarks have successfully defended the philosophy of internal relations from its many hostile critics. My aim here, however, has not been to have Marx's relational conception accepted as much as to have it taken seriously. If, in the course of this discussion, I have raised doubts regarding the validity or relevance of criticisms that suggest that this view is unworthy of scholarly attention, I would consider my job done. If it leads further to a more thorough study of this philosophy than I have been able to undertake, I would consider my efforts well rewarded.

Notes

1. According to Hampshire, failure to comply with this requirement of communicability results in not having any means of pinpointing something, nor of recognizing it, nor of saying what makes it what it is, nor of contradicting a statement in which it appears, nor of investigating its history, nor of distinguishing between truth and falsity (1959, 18ff.).

2. Strawson's discussion of "sophisticated" and "unsophisticated" particulars is another indication of the degree to which he relies on internal relations to bolster his argument against the existence of such relations (1965, 44–45).

3. Ayer continues: "Thus, it may be maintained that it is possible for there to be a language which does not recognize the distinction between particulars and universals, or that physical objects must of necessity be the primary particulars in any universe of discourse which is comparable to our own" (1964, 33). This is a helpful warning against closing our minds to new uses of language by making a priori assumptions from our own use of language as to what must be the case.

4. For a useful account of the difficulty thinkers in the British empiricist tradition have in coming to grips with Marx's epistemology, see Charles Taylor's "Marxism and Empiricism" (1966, 233ff.). Empiricists hold that knowledge consists of impressions made on our minds by the external world and that the form of these impressions is necessarily the same for all people. On this view, what we know about the world is entirely built upon these impressions, conception coming after perception. Consequently, different ways of viewing the world are thought to be reducible to the perceptible units that are the basic elements in each. But if conceptualization occurs at the time of perception, then the units into which we break down different worldviews are not commensurable. Thinking that they are makes it difficult to admit that Marx—unlike most of us—actually conceived of each element in the real world, upon perception, as a Relation.

STEP 3

CHAPTER 5

Putting Dialectics to Work: The Process of Abstraction in Marx's Method

The Problem: How to Think Adequately about Change and Interaction

Is there any part of Marxism that has received more abuse than his dialectical method? And I am not just thinking about enemies of Marxism and socialism but also about scholars who are friendly to both. It is not Karl Popper but George Sorel, in his Marxist incarnation, who refers to dialectics as "the art of reconciling opposites through hocus pocus" (1950, 171) and the English socialist economist Joan Robinson who, on reading *Capital,* objects to the constant intrusion of "Hegel's nose" between her and Ricardo (1953, 23). But perhaps the classic complaint is fashioned by the American philosopher William James, who compares reading about dialectics in Hegel—it could just as well have been Marx—to getting sucked into a whirlpool (1978, 174).

Yet other thinkers have considered Marx's dialectical method among his most important contributions to socialist theory, and Lukács goes so far as to claim that orthodox Marxism relies solely upon adherence to his method (1971, 1). Though Lukács may be exaggerating to make his point, it is not—in my view—by very much. The reasons for such widespread disagreement on the meaning and value of dialectics are many, but what stands out is the inadequate attention given to the nature of its subject matter. What, in other words, is dialectics about? What questions does it deal with, and why are they important? Until there is more clarity, if not consensus, on its basic task, treatises on dialectics will only succeed in piling one layer of obscurity upon another. So this is where we must begin.

First and foremost, and stripped of all qualifications added by this or that dialectician, the subject of dialectics is change, all change, and interaction, all kinds and degrees of interaction. This is not to say that dialectical thinkers recognize the existence of change and interaction while nondialectical thinkers do not. That would be foolish. Everyone recognizes that everything in the world changes, somehow and to some degree, and that the same holds true for interaction. The problem is how to think adequately about them, how to capture them in thought. How, in other words, can we think about change and interaction so as not to miss or distort the real changes and interactions that we know, in a general way at least, are there (with all the implications this has for how to study them and to communicate what we find to others)? This is the key problem addressed by dialectics, this is what all dialectics is about, and it is in helping to resolve this problem that Marx turns to the process of abstraction.

The Solution Lies in the Process of Abstraction

In his most explicit statement on the subject, Marx claims that his method starts from the "real concrete" (the world as it presents itself to us) and proceeds through "abstraction" (the intellectual activity of breaking this whole down into the mental units with which we think about it) to the "thought concrete" (the reconstituted and now understood whole present in the mind) (1904, 293–94). The real concrete is simply the world in which we live, in all its complexity. The thought concrete is Marx's reconstruction of that world in the theories of what has come to be called "Marxism." The royal road to understanding is said to pass from the one to the other through the process of abstraction.

In one sense, the role Marx gives to abstraction is simple recognition of the fact that all thinking about reality begins by breaking it down into manageable parts. Reality may be in one piece when lived, but to be thought about and communicated it must be parceled out. Our minds can no more swallow the world whole at one sitting than can our stomachs. Everyone then, and not only Marx and Marxists, begins the task of trying to make sense of his or her surroundings by distinguishing certain features and focusing on and organizing them in ways deemed appropriate. "Abstract" comes from the Latin abstrahere, which means "to pull from." In effect, a piece has been pulled from or taken out of the whole and is temporarily perceived as standing apart.

We "see" only some of what lies in front of us, "hear" only part of the noises in our vicinity, "feel" only a small part of what our body is in contact with, et cetera, through the rest of our senses. In each case, a focus is established and a kind of boundary set within our perceptions distinguishing what is relevant from what is not. It should be clear that "What did you see?" (What caught your eye?) is a different question from "What did you *actually* see?" (What came into your line of vision?). Likewise, in thinking about any subject, we focus on only some of its qualities and relations. Much that could be included—that may in fact be included in another person's view or thought and may on another occasion be included in our own—is left out. The mental activity involved in establishing such boundaries, whether conscious or unconscious—though it is usually an amalgam of both—is the process of abstraction.

Responding to a mixture of influences that includes the material world and our experiences in it as well as to personal wishes, group interests, and other social constraints, it is the process of abstraction that establishes the specificity of the objects with which we interact. In setting boundaries, in ruling this far and no further, it is what makes something one (or two, or more) of a kind and lets us know where that kind begins and ends. With this decision as to units, we also become committed to a particular set of relations between them—relations made possible and even necessary by the qualities that we have included in each—a register for classifying them and a mode for explaining them.

In listening to a concert, for example, we often concentrate on a single instrument or recurring theme and then redirect our attention elsewhere. Each time this occurs, the whole music alters, new patterns emerge, and each sound takes on a different value. How we understand the music is largely determined by how we abstract it. The same applies to what we focus on when watching a play, whether on a person, a combination of persons, or a section of the stage. The meaning of the play and what more is required to explore or test that meaning alters, often dramatically, with each new abstraction. In this way, too, how we abstract literature, where we draw the boundaries, determines what works and what parts of each work will be studied, with what methods, in relation to what other subjects, in what order, and even by whom. Abstracting literature to include its audience, for example, leads to a sociology of literature, while an abstraction of literature that excludes everything but its forms calls forth various structural approaches, and so on.

From what has been said so far, it is clear that "abstraction" is itself an abstraction. I have abstracted it from Marx's dialectical method, which in turn was abstracted from his broad theories, which in turn were abstracted from his life and work. The mental activities that we have collected and brought into focus as "abstraction" are more often associated with the processes of perception, conception, defining, remembering, dreaming, reasoning, and even thinking. It is not surprising, therefore, if the process of abstraction strikes many people as both foreign and familiar at the same time. Each of these more familiar processes operates in part by separating out, focusing, and putting emphasis on only some aspects of that reality with which they come into contact. In "abstraction" we have simply separated out, focused, and put emphasis on certain common features of these other processes. Abstracting "abstraction" in this way is neither easy nor obvious, and therefore relatively few people have done it. Consequently, though everyone abstracts, of necessity, only a few are aware of it as such. This philosophical impoverishment is reinforced by the fact that most people are lazy abstractors, simply and uncritically accepting the mental units with which they think as part of their cultural inheritance.

A further complication in grasping "abstraction" arises from the fact that Marx uses the term in four different, though closely related, senses. First and most important, it refers to the mental activity of subdividing the world into the mental constructs with which we think about it, which is the process that we have been describing. Second, it refers to the results of this process, the actual parts into which reality has been apportioned. That is to say, for Marx, as for Hegel before him, "abstraction" functions as a noun as well as a verb, the noun referring to what the verb has brought into being. In these senses, everyone can be said to abstract (verb) and to think with abstractions (noun). But Marx also uses "abstraction" in a third sense, where it refers to a suborder of particularly ill-fitting mental constructs. Whether because they are too narrow, take in too little, focus too exclusively on appearances, or are otherwise badly composed, these constructs do not allow an adequate grasp of their subject matter.

Taken in this third sense, abstractions are the basic unit of ideology, the inescapable ideational result of living and working in alienated society. "Freedom," for example, is said to be such an abstraction whenever we remove the real individual from "the conditions of existence within which these individuals enter into contact" (Marx 1973, 164). Omitting the conditions that make freedom possible (or impossible)—including the real alternatives available, the role of money, the socialization of the person choosing, et cetera—from the meaning of "freedom" leaves a notion that can only distort and obfuscate even that part of reality it sets out to convey. A lot of Marx's criticism of ideology makes use of this sense of "abstraction."

Finally, Marx uses the term "abstraction" in a fourth still different sense, where it refers to a particular organization of elements in the real world—having to do with the functioning of capitalism—that provides the objective underpinnings for most of the ideological abstractions mentioned above. Abstractions in this fourth sense exist in the world and not, as in the case with the other three, in the mind. In these abstractions, certain spatial and temporal boundaries and connections stand out, just as others are obscure and even invisible, making what is in practice inseparable appear separate and the historically specific features of things disappear behind their more general forms. It is in this way that labor, commodities, value, money, capital, profit, rent, interest, and wage-labor are likely to be misconstrued from the start. Marx labels these objective results of capitalist functioning "real abstractions," and it is chiefly real abstractions that incline the people who have contact with them to construct ideological abstractions. It is also real abstractions to which he is referring when he says that in capitalist society "people are governed by abstractions" (1973, 164). Such remarks, however, must not keep us from seeing that Marx also abstracts in the first sense given above and, like everyone else, thinks with abstractions in the second sense, and that the particular way in which he does both goes a long way in accounting for the distinctive character of Marxism.

Despite several explicit remarks on the centrality of abstraction in Marx's work, the process of abstraction has received relatively little attention in the literature on Marxism. Serious work on Marx's dialectical method can usually be distinguished on the basis of which of the categories belonging to the vocabulary of dialectics is treated as pivotal. For Lukács, it is the concept of "totality" that plays this role (1971); for Mao, it is "contradiction" (1968); for Raya Dunayevskaya, it is the "negation of negation" (1982); for Scott Meikle, it is "essence" (1985); and for the Ollman of *Alienation*, it is "internal relations" (1971). Even when abstraction is discussed—and no serious work dismisses it altogether—the main emphasis is usually on what it is in capitalism that is responsible for the particular abstractions made, and not on the process of abstraction as such and on what exactly Marx does and how he does it.[1] Consequently, the implications of Marx's abstracting practice for the theories of Marxism remain clouded, and those wishing to develop these theories and where necessary revise them receive little help in their efforts to abstract in the manner of Marx. In what follows, it is just this process of abstraction, how it works and particularly how Marx works it, that serves as the centerpiece for our discussion of dialectics.

After describing how Marx's abstractions differ from those of most other people, we will go on to examine the underlying philosophy of internal relations that allowed and even required him to abstract in this manner along with some of the criticisms that this philosophy has occasioned. The rest of the chapter is devoted to the three kinds of boundary setting and focusing involved in establishing the units out of which Marx constructed his major theories. My aim here is not only to show what Marx does and how he does it but how we—if we wish—can do as much. An attempt to relate the one-sided use of Marx's abstractions to some of the major debates over the meaning of Marxism will serve as my conclusion.

How Marx's Abstractions Differ

What, then, is distinctive about Marx's abstractions? To begin with, it should be clear that Marx's abstractions do not and cannot diverge completely from the abstractions of other thinkers both then and now. There has to be a lot of overlap. Otherwise, he would have constructed what philosophers call a "private language," and any communication between him and the rest of us would be impossible. How close Marx came to falling into this abyss and what can be done to repair some of the damage already done are questions I hope to deal with in a later work. Second, in depicting Marx's process of abstraction as a predominantly conscious and rational activity, I do not mean to deny the enormous degree to which what results accurately reflects the real world. However, the realist foundations of Marx's thinking are sufficiently (though by no means adequately) understood to be taken for granted here while we concentrate on the process of abstraction as such.[2]

Keeping these two qualifications clearly in mind, we can now say that what is most distinctive about Marx's abstractions, taken as a group, is that they focus on and incorporate both change and interaction (or system) in the particular forms in which these occur in the capitalist era. It is important to underline from the start that Marx's main concern was with capitalism. He sought to discover what it is and how it works as well as how it emerged and where it is tending. We shall call the organic and historical processes involved here the double movement of the capitalist mode of production. Each movement affects the other, and how one grasps either affects one's understanding of both. But how does one study the history of a system or the systemic functioning of evolving processes where the main determinants of change lie within the system itself? For Marx, the first and most important step was to incorporate the general form of what he was looking for—to wit, change and interaction—into all the abstractions he constructed as part of his research. Marx's understanding of capitalism, therefore, is not restricted to the theories of Marxism, which relate the components of the capitalist system, but some large part of it is found within the very abstractions with which these theories have been constructed.

Beginning with historical movement, Marx's preoccupation with change and development is undisputed. What is less known, chiefly because it is less clear, is how he thought about change, how he abstracted it, and how he integrated these abstractions into his study of a changing world. The underlying problem is as old as philosophy itself. The ancient Greek philosopher Heraclitus provides us with its classic statement when he asserts that a person cannot step into the same river twice. Enough water has flowed between the two occasions so that the river we step into the second time is not the same river we walked into earlier. Yet our common sense tells us that it is, and our naming practice reflects this view. The river is still called the "Hudson," or the "Rhine," or the "Ganges." Heraclitus, of course, was not interested in rivers but in change. His point is that change goes on everywhere and all the time, but that our manner of thinking about it is sadly inadequate. The flow, the constant alteration of movement away from something and toward something else, is generally missing. Usually, where change takes place very slowly or in small increments, its impact can be safely neglected. Depending on the context and on our purpose in it, however, even such change—because it occurs outside our attention—may occasionally startle us and have grave consequences for our lives.

Even today few are able to think about the changes they know to be happening in ways that don't distort—usually by underplaying—what is actually going on. From the titles of so many works in the social sciences it would appear that a good deal of effort is being directed to studying change of one kind or another. But what is actually taken as "change" in most of these works? It is not the continuous evolution and alteration that goes on in their subject matter, the social equivalent of the flowing water in Heraclitus's river. Rather, almost invariably it is a comparison of two or more differentiated states in the development of the object or condition or group under examination. As the sociologist James Coleman, who defends this approach, admits, "The concept of change in science is a rather special one, for it does not immediately follow from our sense impressions. . . . It is based on a comparison, or difference between two sense impressions, and simultaneously a comparison of the times at which the sense impressions occurred." Why? Because, according to Coleman, "the concept of change must, as any concept, itself reflect a state of an object at a point in time" (1968, 429). Consequently, a study of the changes in the political thinking of the American electorate, for example, gets translated into an account of how people voted (or responded to opinion polls) in 1956, 1960, 1964, et cetera, and the differences found in a comparison of these static moments is what is called "change." It is not simply, and legitimately, that the one, the difference between the moments, gets taken as an indication of or evidence for the other, the process; rather, it stands in for the process itself.

In contrast to this approach, Marx sets out to abstract things, in his words, "as they really are and happen," making how they happen part of what they are (Marx and Engels 1964, 57). Hence, capital (or labor, or money) is not only how capital appears and functions but also how it develops; or rather, how it develops, its real history, is also part of what it is. It is also in this sense that Marx could deny that nature and history "are two separate things" (Marx and Engels 1964, 57). In the view that currently dominates the social sciences, things exist *and* undergo change. The two are logically distinct. History is something that happens to things; it is not part of their nature. Hence, the difficulty of examining change in subjects from which it has been removed at the start. Whereas Marx, as he tells us, abstracts "every historical social form as in fluid movement, and therefore takes into account its transient nature *not less* than its momentary existence" (1958, 20 [emphasis added]).

But history for Marx refers not only to time past but to time future. So that whatever something is becoming—whether we know what that will be or not— is in some important respects part of what it is along with what it once was. For example, capital, for Marx, is not simply the material means of production used to produce wealth, which is how it is abstracted in the work of most economists. Rather, it includes the early stages in the development of these particular means of production, or "primitive accumulation," indeed, whatever has made it possible for it to produce the kind of wealth it does in just the way it does (namely, permits wealth to take the form of value, something produced not because it is useful but for purposes of exchange). Furthermore, as part of its becoming, capital incorporates the accumulation of capital that is occurring now together with its tendency toward concentration and centralization and the effect of this tendency on both the development of a world market and an eventual transition to socialism. According to Marx, the tendency to expand surplus-value and with it production, and therefore to create a world market, is "directly given in the concept of capital itself" (1973, 408).

That capital contains the seeds of a future socialist society is also apparent in its increasingly socialized character and in the growing separation of the material means of production from the direct control of capitalists, making the latter even more superfluous than they already are. This "history" of capital is part of capital, contained within the abstraction that Marx makes of capital, and part of what he wants to convey with its covering concept. All of Marx's main abstractions—labor, value, commodity, money, et cetera—incorporate process, becoming, history in just this way. Our purpose here is not to explain Marx's political economy but simply to use some of his claims in this area to illustrate how he integrates what most readers would take to be externally related phenomena, in this case its real past and likely future, into his abstraction of its present form.

Marx often uses the qualifying phrase "in itself" to indicate the necessary and internal ties between the future development of anything and how it presents itself at this moment. Money and commodity, for example, are referred to as "in themselves" capital (1963, 396). Given the independent forms in which they confront the worker in capitalist society—something separate from the worker but something he or she must acquire in order to survive—money and commodity ensure the exchange of labor power and through it their own transformation into means of production used to produce new value. Capital is part of what they are becoming, part of their future, and hence part of them, just as money and commodity as parts of what capital once was are also parts of what it is now. Elsewhere, Marx refers to money and commodity as "potential capital" (1971, 465), as capital "only in intention, in their essence, in what they were destined to be" (1963, 399–400). Similarly, all labor is abstracted as wage-labor and all means of production as capital, because this is the direction in which they are evolving in capitalist society (1963, 409–10).

To consider the past and likely future development of anything as integral to what it is, to grasp this whole as a single process, does not keep Marx from abstracting out some part or instant of this process for a particular purpose and from treating it as relatively autonomous. Aware that the units into which he has subdivided reality are the results of his abstractions, Marx is able to reabstract this reality, restricting the area brought into focus in line with the requirements of his current study. But when he does this, he often underscores its character as a temporally stable part of a larger and ongoing process by referring to it as a "moment." In this way, commodity is spoken of as a "moment in exchange," money (in its aspect as capital) as a "moment" in the process of production, and circulation in general as a "moment in the system of production" (1973, 145 and 217). Marx's naming practice here reflects the epistemological priority he gives to movement over stability, so that stability—whenever it is found—is viewed as temporary and/or only apparent, or, as he says on one occasion, as a "paralysis" of movement (1971, 212). With stability used to qualify change rather than the reverse, Marx—unlike most modern social scientists—did not and could not study why things change (with the implication that change is external to what they are, something that happens to them). Given that change is always a part of what things are, his research problem could only be how, when, and into what they change and why they sometimes appear not to (ideology).

Before concluding our discussion of the place of change in Marx's abstractions, it is worth noting that thinking in terms of processes is not altogether alien to common sense. It occurs in abstractions of actions, such as eating, walking, fighting, et cetera, indeed, whenever the gerund form of the verb is used. Likewise, event words, such as "war" and "strike," indicate that to some degree at least the processes involved have been abstracted as such. On the other hand, it is also possible to think of war and strike as a state or condition, more like a photo than a motion picture, or if the latter, then a single scene that gets shown again and again, which removes or seriously underplays whatever changes are taking place. And unfortunately, the same is true of most action verbs. They become action "things." In such cases, the real processes that go on do not get reflected—certainly not to any adequate degree—in our thinking about them. It is my impression that in the absence of any commitment to bring change itself into focus, in the manner of Marx, this is the more typical outcome.

Earlier we said that what distinguishes Marx's abstractions is that they contain not only change or history but also some portion of the system in which it occurs. Since change in anything only takes place in and through a complex interaction between internally related elements, treating change as intrinsic to what anything is requires that we treat the interaction through which it occurs in the same way. With a static notion of anything it is easy to conceive of it as also discrete, logically independent of, and easily separable from its surrounding conditions. They do not enter directly into what it is, while viewing the same thing as a process makes it necessary to extend the boundaries of what it is to include at least some part of the surrounding conditions that enter into this process. In sum, as far as abstractions are concerned, change brings mutual dependence in its wake. Instead of a mere sequence of events isolated from their context, a kind of one-note development, Marx's abstractions become phases of an evolving and interactive system.

Hence, capital, which we examined earlier as a process, is also a complex Relation encompassing the interaction between the material means of production, capitalists, workers, value, commodity, money, and more—and all this over time. Marx says, "the concept of capital contains the capitalist" (1973, 512); he refers to workers as "variable capital" (1958, 209) and says that capital is "nothing without wage-labor, value, money, price, etc." (1904, 292). Elsewhere, the "processual" character of these aspects of the capital Relation is emphasized in referring to them as "value in process" and "money in process" (1971, 137). If capital, like all other important abstractions in Marxism, is both a process and a Relation, viewing it as primarily one or the other could only be a way of emphasizing either its historical or systemic character for a particular purpose.

As in his abstractions of capital as a process, so too in his abstractions of it as a Relation, Marx can focus on but part of what capital contains. While the temporally isolated part of a process is generally referred to as a "moment," the spatially isolated aspect of a Relation is generally referred to as a "form" or "determination." With "form," Marx usually brings into focus the appearance and/ or function of any Relation, that by which we recognize it, and most often it is its form that is responsible for the concept by which we know and communicate it. Hence, value (a Relation) in its exchangeable form is called "money," while in the form in which it facilitates the production of more value, it is called "capital," et cetera. "Determination," on the other hand, enables Marx to focus on the transformational character of any relational part, on what best brings out its mutual dependence and changeability within the interactive system. Upon analysis, moments, forms, and determinations all turn out to be Relations. So that after referring to the commodity as a moment in wealth, Marx immediately proceeds to pick it apart as a Relation (1973, 218). Elsewhere, he refers to interest, profit, and rent as forms that through analysis lose their "apparent independence" and are seen to be Relations (1971, 429).

Earlier, we saw that some abstractions that contain processes could also be found in what we called common sense. The same is true of abstractions that focus on Relations. Father, which contains the relation between a man and a child, is one. Buyer, which contains the relations between a person and something sold or available for sale, is another. But compared to the number and scope of relations in the world, such examples are few and meager in their import. Within the common sense of our time and place, most social ties are thought about in abstractions that focus on the parts one at a time, separately as well as statically. Marx, however, believes that in order to adequately grasp the systemic connections that constitute such an important part of reality one has to incorporate them—along with the ways in which they change—into the very abstractions in and with which one thinks about them. All else is make-do patchwork, a one-sided, lopsided way of thinking that invites the neglect of essential connections together with the distortion of whatever influence they exert on the overall system.

Where have we arrived? Marx's abstractions are not things but processes. These processes are also, of necessity, systemic Relations in which the main processes with which Marx deals are all implicated. Consequently, each process serves as an aspect, or subordinate part, of other processes, grasped as clusters of relations, just as they do in it. In this way, Marx brings what we have called the double movement of the capitalist mode of production (its history and organic movement) together in the same abstractions, uniting in his thinking what is united in reality. And whenever he needs to focus on but part of this complex, he does so as a moment, a form or a determination.

Marx's abstractions seem to be very different, especially as regards the treatment of change and interaction, from those in which most people think about society. But if Marx's abstractions stand out as much as our evidence suggests they do, it is not enough to display them. We also need to know what gives Marx the philosophical license to abstract as he does. Whence comes his apparent facility in making and changing abstractions? And what is the relation between his abstractions and those of common sense? It is because most readers cannot see how Marx could possibly abstract as he does that they continue to deny—and perhaps not even notice—the widespread evidence of his practice. Therefore, before making a more detailed analysis of Marx's process of abstraction and its place and role in his dialectical method and broader theories, a brief detour through his philosophical presuppositions is in order.

The Philosophy of Internal Relations

According to Marx, "The economists do not conceive of capital as a Relation. They cannot do so without at the same time conceiving of it as a historical transitory, i.e., a relative—not an absolute—form of production" (1971, 274). This is not a comment about the content of capital, about what it is, but about the *kind* of thing it is—to wit, a Relation. To grasp capital, as Marx does, as a complex Relation that has at its core internal ties between the material means of production and those who own them, those who work on them, their special product, value, and the conditions in which owning and working go on is to know capital as a historical event, as something that emerged as a result of specific conditions in the lifetime of real people and that will disappear when these conditions do. Viewing such connections as external to what capital is—which, for them, is simply the material means of production or money used to buy such—the economists fall into treating capital as an ahistorical variable. Without saying so explicitly and certainly without ever explicitly defending this position, capital becomes something that has always been and will always be.

The view held by most people, scholars and others, in what we've been calling the commonsense view, maintains that there are things and there are relations and that neither can be subsumed in the other. This position is summed up in Bishop Butler's statement, which G. E. Moore adopts as a motto: "Everything is what it is, and not another thing" (1903, title page), taken in conjunction with Hume's claim, "All events seem entirely loose and separate" (1955, 85). On this view, capital may be found to have relations with labor, value, et cetera, and it may even be that accounting for such relations plays an important role in explaining what capital is; but capital is one thing, and its relations are quite another. Marx, however, follows Hegel's lead in this matter and rejects what is, in essence, a logical dichotomy. For him, as we have seen, capital is itself a Relation in which the ties of the material means of production to labor, value, commodity, et cetera, are interiorized as parts of what capital is. Marx refers to "things themselves" as "their interconnections" (Marx and Engels 1950, 488). Moreover, these relations extend backward and forward in time, so that capital's conditions of existence as they have evolved over the years and its potential for future development are also viewed as parts of what it is.

On the commonsense view, any element related to capital can change without capital itself changing. Workers, for example, instead of selling their labor-power to capitalists, as occurs in capitalism, could become slaves, or serfs, or owners of their own means of production, and in every case their instruments of work would still be capital. The tie between workers and the means of production here is contingent, a matter of chance, and therefore external to what each really is. In Marx's view, a change of this sort would mean a change in the character of capital itself, in its appearance and/or functioning no matter how far extended. The tie is a necessary and essential one; it is an internal relation. Hence, where its specific relationship to workers has changed, the means of production become something else, something that is best captured by a concept other than "capital." Every element that comes into Marx's analysis of capitalism is a Relation of this sort. It is this view that underlies and helps explain his practice of abstraction and the particular abstractions that result, along with all the theories raised on them.

It appears that the problem non-Marxists have in understanding Marx is much more profound than is ordinarily thought. It is not simply that they don't grasp what Marx is saying about capital (or labor, or value, or the state) because his account is unclear or confused, or that the evidence for his claims is weak or undeveloped. Rather, it is that the basic form, the Relation, in which Marx thinks about each of the major elements that come into his analysis is unavailable, and therefore its ideational content is necessarily misrepresented, if only a little (though usually it is much more). As an attempt to reflect the relations in capitalist society by incorporating them into its core abstractions, Marxism suffers the same distorting fate as these relations themselves.

In the history of ideas, the view that we have been developing is known as the philosophy of internal relations. Marx's immediate philosophical influences in this regard were Leibniz, Spinoza, and particularly Hegel. What all had in common is the belief that the relations that come together to make up the whole get expressed in what are taken to be its parts. Each part is viewed as incorporating in what it is all its relations with other parts up to and including everything that comes into the whole. To be sure, each of these thinkers had a distinctive view of what the parts are. For Leibniz, it was monads; for Spinoza, modes of nature or God; and for Hegel, ideas. But the logical form in which they construed the relation between parts and the whole was the same.

Some writers on Marx have argued for a restricted form of internal relations that would apply only to society and not to the natural world (Rader 1979, chap. 2). But reality doesn't allow such absolute distinctions. People have bodies as well as minds and social roles. Alienation, for example, affects all three, and in their alienated forms each is internally related to the others. Likewise, capital, commodities, money, and the forces of production all have material as well as social aspects. To maintain that the philosophy of internal relations does not respect the usual boundaries between nature and society does not mean that Marx cannot for certain purposes abstract units that fall primarily or even wholly on one or the other side of this divide. Whenever he speaks of a "thing" or, as is more frequent, of "social relations," this is what occurs, but in every case what has been momentarily put aside is internally related to what has been brought into focus. Consequently, he is unlikely to minimize or dismiss, as many operating with external relations do, the influences of either natural or social phenomena on the other.

What is the place of such notions as "cause" and "determine" within a philosophy of internal relations? Given the mutual interaction Marx assumes between everything in reality, now and forever, there can be no cause that is logically prior to and independent of that to which it is said to give rise and no determining factor that is itself not affected by that which it is said to determine. In short, the commonsense notions of "cause" and "determine" that are founded on such logical independence and absolute priority do not and cannot apply. In their stead we find frequent claims of the following kind: the propensity to exchange is the "cause or reciprocal effect" of the division of labor, and interest and rent "determine" market prices and "are determined" by it (Marx 1959b, 134; 1971, 512). In any organic system viewed over time, all the processes evolve together. Hence, no process comes first, and each one can be said to determine and be determined by the others. However, it is also the case that one process often has a greater effect on others than they do on it, and Marx also uses "cause" and especially "determine" to register this asymmetry. Thus, in the interaction between production, distribution, exchange, and consumption—particularly though not exclusively in capitalism—production is held to be more determining (1904, 274ff.). A good deal of Marx's research is devoted to locating and mapping whatever exercises a greater or special impact on other parts of the capitalist system, but, whether made explicit or not, this always takes place on a backdrop of reciprocal effect. (Another complementary sense of "cause" and "determine" will be presented later.)

Returning to the process of abstraction, it is the philosophy of internal relations that gives Marx both license and opportunity to abstract as freely as he does, to decide how far into its internal relations any particular will extend. Making him aware of the need to abstract—since boundaries are never given and when established never absolute—it also allows and even encourages reabstraction, makes a variety of abstractions possible, and helps to develop his mental skills and flexibility in making abstractions. If "a relation," as Marx maintains, "can obtain a particular embodiment and become individualized only by means of abstraction," then learning how to abstract is the first step in learning how to think (1973, 142).

Operating with a philosophy of external relations doesn't absolve others from the need to abstract. The units in and with which one thinks are still abstractions and products of the process of abstraction as it occurs during socialization and, particularly, in the acquisition of language. Only, in this case, one takes boundaries as given in the nature of reality as such, as if they have the same ontological stature as the qualities perceived. The role played by the process of

abstraction is neither known nor appreciated. Consequently, there is no awareness that one can—and often should—reabstract, and the ability and flexibility
for doing so is never acquired. Whatever reabstraction goes on, of necessity, as
part of learning new languages or new schools of thought or as a result of important new experiences, takes place in the dark, usually unconsciously, certainly
unsystematically, and with little understanding of either assumptions or implications. Marx, on the other hand, is fully aware that he abstracts and of its
assumptions and implications both for his own thinking and that of others—
hence the frequent equation of ideology in those he criticizes with their inadequate abstractions.

In order to forestall possible misunderstandings it may be useful to assert that
the philosophy of internal relations is not an attempt to reify "what lies between." It is simply that the particular ways in which things cohere become essential attributes of what they are. The philosophy of internal relations also does
not mean—as some of its critics have charged—that investigating any problem
can go on forever (to say that boundaries are artificial is not to deny them an
existence, and, practically speaking, it is simply not necessary to understand
everything in order to understand anything); or that the boundaries that are
established are arbitrary (what actually influences the character of Marx's or
anyone else's abstractions is another question); or that we cannot mark or work
with some of the important objective distinctions found in reality (on the contrary, such distinctions are a major influence on the abstractions we do make);
or, finally, that the vocabulary associated with the philosophy of internal relations—particularly "totality," "relation," and "identity"—cannot also be used
in subsidiary senses to refer to the world that comes into being after the process of abstraction has done its work.

In the philosophy of internal relations, "totality" is a logical construct that
refers to the way the whole is present through internal relations in each of its
parts. Totality, in this sense, is always there, and adjectives like "more" and "less"
don't apply. But Marx's work also contains constructed or emergent totalities,
which are of a historical nature, and great care must be taken not to confuse the
two. In the latter case, a totality, or whole, or system is built up gradually as its
elements emerge, cohere, and develop over time. "The circumstances under
which a relation occurs for the first time," Marx says, "by no means shows us
that relation either in its purity or in its totality" (1971, 205). Here, too, unlike
logical totalities, some systems can be said to be more or less complete than
others, or than itself at an earlier stage. There is nothing in the philosophy of
internal relations that interferes with the recognition of such totalities. All that
is required is that at every stage in its emergence each part be viewable as a relational microcosm of the whole, including its real history and potential for
future development.

The advantages of using any relational part as a starting point for reconstructing the interconnections of the whole, of treating it as a logical totality, will in-

crease, of course, as its social role grows and its ties with other parts become more complex, as it becomes, in other words, more of an emergent totality. One would not expect the commodity, for example, to serve as a particularly useful starting place from which to reconstruct slave society or feudalism, where it exists but only on the fringes (to the extent that there is some wage-labor and/ or some trade between different communities), but it offers an ideal starting place from which to reconstruct the capitalist system in which it plays a central role (Marx 1971, 102–3).

A somewhat similar problem exists with the concept of "relation." Perhaps no word appears more frequently in Marx's writings than *Verhältnis* (relation). The crucial role played by *Verhältnis* in Marx's thinking is somewhat lost to non-German-language readers of his works as a result of translations that often substitute "condition," "system," and "structure" for "relation." *Verhältnis* is usually used by Marx in the sense given to it by the philosophy of internal relations, where parts such as capital, labor, et cetera, are said to be Relations containing within themselves the very interactions to which they belong. But Marx also uses *Verhältnis* as a synonym for *Beziehung* (connection), as a way of referring to ties between parts that are momentarily viewed as separate. Taken in this sense, two parts can be more or less closely related, have different relations at different times, and have their relations distorted or even broken. These are, of course, all important distinctions, and it should be obvious that none of them are foreign to Marx's writings. Yet, if the parts are themselves Relations, in the sense of internal relations, possessing the same logical character no matter what changes they undergo, it would seem that such distinctions could not be made. And, indeed, this belief lies behind a lot of the criticism directed at the philosophy of internal relations.

The two different senses of "relation" found in Marx's writings, however, simply reflect two different orders of relation in his understanding. The first comes out of his philosophy of internal relations and applies to how he views anything. The second is of a practical, empirical sort and applies to what is actually found between two or more elements (each also Relations in the first sense) that are presently viewed as separate. How Marx separates out parts that are conceived of as logically internal to one another is, of course, the work of the process of abstraction. Once abstracted, all manner of relations between these parts can be noted and are in fact noted whenever relevant. Refusing to take the boundaries that organize our world as given and natural, the philosophy of internal relations admits a practice of abstraction that allows for an even greater variety of second-order relations than exists on the commonsense view.

Three Modes of Abstraction: Extension

Once we recognize the crucial role abstraction plays in Marx's method, how different his own abstractions are, and how often and easily he reabstracts, it becomes clear that Marx constructs his subject matter as much as he finds it. This is not to belittle the influence of natural and social (particularly capitalist) conditions on Marx's thinking but rather to stress how, given this influence, the results of his investigations are prescribed to a large degree by the preliminary organization of his subject matter. Nothing is made up of whole cloth, but at the same time Marx only finds what his abstractions have placed in his way. These abstractions do not substitute for the facts but give them a form, an order, and a relative value, just as frequently changing his abstractions does not take the place of empirical research but does determine, albeit in a weak sense, what he will look for, even see, and of course emphasize. What counts as an explanation is likewise determined by the framework of possible relationships imposed by Marx's initial abstractions.

So far we have been discussing the process of abstraction in general, our main aim being to distinguish it from other mental activities. Marx's own abstractions were said to stand out in so far as they invariably include elements of change and interaction, while his practice of abstracting was found to include more or less of each as suited his immediate purpose. Taking note of the importance Marx gives to abstractions in his critique of ideology, we proceeded to its underpinnings in the philosophy of internal relations, emphasizing that it is not a matter of this philosophy making such moves possible—since everybody abstracts—but of making them easier and enabling Marx to acquire greater control over the process. What remains is to analyze in greater detail what actually occurs when Marx abstracts and to trace its results and implications for some of his major theories.

The process of abstraction, which we have been treating as an undifferentiated mental act, has three main aspects or modes, which are also its functions vis-à-vis the part abstracted, on the one hand, and the system to which the part belongs and that it in turn helps to shape, on the other hand. That is, the boundary setting and bringing into focus that lies at the core of this process occurs simultaneously in three different, though closely related, senses. These senses have to do with extension, level of generality, and vantage point. First, each abstraction can be said to achieve a certain extension in the part abstracted, and this applies both spatially and temporally. In abstracting boundaries in space, limits are set in the mutual interaction that occurs at a given point of time. While in abstracting boundaries in time, limits are set in the distinctive history and potential development of any part, in what it once was and is yet to become. Most of our examples of abstraction so far have been drawn from what we shall now call "abstraction of extension."

Second, at the same time that every act of abstraction establishes an extension, it also sets a boundary around and brings into focus a particular level of generality for treating not only the part but the whole system to which it belongs. The movement is from the most specific, or that which sets it apart from everything else, to its most general characteristics, or what makes it similar to other entities. Operating rather like a microscope that can be set at different degrees of magnification, this mode of abstraction enables us to see the unique qualities of any part, or the qualities associated with its function in capitalism, or the qualities that belong to it as part of the human condition (to give only the most important of these levels of generality). In abstracting capital, for example, Marx gives it an extension in both space and time as well as a level of generality such that only those qualities associated with its appearance and functioning as a phenomenon of capitalism are highlighted (i.e., its production of value, its ownership by capitalists, its exploitation of workers, etc.). The qualities a given capital may also possess as a Ford Motor Company assembly line for making cars or as a tool in general—that is, qualities that it has as a unique object or as an instance of something human beings have always used—are not brought into the picture. They are abstracted out. This aspect of the process of abstraction has received least attention not only in our own discussion but in other accounts of dialectics. In what follows, we shall refer to it as "abstraction of level of generality."

Third, at the same time that abstraction establishes an extension and a level of generality, it also sets up a vantage point or place within the relationship from which to view, think about, and piece together the other components in the relationship; meanwhile, the sum of their ties (as determined by the abstraction of extension) also becomes a vantage point for comprehending the larger system to which it belongs, providing both a beginning for research and analysis and a perspective in which to carry it out. With each new perspective, there are significant differences in what can be perceived, a different ordering of the parts, and a different sense of what is important. Thus, in abstracting capital, Marx not only gives it an extension and a level of generality (that of capitalism), he also views the interrelated elements that compose it from the side of the material means of production and, simultaneously, transforms this configuration itself into a vantage point for viewing the larger system in which it is situated, providing himself with a perspective that influences how all other parts of the system will appear (one that gives to capital the central role). We shall refer to this aspect of abstraction as "abstraction of vantage point." By manipulating extension, level of generality, and vantage point, Marx puts things into and out of focus, into better focus, and into different kinds of focus, enabling himself to see more clearly, investigate more accurately, and understand more fully and more dynamically his chosen subject.

As regards the abstraction of extension, Marx's general stand in favor of large units is evident from such statements as, "In each historical epoch, property has developed differently and under a set of entirely different social relations. Thus, to define bourgeois property is nothing else than to give an exposition of all these social relations of bourgeois production. . . . To try to give a definition of property an independent relation, a category apart, an abstraction and eternal idea, can be nothing but an illusion of metaphysics and jurisprudence" (n.d., 154).

Obviously, large abstractions are needed to think adequately about a complex, internally related world.

The specifics of Marx's position emerge from his frequent criticisms of the political economists for offering too narrow abstractions (narrow in the double sense of including too few connections and too short a time period) of one or another economic form. Ricardo, for example, is reproached for abstracting too short a period in his notions of money and rent and for omitting social relations in his abstraction of value (Marx 1968, 125; 1971, 131). One of the most serious distortions is said to arise from the tendency among political economists to abstract processes solely in terms of their end results. Commodity exchange, for example, gets substituted for the whole of the process by which a product becomes a commodity and eventually available for exchange (Marx 1973, 198). As Amiri Baraka so colorfully points out: "Hunting is not those heads on the wall" (1966, 73). By thinking otherwise for the range of problems with which they are concerned, the political economists avoid seeing the contradictions in the capitalist-specific processes that give rise to these results.

The same narrowing of abstractions obtains a similar ideological result in thinking about human beings. In order to maximize individual freedom, Max Stirner sought to abstract an "I" without any messy presuppositions, whether natural or social. Marx's response is that by excluding all that brought it into existence and the full context in which it acts, this "I" is not a particularly helpful abstraction for understanding anything about the individual, least of all his freedom (Marx and Engels 1964, 477–82). Yet something like Stirner's "I," in the person of the isolated individual, has become the standard way of thinking about human nature in capitalist society. It is the preferred abstraction of extension in which bourgeois ideology treats human beings.

Granted the unusually large extensions Marx gives his abstractions, we need to know how this practice affects his work. What do such abstractions make possible, perhaps even necessary, and what do they make difficult and even impossible? Consider all that a wide-angle photograph does in giving value to what is included, to what crowds the edges as well as to what appears at the center. Notice the relations it establishes as important, or at least relevant, and even the explanations that are implicit in what is included and what is left out. Something very similar occurs through the extension given to units of thinking in the process of abstraction. It is by placing so much in his abstractions—and by altering them as often as he does—that Marx greatly facilitates his analysis of what we've called the double motion of the capitalist mode of production. In particular, Marx's practice in abstracting extension serves as the basis for his theory of identity; it underlies his criticism of existing systems of classification and their replacement by the various classificatory schemes that distinguish his theories, that is, the class division of society, forces/relations of production, appearance/essence, et cetera; and it enables him to capture in thinking the real movements that go on in both nature and society.

As regards identity, Marx claims, "It is characteristic of the entire crudeness of 'common sense,' which takes its rise from the 'full life' and does not cripple its natural features by philosophy or other studies, that where it succeeds in seeing a distinction it fails to see a unity, and where it sees a unity it fails to see a distinction. If 'common sense' establishes distinction determinations, they immediately petrify surreptitiously and it is considered the most reprehensible sophistry to rub together these conceptual blocks in such a way that they catch fire" (Marx and Engels 1961, 339). According to the commonsense approach, things are either the same (the sense in which Marx uses "unity" here) or different. A frequent criticism Marx makes of the political economists is that they see only identity or difference in the relations they examine (1971, 168, 497, and 527). Marx has it both ways—he is forever rubbing these blocks together to make fire. Most striking are his numerous references to what most people take as different subjects as identical. Such is his claim that "the social reality of nature and human natural science, or natural science about man are identical terms" (1959b, 111). Demand and supply (and in a "wider sense" production and consumption) are also said to be identical (1968, 505). And the list of such claims, both with and without the term "identity," is very long. An example of the latter is his reference to "Bourgeoisie, i.e., capital" (Marx and Engels 1945, 21).

In one place, Marx says that by "identity" he means a "different expression of the same fact" (1968, 410). This appears straightforward enough, but in Marx's case, this "fact" is relational, composed of a system of mutually dependent parts. Viewing this mutual dependence within each of the interacting parts, viewing the parts as necessary aspects of each other, they become identical in expressing the same extended whole. Consequently, Marx can claim that labor and capital are "expressions of the same relation, only seen from opposite poles" (1971, 491). Underlying all such claims are abstractions of extension that are large enough to contain whatever is held to be identical.

Marx's theory of identity also helps us understand the pivotal role he gives to the notion of form. A form, we will recall, is that aspect of a relation, centering either on appearance or function, from which its covering concept is usually drawn. But "form" is also Marx's chief way of telling us that he has found an identity in difference, as when he says that rent, profit, and interest, which are obviously different in many respects, are identical as forms of surplus-value (Marx and Engels 1941, 106). What is called "Marxism" is largely an investigation of the different forms human productive activity takes in capitalist society, the changes these forms undergo, how such changes are misunderstood, and the power acquired by these changed and misunderstood forms over the very people whose productive activity brought them into existence in the first place. Value, commodity, capital, and money could only be grasped as forms of labor (and, eventually, of each other) and investigated as such because Marx abstracts each of these units large enough to contain all these elements in their distinctive relations. Marx's theories of alienation and of the metamorphosis of value, in particular, offer many examples of this practice. Abstracted more narrowly, as typically occurs in bourgeois ideology, the identity of such elements gives way to similarity and other vague kinds of connection, with the result that some part of the effect and/or influence brought into focus by Marx's encompassing abstractions is lost or seriously distorted.

In adhering to a philosophy of internal relations, the commitment to view parts as identical exists even before they have been abstracted from the whole, so that one can say that, in a sense, identity precedes difference, which only appears with the abstraction of parts based on some appreciation of their distinctiveness. Such differences, when found, do nothing to contradict the initial assumption of identity, that each part through internal relations can express the same whole. Hence, the coexistence of identity and difference.

It was noted earlier that Marx uses "totality" and "relation" in two senses, a logical sense having to do with how he views all reality and a reconstructed or emergent sense that applies to particular kinds of ties uncovered in his research between parts that had already been abstracted as separate parts. "Identity," as we have been using it so far, belongs to this logical vocabulary and "difference" to the reconstructed one. However, "identity," like "totality" and "relation," is sometimes used in this second, subsidiary sense to highlight closely related aspects of parts whose different appearances or functions have already led to their abstraction as separate parts. In which case, one can also speak of things as being more or less identical.

Besides its effect on the relation of identity, Marx's practice in abstracting extension also has major implications, as I have indicated, for the various classificatory schemes that frame his theories. Every school of thought stands out in large measure by the distinctions it makes and doesn't make and by those it singles out as being in some respect the most important. Marxism is no exception. Among the better-known classifications found in Marx's work are the juxtapositions of forces and relations of production, base and superstructure, materialism and idealism, nature and society, objective and subjective conditions, essence and appearance, the periodization of history based on different modes of production, and the class division of society (particularly the split between workers and capitalists).

Most accounts of Marxism try very hard to establish where one element in each of these classifications ends and the next one begins, to define neatly and permanently the boundaries that subdivide the structures into which Marx organizes human existence. However, given what has just been said about Marx's practice of abstracting extension and his philosophy of internal relations, it should be clear that this is a fruitless exercise. It is only because they assume that Marx is operating with a philosophy of external relations in which the boundaries between things are taken to be of the same order as their other sense-perceptible qualities (hence determined and discoverable once and for all) that these critics can so consistently dismiss the overwhelming evidence of Marx's practice. Not only does Marx often redraw the boundaries of each of these units, but with every classification there are instances where his abstractions are large enough to contain most or even all of the qualities that seemed to fall into other contrasting units.

Marx's materialist conception of history, for example, is characterized by a set of overlapping contrasts between mode of production and "social, political, and intellectual life processes," base and superstructure, forces and relations of production, economic structures (or foundations) and the rest of society, and material and social existence (1904, 11–12). Since Marx did not take much care to distinguish these different formulations, there is a lot of dispute over which one to stress in giving an account of his views, but on two points there is widespread agreement: (1) that the first term in each pairing is in some sense determinant of the latter, and (2) that the boundaries between the terms in each case are more or less set and relatively easy to establish. But how clear-cut can such boundaries be if Marx can refer to "religion, family, state, law, morality, science, art, etc." as "particular modes of production" (1959b, 103), community and the "revolutionary class" as forces of production (which also has "the qualities of individuals" as its subjective side [1973, 495]), theory "in so far as it gets ahold of people" as a "material force" (n.d., 196), and can treat laws regarding private property (which would seem to be part of the superstructure) as part of the base and class struggle (which would seem to be part of political life) as part of the economic structure (1970, 137; see also Acton, 1962, 164)? It is worth noting, too, that Engels could even refer to race as an economic factor (Marx and Engels 1951, 517).

To be sure, these are not the main uses to which Marx put these categories, but they do indicate something of their elasticity, something about how encompassing he could make his abstractions if he wanted to. And it does show how futile it is to try to interpret the sense in which one half of each of these dichotomies is said to determine the other before coming to grips with the practice that arranges and rearranges the boundaries between them.

A similar problem awaits any reader of Marx who insists on looking for a single fixed boundary between essence and appearance. As Marx's investigation into capitalism is largely a study of essential connections, the importance of this distinction is not in doubt. The abstraction of appearance is relatively easy to determine. It is simply what strikes us when we look; it is what's on the surface, what's obvious. Essence is more problematical. It includes appearance but goes beyond it to take in whatever gives any appearance its special character and importance. As such, essence generally introduces systemic and historical connections (including where something seems to be heading as well as where it has come from) as parts of what it is. It brings into focus an extended set of internal relations. But what gives appearances their special importance on any occasion is tied to the particular problem Marx is working on. Hence, what he calls the essence of anything varies somewhat with his purpose. So it is that the essence of man, for example, is said to be, in turn, his activity, his social relations, and the part of nature that he appropriates (Marx 1959b, 75; Marx and Engels 1964, 198; Marx 1959b, 106). The answer that it is all these in their interconnection, an answer that would secure a fixed if not necessarily permanent essence for human beings, misses the point that it is with "essence" that Marx wishes to single out one set of connections as crucial.

In the present discussion, what needs to be stressed is that an approach that focuses on appearances and constructs its explanations on this same plane is based on abstractions of extension composed only of appearances. Relevance ends at the horizon marked off by our sense perceptions. The rest, if not unreal, is trivialized as unnecessary for understanding or dismissed as mystical. A major ideological result of the single-minded attention to appearances is an imaginary reversal of real relations, as what strikes us immediately gets taken as responsible for the more or less hidden processes that have given rise to it. Marx refers to mistaking appearance for essence as "fetishism" and sees it operating throughout society, its best-known example being the fetishism of commodities, where the price of things (something everyone can observe in the market) gets substituted for the relations between the people who made them (something that can only be grasped through analysis).

Marx, on the other hand, was aided in his investigation of essences by his practice of abstracting units large enough to contain them. For him the absolute division of reality into appearance and essence does not exist, since his main units of analysis include both appearance and essence. Thus, according to Marx, "only when labor is grasped as the essence of private property can the economic process as such be penetrated in its actual concreteness" (1959b, 129). Labor, by which Marx means the particular kind of productive activity that goes on in capitalism, not only brings private property into existence but gives it its most distinctive qualities and hence is essential to what it is. It is only by going beyond the apparent thing like qualities of private property, only by seizing its essence in labor (which, again, is dependent on constructing an abstraction that is large enough to contain both in their internal relation) that we can truly grasp private property and the capitalist mode of production in which it plays such a crucial part.

Perhaps the classification that has suffered the greatest misunderstanding as a result of readers' efforts to arrive at permanent boundaries is Marx's class division of society. Marx's abstraction of extension for class brings together many people but not everything about them. Its main focus is on whatever it is that both enables and requires them to perform a particular function in the prevailing mode of production. Hence, Marx's frequent reference to capitalists as the "personification" (or "embodiment") of capital, grasped as the function of wealth to expand through the exploitation of wage-labor (1958, 10, 85, and 592). As a complex Relation, however, class contains other aspects, such as distinguishing social and economic conditions (ones that generally accompany its position in the mode of production), a group's opposition to other similarly constituted groups, its cultural level, its state of mind (encompassing both ideology and degree of consciousness of itself as a class), and forms of inner-class communication and of interclass political struggle. But how many of these aspects Marx actually includes in abstracting the extension of class or of any one of the classes into which he divides a society varies with his problem and purpose at the time. Likewise, since all of these aspects in their peculiar configuration have evolved over time, there is also a decision to make regarding temporal extension, over how much of this evolution to abstract in. How much Marx's decisions in these matters may differ can be seen from such apparently contradictory claims as, "All history is the history of class struggle" (where class contains a bare minimum of its aspects) and, "Class is the product of the bourgeoisie" (where class is abstracted as a sum of all these aspects) (Marx and Engels 1945, 11; 1964, 93).

What class any person belongs to and even the number of classes in society are also affected by where exactly Marx draws his boundaries. Thus, "working class," for example, can refer to everyone who is employed by capitalists and the institutions that serve them, such as the state, or to all the people who work for capitalists but also produce value (a smaller group), or to all the people who not only work for capitalists and produce value but are also organized politically as a class (a smaller group still). As regards temporal extension, Marx can also abstract a particular group to include where they seem to be heading, together with the new set of relations that await them but which they have not yet fully acquired. In the case of peasants who are rapidly losing their land and of small businessmen who are being driven into bankruptcy, this translates into becoming wage-laborers (Marx and Engels 1945, 16). Hence, the class of workers is sometimes abstracted broadly enough to include them as well, that is, people in the process of becoming workers along with those who function as workers at this moment. Marx's well-known reference to capitalism as a two-class society is based on his abstracting all groups into either workers or capitalists depending on where they seem to be heading, the landlords being the major group that is moving toward becoming capitalists. Abstracting such large spatial and temporal extensions for class is considered helpful for analyzing a society that is rapidly developing toward a situation where everyone either buys labor-power or sells it.

At the same time, Marx could abstract much more restricted extensions, which allowed him to refer to a variety of classes (and fragments of classes) based on as many social and economic differences between these groups. In this way, bankers, who are usually treated as a fragment of the capitalist class, are sometimes abstracted as a separate moneyed or financial class (Marx 1968, 123). This helps explain why Marx occasionally speaks of "ruling classes" (plural), a designation that also usually includes landlords, narrowly abstracted (Marx and Engels 1964, 39).

Obviously, for Marx, arriving at a clear-cut, once-and-for-all classification of capitalist society into classes is not the aim, which is not to deny that one such classification (that of capitalists/landlords/workers) enjoys a larger role in his work or that one criterion for determining class (a group's relationship to the prevailing mode of production) is more important. Much to the annoyance of his critics, Marx never defines "class" or provides a full account of the classes in capitalist society. *Capital* III contains a few pages where Marx appears to have begun such an account, but it was never completed (1959a, 862–63). In my view, had he finished these pages, most of the problems raised by his theory of class would remain, for the evidence of his flexibility in abstracting class is clear and unambiguous. Thus, rather than looking for what class a person or group belongs to or how many classes Marx sees in capitalist society—the obsession of most critics and of not a few of his followers—the relevant question is: "Do we know on any given occasion when Marx uses 'class,' or the label associated with any particular class, who he is referring to and why he refers to them in this way?" Only then can the discussion of class advance our understanding, not of everything, but of what it is Marx is trying to explain. It cannot be repeated too often that Marx is chiefly concerned with the double movement of the capitalist mode of production, and arranging people into classes based on different though interrelated criteria is a major means for uncovering this movement. Rather than simply a way of registering social stratification as part of a flat description or as a prelude to rendering a moral judgment (things Marx never does), which *would* require a stable unit, class helps Marx to analyze a changing situation in which it is itself an integral and changing part (Ollman 1979, chap. 2).

Besides making possible his theory of identity and the various classifications that mark his theories, Marx's practice of abstracting broad extensions for his units also enables him to capture in thought the various real movements that he sets out to investigate. In order to grasp things "as they really are and happen," Marx's stated aim, in order to trace their happening accurately and give it its due weight in the system(s) to which it belongs, Marx extends his abstractions—as we have seen—to include how things happen as part of what they are (Marx and Engels 1964, 57). Until now, change has been dealt with in a very general way. What I have labeled the double movement (organic and historical) of the capitalist mode of production, however, can only be fully understood by breaking it down into a number of submovements, the most important of which are quantity/quality, metamorphosis, and contradiction.[3] These are some of the main ways in which things move or happen; they are forms of change. Organizing becoming and time itself into recognizable sequences, they are some of the pathways that bring order to the flow of events. As such, they help structure all of Marx's theories and are indispensable to his account of how capitalism works, how it developed, and where it is tending.

Quantity/quality change is a historical movement encompassing both buildup and what it leads to. One or more of the aspects that constitute any process-cum-Relation gets larger (or smaller), increases (or decreases) in number, et cetera. Then, with the attainment of a critical mass—which is different for each entity studied—a qualitative transformation occurs, understood as a change in appearance and/or function. In this way, Marx notes, money becomes capital, that is, it acquires the ability to buy labor-power and produce value only when it reaches a certain amount (1958, 307–8). In order for such change to appear as an instance of the transformation of quantity into quality, Marx's abstractions have to contain the main aspects whose quantitative change is destined to trigger off the coming qualitative change as well as the new appearances and/or functions embodied in the latter, and all this for the time it takes for this to occur. Abstracting anything less runs the risk of first dismissing and then missing the coming qualitative change and/or misconstruing it when it happens, three frequent errors associated with bourgeois ideology.

Metamorphosis is an organic movement of interaction within a system in which qualities (occasionally appearances but usually functions) of one part get transferred to other parts so that the latter can be referred to as forms of the former. In the key distinguishing movement in Marx's labor theory of value, value—through its production by alienated labor and entry into the market—gets metamorphosed into commodity, money, capital, wages, profit, rent, and interest. The metamorphosis of value takes place in two circuits. What Marx calls the "real metamorphosis" occurs in the production process proper, where commodities are transformed into capital and means of subsistence, both forms of value, which are then used to make more commodities. A second circuit, or "formal metamorphosis," occurs where the commodity is exchanged for money, another form of value; and, on one occasion, Marx goes so far as to equate "metamorphosed into" and "exchanged for" (1973, 168). The value over and above what gets returned to the workers as wages, or what Marx calls "surplus-value," undergoes a parallel metamorphosis as it gets transferred to groups with various claims on it, appearing as rent, interest, and profit. In both real and formal metamorphosis, new forms are signaled by a change in who possesses the value and in how it appears and functions for them, that is, as a means of subsistence, a means of producing more value, a means of buying commodities, et cetera.

In metamorphosis, a process is abstracted that is large enough to include both what is changing and what it is changing into, making the transformation of one into the other an internal movement. Thus, when value metamorphoses into commodity or money, for example, the latter assume some of the alienated relationships embodied in value—somewhat altered due to their new location—as their own, and this is seen as a later stage in the development of value itself. Otherwise, operating with smaller abstractions, commodity or money could never actually become value, and speaking of them as "forms" of value could only be understood metaphorically.

The essentially synchronic character of metamorphosis, no matter the number of steps involved, is also dependent on the size of the abstraction used. To some it may appear that the various phases in the metamorphosis of value occur one after another, serially, but this is to assume a brief duration for each phase. When, however, all the phases of this metamorphosis are abstracted as ongoing, as Marx does in the case of value—usually as aspects of production abstracted as reproduction—then all phases of the cycle are seen as occurring simultaneously (1971, 279–80). Events occur simultaneously or in sequence depending on the temporal extension of the units involved. When Marx refers to all the production that goes on in the same year as simultaneous production, all its causes and effects are viewed as taking place at the same time, as parts of a single interaction (1968, 471). To grasp any organic movement as such, it is simply that one must allow enough time for the interactions involved to work themselves out. Stopping too soon, which means abstracting too short a period for each phase, leaves one with an incompleted piece of the interaction and inclines one to mistake what is an organic tie for a causal one.

In sum, metamorphosis, as Marx understands it, is only possible on the basis of an abstraction of extension that is sufficiently large to encompass the transfer of qualities from one element in an interaction to others over time, which assumes a particular theory of forms (movement is registered through elements becoming forms of one another), which assumes in turn a particular theory of identity (each form is both identical to and different from the others) that is itself a necessary corollary of the philosophy of internal relations (the basic unit of reality is not a thing but a Relation).

If quantity/quality is essentially a historical movement and metamorphosis an organic one, then contradiction has elements of both. As a union of two or more processes that are simultaneously supporting and undermining one another, a contradiction combines five distinct though closely intertwined movements. But before detailing what they are, it is worth stressing once again the crucial role played by Marx's philosophy of internal relations. As regards contradictions, Engels says, "So long as we consider things as static and lifeless, each one by itself, alongside of and after each other, it is true that we do not run up against any contradiction in them. We find certain qualities which are partly common to, partly diverse from, and even contradictory to each other, *but which in this case are distributed among different objects and therefore contain no contradiction.* . . . But the position is quite different as soon as we consider things in their motion, their change, their life, their reciprocal influence on one another. Then we immediately become involved in contradictions" (1934, 135 [emphasis added]). Elsewhere, referring to the bourgeois economists' treatment of rent, profit, and wages, Marx asserts where there is "no inner connection," there can be no "hostile connection," no "contradiction" (1971, 503). Only when apparently different elements are grasped as aspects of the same unit as it evolves over time can certain of their features be abstracted as a contradiction.

Of the five movements found in contradiction, the two most important are the movements of mutual support and mutual undermining. Pulling in opposite directions, each of these movements exercises a constant, if not even or always evident, pressure on events. The uneasy equilibrium that results lasts until one or the other of these movements predominates.

In the contradiction between capital and labor, for example, capital, being what it is, helps bring into existence labor of a very special kind, that is, alienated labor, which will best serve its needs as capital, while labor, as the production of goods intended for the market, helps fashion capital in a form that enables it to continue its exploitation of labor. However, capital and labor also possess qualities that exert pressure in the opposite direction. With its unquenchable thirst for surplus-value, capital would drive labor to exhaustion, while labor, with its inherent tendencies toward working less hours, in better conditions, et cetera, would render capital unprofitable. To avoid the temptation of misrepresenting contradiction as a simple opposition, tension, or dysfunction (common ideological errors), it is essential that the chief movements that reproduce the existing equilibrium as well as those that tend to undermine it be brought into the same overarching abstraction.

A third movement present in contradictions is the immanent unfolding of the processes that make up the "legs" of any contradiction. In this way, a contradiction becomes bigger, sharper, more explosive; both supporting and undermining movements become more intense, though not necessarily to the same degree. According to Marx, the capitalist contradictions "of use-value and exchange-value, commodity and money, capital and wage-labor, etc., assume ever greater dimensions as productive power develops" (1971, 55). The very growth of the system that contains these contradictions leads to their own growth.

A fourth movement found in contradictions is the change in overall form that many undergo through their interaction with other processes in the larger system of which they are part. Of the contradiction between use and exchange-value, Marx says that it "develops further, presents itself and manifests itself in the duplication of the commodity into commodity and money. This duplication appears as a process in the metamorphosis of commodity in which selling and buying are different aspects of a single process and each act of this process simultaneously includes its opposite" (1971, 88). The same contradictions seem to undergo still another metamorphosis: the contradictions in commodity and money, which develop in circulation, are said "to reproduce themselves" in capital (1968, 512). The contradiction between use and exchange-value with which we began has moved, been transferred, into the relation between commodity and money, and from there into capital. This movement is similar to what occurs in the metamorphosis of value—the systemic interactions are the same. Except here it is an entire contradiction that gets metamorphosed.

The fifth and final movement contained in contradiction occurs in its resolution, when one side overwhelms what has hitherto been holding it in check, transforming both itself and all its relationships in the process. The resolution of a contradiction can be of two sorts, either temporary and partial or permanent and total. An economic crisis is an example of the first. Marx refers to crises as "essential outbursts . . . of the immanent contradictions" (1971, 55). The preexisting equilibrium has broken down, and a new one composed of recognizably similar elements, usually with the addition of some new elements, is in the process of replacing it. A partial resolution of a contradiction is more in the order of a readjustment, for it can also be said here that the old contradiction has been raised to a new and higher stage. In the case of simple economic crises, where economic breakdown is followed sooner or later by a renewed burst of accumulation, the initial contradiction is expanded to include more things, a larger area of the globe, more people, and a more highly developed technology. Essentially, the stakes have been raised for the next time around.

A permanent and total resolution occurs when the elements in contradiction undergo major qualitative change, transforming all their relations to one another as well as the larger system of which they are a part. An economic crisis that gives rise to a political and social revolution is an example of this. Here, the initial contradictions have moved well beyond what they once were and are often so different that it may be difficult to reconstruct their earlier forms. What determines whether the resolution of a contradiction will be partial or total, of course, is not its dialectical form, the fact that differences get abstracted as contradictions, but its real content. However, such content is unlikely to reveal its secret to anyone who cannot read it as a contradiction. By including the undermining interaction of mutually dependent processes in the same unit, by expanding this unit to take in how such interaction has developed and where it is tending (its metamorphosis through different forms and eventual resolution), it is Marx's broad abstractions of extension that make it possible to grasp these varied movements as internal and necessary elements of a single contradiction.

Finally, Marx's large abstractions of extension also account for how the same factor, as indicated by its proper name, can contain two or more contradictions. Commodity, for example, is said to embody the contradiction between use and exchange-value as well as the contradiction between private and social labor. To contain both contradictions, commodity must be given a large enough extension to include the interaction between the two aspects of value as well as the interaction between the two aspects of labor, and both of them as they develop over time (Marx 1971, 130).

Level of Generality

The second main aspect of Marx's process of abstraction, or mode in which it occurs, is the abstraction of level of generality. In his unfinished introduction to the *Critique of Political Economy*, Marx's only systematic attempt to present his method, great care is taken to distinguish "production" from "production in general" (1904, 268–74). The former takes place in a particular society, capitalism, and includes all the relations of this society that enable it to appear and function as it does. "Production in general," on the other hand, refers to whatever it is that work in all societies has in common—chiefly the purposive activity of human beings in transforming nature to satisfy human needs—leaving out everything that distinguishes different social forms of production from one another.

Marx makes a further distinction within capitalist production between "production as a whole," what applies to all kinds of production within capitalism, and "production as a specific branch of industry," or what applies only to production in that industry (1904, 270). It is clear that more than a change in extension is involved in making these distinctions, especially the first one. The relations of productive activity with those who engage in it as well as with its product are *internal* relations in both cases, but production in capitalism is united with the distinctive capitalist forms of producers and their products, while production in general is united with them in forms that share its own quality as a lowest common denominator.

The abstraction Marx makes in moving from capitalist production to production in general, then, is not one of extension but one of level of generality. It is a move from a more specific understanding of production that brings into focus the whole network of equally specific qualities in which it functions (and with it the period of capitalism in which all this takes place) to a more general understanding of production that brings into focus the equally general state of those conditions in which it occurs (along with the whole of human history as the period in which these qualities are found).

Something similar is involved in the distinction Marx makes between "production as a whole" and "production in a particular branch of industry," though the movement here is away from what is more general in the direction of what is more specific. How a particular branch of industry—car manufacturing, for example—appears and functions involves a set of conditions that fall substantially short of applying to the entire capitalist epoch. What appears superficially like a whole-part distinction is—like the earlier distinction between "capitalist production" and "production in general"—one of levels of generality. Both capitalist production (or production as a whole) and production in a particular industry are internally related to the rest of society, but each brings into focus a different period of history, the capitalist epoch in one case and what might be called "modern capitalism," or that period in which this branch of production has functioned in just this way, in the other case.

In this Introduction, Marx comes out in favor of concentrating on production in its current historical forms, that is, on capitalist and modern capitalist production, and criticizes the political economists for contenting themselves with production in general when trying to analyze what is happening here and now. Then, falling for the all-too-common error of mistaking what is more general for what is more profound, the political economists treat the generalizations they have derived from examining different social formations as the most important truths about each particular society in turn, and even as the cause of phenomena that are peculiar to each one. In this way, for example, the general truth that production in any society makes use of material nature, the most general form of property, is offered as an explanation and even a justification for how wealth gets distributed in capitalist society, where people who own property claim a right to part of what gets produced with its help (1904, 271–72).

While Marx's discussion of the political economists in this introduction oscillates between modern capitalism, capitalism as such, and the human condition, much of what he says elsewhere shows that he can operate on still other levels of generality, and therefore that a more complex breakdown of what are in fact degrees of generality is required. Before offering such a breakdown, I want to make it clear that the boundary lines that follow are all suggested by Marx's own practice in abstracting, a practice that is largely determined by his aim of capturing the double movement of the capitalist mode of production. In other words, there is nothing absolute about the particular divisions I have settled on. Other maps of levels of generality could be drawn, and for other kinds of problems they might be very useful.

Keeping this in mind, there are seven major levels of generality into which Marx subdivides the world, seven plains of comprehension on which he places all the problems he investigates, seven different foci for organizing everything that is. Starting from the most specific, there is the level made up of whatever is unique about a person and situation. It's all that makes Joe Smith different from everyone else, and so too all his activities and products. It's what gets summed up in a proper name and an actual address. With this level—let's call it level one—the here and now, or however long what is unique lasts, is brought into focus.

Level two distinguishes what is general to people, their activities, and products because they exist and function within modern capitalism, understood as the last twenty to fifty years. Here, the unique qualities that justify using proper names, such as Joe Smith, are abstracted out of focus (we no longer see them), and abstracted into focus are the qualities that make us speak of an individual as an engineer or in terms of some other occupation that has emerged in modern capitalism. Bringing these slightly more general qualities into sight, we also end up considering more people—everyone to whom such qualities apply—and a longer period, the entire time during which these qualities have existed. We also bring into focus a larger area, usually one or a few countries, with whatever else has occurred there that has affected or been affected by the qualities in question during this period. Marx's abstraction of a "particular branch of production" belongs to this level.

Capitalism as such constitutes level three. Here, everything that is peculiar to people, their activity, and products due to their appearance and functioning in capitalist society is brought into focus. We encountered this level earlier in our discussion of "production as a whole." The qualities that Joe Smith possesses that mark him as Joe Smith (level one) and as an engineer (level two) are equally irrelevant. Front and center now are all that makes him a typical worker in capitalism, including his relations to his boss and product. His productive activity is reduced to the denominator indicated by calling it "wage-labor" and his product to the denominator indicated by calling it "commodity" and "value." Just as level two widens the area and lengthens the time span brought into focus as compared to level one, level three widens the focus so that it now includes everyone who partakes of capitalist relations anywhere that these relations obtain and the entire four hundred or so years of the capitalist era.

After capitalism, still moving from the specific to the general, there is the level of class society, level four. This is the period of human history during which societies have been divided up into classes based on the division of labor. Brought into focus are the qualities people, their activities, and products have in common across the five to ten thousand years of class history, or whatever capitalism, feudalism, and slavery share as versions of class society, and wherever these qualities have existed. Next—level five—is human society. It brings into focus—as we saw in the case of the political economists above—qualities people, their activities, and products have in common as part of the human condition. Here, one is considering all human beings and the entire history of the species.

To make this scheme complete, two more levels will be added, but they are not nearly as important as the first five in Marx's writings. Level six is the level of generality of the animal world, for just as we possess qualities that set us apart as human beings (level five), we have qualities (including various life functions, instincts, and energies) that are shared with other animals. Finally, there is level seven, the most general level of all, which brings into focus our qualities as a material part of nature, including weight, extension, movement, et cetera.

In acquiring an extension, all Marx's units of thought acquire in the same act of abstraction a level of generality. Thus, all the Relations that are constituted as such by Marx's abstractions of extension, including the various classifications and movements they make possible, are located on one or another of these levels of generality. And though each of these levels brings into focus a different time period, they are not to be thought of as "slices of time," since the whole of history is implicated in each level, including the most specific. Rather, they are ways of organizing time, placing the period relevant to the qualities brought into focus in the front and treating everything that comes before as what led up to it, as origins.

It is important, too, to underline that all the human and other qualities discussed above are present simultaneously and are equally real but that they can only be perceived and therefore studied when the level of generality on which they fall has been brought into focus. This is similar to what occurs in the natural sciences, where phenomena are abstracted on the basis of their biological or chemical or atomic properties. All such properties exist together, but one cannot see or study them at the same time. The significance of this observation is evident when we consider that all the problems from which we suffer and everything that goes into solving them or keeping them from being solved is made up of qualities that can only be brought into focus on one or another of these different levels of generality. Unfolding as they do over time, these qualities can also be viewed as movements and pressures of one sort or another—whether organized into tendencies, metamorphoses, or contradictions—that, taken together, pretty well determine our existence. Consequently, it is essential, in order to understand any particular problem, to abstract a level of generality that brings the characteristics chiefly responsible for this problem into focus. We have already seen Marx declare that because the classical political economists abstract production at the level of generality of the human condition (level five) they cannot grasp the character of distribution in capitalist society (level three).

A similar situation exists today with the study of power in political science. The dynamics of any power relationship lies in the historically specific conditions in which the people involved live and work. To abstract the bare relation of power from these conditions in order to arrive at conclusions about "power in general" (level five), as many political scientists and an increasing number of social movement theorists have done, ensures that every particular exercise of power will be out of focus and its distinctive features undervalued and/or misunderstood.

Given Marx's special interest in uncovering the double movement of the capitalist mode of production, most of what he writes on man and society falls on level three. Abstractions such as "capital," "value," "commodity," "labor," and "working class," whatever their extensions, bring out the qualities that these people, activities, and products possess as part of capitalism. Pre- and postcapitalist developments come into the analysis on this level as the origins and likely futures of these capitalist qualities. What Marx refers to in his *Grundrisse* as "pre-capitalist economic formations" (the apt title of an English translation of some historical material taken from this longer work) are just that (1973, 471–513). The social formations that preceded capitalism are mainly viewed and studied here as early moments of capitalism abstracted as a process, as its origins extending back before enough of its distinctive structures had emerged to justify the use of the label "capitalism."

Marx also abstracts his subject matter on levels two (modern capitalism) and four (class society), though this is much less frequent. Where Marx operates on the level of generality of class society, capitalism, feudalism, and slave society are examined with a view to what they have in common. Studies in feudalism on this level of generality emphasize the division of labor and the struggle between the classes that it gives rise to, as compared to the breakdown of the conditions underlying feudal production that gets most of the attention when examining feudalism as part of the origins of capitalism, that is, on level three (Marx 1958, pt. 8).

An example of Marx operating on level two, modern capitalism, can be found in his discussion of economic crisis. After examining the various ways that the capitalist system, given what it is and how it works, could break down, that is, after analyzing it on the level of capitalism as such (level three), he then shows how these possibilities got actualized in the immediate past, in what was for him modern or developed capitalism (1968, 492–535). To explain why the last few crises occurred in just the ways they did, he has to bring into focus the qualities that apply to this particular time period and these particular places, that is, recent economic, social, and political history in specific countries. This is also an example of how Marx's analysis can play off two or more different levels of generalization, treating what he finds on the more specific level as the actualization of one among several possibilities present on the more general level(s).

It is instructive to compare Marx's studies of man and society conducted on levels two, three, and four (chiefly three, capitalism) with studies in the social sciences and also with commonsense thinking about these subjects, which typically operate on levels one (the unique) and five (the human condition). Where Marx usually abstracts human beings, for example, as classes (as a class on level four, as one of the main classes that emerge from capitalist relations of production—workers, capitalists, and sometimes landowners—on level three, and as one of the many classes and fragments of classes that exist in a particular country in the most recent period on level two), most non-Marxists abstract people as unique individuals, where everyone has a proper name (level one), or as a member of the human species (level five). In proceeding in their thinking directly from level one to level five, they may never even perceive, and hence have no difficulty in denying, the very existence of classes.

But the question is not which of these different abstractions is true. They all are in so far as people possess qualities that fall on each of these levels of generality. The relevant question is: which is the appropriate abstraction for dealing with a particular set of problems? For example, if social and economic inequality, exploitation, unemployment, social alienation, and imperialist wars are due in large part to conditions associated with capitalist society, then they can only be understood and dealt with through the use of abstractions that bring out their capitalist qualities. And that involves, among other things, abstracting people as capitalists and workers. Not to do so, to insist on sticking to levels one and five, leaves one blaming particular individuals (a bad boss, an evil president) or human nature as such for these problems.

To complete the picture, it must be admitted that Marx occasionally abstracts phenomena, including people, on levels one and five. There are discussions of specific individuals, such as Napoleon III and Palmerston, where he focuses on the qualities that make these people different, and some attention is given, especially in his earliest writings, to qualities that all human beings have in common, to human nature in general. But not only are such digressions an exception, what is more important for our purposes is that Marx seldom allows the qualities that come from these two levels to enter into his explanation of social phenomena. Thus, when G. D. H. Cole faults Marx for making classes more real than individuals (1966, 11), or when Carol Gould says that individuals enjoy an ontological priority in Marxism (1980, 33), or, conversely, when Louis Althusser denies the individual any theoretical space in Marxism whatsoever (1966, 225–58), they are all misconstruing the nature of a system that has places—levels of generality—for individuals, classes, and the human species. The very idea of attributing an ontological priority to either individuals, class, or the species assumes an absolute separation between them that is belied by Marx's conception of man as a Relation with qualities that fall on different levels of generality. None of these ways of thinking about human beings is more real or more fundamental than the others. If, despite this, class remains Marx's preferred abstraction for treating human beings, it is only because of its necessary ties to the kind, range, and above all levels of generality of the phenomena he seeks to explain.

It is not only the abstractions in which we think about people but also how we organize our thinking within each of these abstractions that can be set apart on the basis of levels of generality. Beliefs, attitudes, and intentions, for example, are properties of the unique individuals who inhabit level one. Social relations and interests are the main qualities of the classes and fragments of classes who occupy levels two, three, and four. Powers, needs, and behavior belong to human nature as such, while instincts apply to people as part of human nature but also in their identity as animals. Though there is some movement across level boundaries in the use of these concepts—and some concepts, such as "consciousness," that apply in a somewhat different sense on several levels—their use is usually a good indication of the level of generality on which a particular study falls and hence, too, of the kind of problems that can be addressed. An integrated conception of human nature that makes full use of all these concepts, which is to say that organically connects up the study of people coming from each of these levels of generality, remains to be done.

By focusing on different qualities of people, each level of generality also contains distinctive ways of dividing up humanity and with that its own kinds of oppression based on these divisions. Exploitation, for example, refers to the extraction of surplus-value from workers by capitalists that is based on a level three division of society into workers and capitalists. Therefore, as a form of oppression, it is specific to capitalism (though, with a more limited abstraction of extension, "exploitation" is occasionally used to refer to the extraction of the surplus—surplus in general—that takes place in all class societies [level four]). The human condition, level five, brings out what all people share as members of our species. The only kind of oppression that can exist here comes from outside the species and is directed against everyone. The destruction of the ecological conditions necessary for human life is an example of an oppression against people that falls on this level of generality. Where certain classes—such as the capitalists through their single-minded pursuit of profit—contribute to this destruction, this only signals that this particular oppression must be studied and fought on two or more levels.

Level four, which is marked by a whole series of distinctions between people that are rooted in the division between mental and manual work, enables us to see the beginning of oppressions based on class, nation, race, religion, and gender. Though racial and gender differences obviously existed before the onset of class society, it is only with the division between those who produce wealth and those who direct its production that these differences become the basis for the distinctive forms of oppression associated with racism and patriarchy. With the appearance of different relationships to the prevailing mode of production and the contradictory interests they generate, with mutual indifference replacing the mutual concern that was characteristic of an earlier time when everything was owned in common, and with the creation of a growing surplus that everyone wishes to possess (because no one has enough), all manner of oppressions based on both the existing and new divisions of society become possible and for the ruling economic class extremely useful. Racism, patriarchy, religion, caste, regionalism, and nationalism become the most effective ways of rationalizing these oppressive economic practices, whose underlying conditions they help over time to reproduce. Upon frequent repetition, they also sink deep roots into people's minds and emotions and acquire a relative autonomy from the situation in which they originated, which makes it increasingly difficult for those affected to recognize the crucial economic role that these different oppressions continue to play.

To be sure, all the oppressions associated with class society also have their capitalist-specific forms and intensities having to do with their place and function in capitalism as a particular form of class society, but the main relations that underlie and give force to these oppressions come from class society as such. Consequently, the abolition of capitalism will not do away with any of these oppressions, only with their capitalist forms. Ending racism, patriarchy, nationalism, et cetera, in all their forms and completely can only occur when class society itself is abolished, and in particular with the end of the division between mental and manual labor, a world historical change that could only occur, Marx believes, with the arrival of full communism.

If all of Marx's abstractions involve—as I have argued—a level of generality as well as an extension, if each level of generality organizes and even prescribes to some degree the analyses made with its help, that is, in its terms, if Marx abstracts this many levels of generality in order to get at different though related problems (even though his abstraction of capitalism as such, level three, is the decisive one)—*then* the conclusions of his studies, the theories of Marxism, are all to be found on one or another of these levels and must be viewed accordingly if they are to be correctly understood, evaluated, and, where necessary, revised.

Marx's labor theory of value, for example, is chiefly an attempt to explain why all the products of human productive activity in capitalist society have a price—not why a particular product costs such and such, but why it costs anything at all. That everything humans produce has a price is an extraordinary phenomenon peculiar to the capitalist era, whose social implications are even more profound because most people view it ahistorically, simply taking it for granted. Marx's entire account of this phenomenon, which includes the history of how a society in which all products have a price has evolved, takes place on the level of generality of capitalism as such, which means that he only deals with the qualities of people, their activities, and products in the forms they assume in capitalism overall. The frequent criticism one hears of this theory—that it doesn't take account of competition in real marketplaces and therefore cannot explain actual prices—is simply off the point, that is, the more general point that Marx is trying to make.

To account for the fact that a given pair of shoes costs exactly fifty dollars, for example, one has to abstract in qualities of both modern capitalism (level two) and the here and now (level one) in a way that takes us well beyond Marx's initial project. In *Capital* III, Marx makes some effort to reabstract the phenomena that enter into his labor theory of value on the level of modern capitalism, and here he does discuss the role of competition among both buyers and sellers in affecting actual prices. Still, the confusion from which innumerable economists have suffered over what has been labeled the "transformation problem" (the transformation of values into prices) disappears once we recognize that it is a matter of relating analyses from two different levels of generality and that Marx gives overriding attention to the first, capitalism, and relatively little attention to the second, which unfortunately is the only level that interests most non-Marxist economists.

The theory of alienation offers another striking example of the need to locate Marx's theories on particular levels of generality if they are not to be distorted. Marx's description of the severed connections between man and his productive activity, products, other people, and the species that lies at the core of this theory falls on two different levels of generality: capitalism (level three) and class society (level four). In his earliest writings, this drama of separation is generally played out in terms of "division of labor" and "private property" (level four). It is clear even from this more general account that alienation reaches its zenith in capitalist society, but the focus is on the class context to which capitalism belongs and not on capitalism as such. Here, capitalism is not so much "it" as the outstanding example of "it." (Incidentally, this conclusion calls for a modification in the subtitle of my earlier work *Alienation*, which has as its subtitle *Marx's Conception of Man in Capitalist Society*.)

In later writings, as Marx's concern shifts increasingly to uncovering the double motion of the capitalist mode of production, the theory of alienation gets raised to the level of generality of capitalism (level three). The focus now is on productive activity and its products in their capitalist-specific forms, that is, on labor, commodity, and value; and the mystification that has accompanied private property throughout class history gets upgraded to the fetishism of commodities (and values). The broader theory of alienation remains in force. The context of class society in which capitalism is situated has not changed its spots, but now Marx has developed a version of the theory that can be better integrated into his analysis of capitalist dynamics. With the introduction of this notion of levels of generality, some of the major disputes regarding Marx's theory of alienation—whether it is mainly concerned with class history or with capitalism, and how and to what degree Marx used this theory in his later writings—are easily resolved.

But it is not only Marx's theories that must be placed on particular levels of generality to be correctly understood. The same applies to virtually all of his statements. For example, what is the relation between the claim we have already met in another context that "all history [later qualified to class history] is the history of class struggle" and the claim that "class is the product of the bourgeoisie" (Marx and Engels 1945, 12; 1964, 77)? If "class" in both instances refers to qualities on the same level of generality, then only one of these claims can be true, that is, either class has existed over the past five to ten thousand years of human history or it only came into existence with capitalism, four to five hundred years ago. However, if we understand Marx as focusing on the qualities common to all classes in the last five to ten thousand years (on level four) in the first claim and on the distinctive qualities classes have acquired in the capitalist epoch (on level three) in the second (that which makes them more fully classes, involving mainly development in organization, communication, alienation, and consciousness), then the two claims are compatible. Because so many of Marx's concepts—"class" and "production" being perhaps the outstanding examples—are used to convey abstractions on more than one level of generality, the kind of confusion generated by such apparent contradictions is all too common.

Marx's remarks on history are especially vulnerable to being misunderstood unless they are placed on one or another of these levels of generality. The role Marx attributes to production and economics generally, for example, differs somewhat, depending on whether the focus is on capitalism (including its distinctive origins), modern capitalism (the same), class societies (the same), or human societies (the same). Starting with human societies, the special importance Marx accords to production is based on the fact that one has to do what is necessary in order to survive before attempting anything else, that production limits the range of material choices available just as, over time, it helps to transform them, and that production is the major activity that gives expression to and helps to develop our peculiarly human powers and needs (Marx 1958, 183–84; Marx and Engels 1964, 117; Ollman 1976, 98–101). In class society, production plays its decisive role primarily through "the direct relationship of the owners of the conditions of production to the direct division of labor that comes into being in this period and producers" (Marx 1959a, 772). It is also on this level that the interaction between the forces and class-based relations of production come into focus. In capitalism, the special role of production is shared by everything that goes into the process of capital accumulation (Marx 1958, pt. 8). In modern capitalism, it is usually what has happened recently in a particular sector of production in a given country (like the development of railroads in India during Marx's time) that is treated as decisive (Marx and Engels n.d., 79).

Each of these interpretations of the predominant role of production applies only to the level of generality that it brings into focus. No single interpretation comes close to accounting for all that Marx believes needs to be explained, which is probably why, on one occasion, he denies that he has any theory of history whatsoever (Marx and Engels 1952, 278). It might be more accurate, however, to say that he has four complementary theories of history, one for history as abstracted on each of these four levels of generality. The effort by most of Marx's followers and virtually all of his critics to encapsulate the materialist conception of history into a single generalization regarding the role of production (or economics) has never succeeded, therefore, because it could not succeed.

Finally, the various movements Marx investigates, some of which were discussed under abstraction of extension, are also located on particular levels of generality. That is, like everything else, these movements are composed of qualities that are unique, or special to modern capitalism, or to capitalism, et cetera, so that they only take shape as movements when the relevant level of generality is brought into focus. Until then, whatever force they exercise must remain mysterious and our ability to use or affect them virtually nil. The movement of the metamorphosis of value, for example, dependent as it is on the workings of the capitalist marketplace, operates chiefly on the levels of generality of capitalism (level three) and modern capitalism (level two). Viewing the products of work on the levels of generality of class society (level four) or the human condition (level five) or concentrating on its unique qualities (level one)—the range of most non-Marxist thinking on this subject—does not keep the metamorphosis of value from taking place, it simply prevents us from perceiving it. Likewise, if "in capitalism," as Marx says, "everything seems and in fact is contradictory" (1963, 218), it is only by abstracting the levels of generality of capitalism and modern capitalism (granted appropriate abstractions of extension) that we can perceive them.

What are called the "laws of the dialectic" are those movements that can be found in one or another recognizable form on every level of generality, that is, in the relations between the qualities that fall on each of these levels, including that of inanimate nature. The transformation of quantity to quality and development through contradiction, which were discussed above, are such dialectical laws. Two other dialectical laws that play important roles in Marx's work are the interpenetration of polar opposites (the process by which a radical change in the conditions surrounding two or more elements or in the conditions of the person viewing them produces a striking alteration, even a complete turnabout, in their relations), and the negation of the negation (the process by which the most recent phase in a development that has gone through at least three phases will display important similarities with what existed in the phase before last).

Naturally, the particular form taken by a dialectical law will vary somewhat depending on its subject and on the level of generality on which this subject falls. The mutually supporting and undermining movements that lie at the core of contradiction, for example, appear very different when applied to the forces of inanimate nature than they do when applied to specifically capitalist phenomena. Striking differences such as these have led a growing band of critics and some followers of Marx to restrict the laws of dialectic to social phenomena and to reject as "un-Marxist" what they label "Engels's dialectics of nature." Their error, however, is to confuse a particular statement of these laws, usually one appropriate to levels of generality where human consciousness is present, for all possible statements. This error is abetted by the widespread practice—one I also have adopted for purposes of simplification and brevity—of allowing the most general statement of these laws to stand in for the others. Quantity/quality changes, contradictions, et cetera, that occur among the unique qualities of our existence (level one), or in the qualities we possess as workers and capitalists (levels two and three), or in those we possess as members of a class and as human beings (levels four and five), however, are not simply illustrations for and the working out of still more general dialectical laws. To be adequately apprehended, such movements on each level of generality must be seen as expressions of laws that are specific to that level as well as versions of more general laws. Most of the work of drafting such multilevel statements of the laws of the dialectic remains to be done.

The importance of the laws of the dialectic for grasping the pressures at work on different levels of generality will also vary. We have just seen Marx claim that capitalism in particular is full of contradictions. Thus, viewing conditions and events in terms of contradictions is far more important for understanding their capitalist character than it is for understanding their qualities as human, or natural, or unique conditions and events. Given Marx's goal to explain the double movement of the capitalist mode of production, no other dialectical law receives the attention given to the law of development through contradiction. Together with the relatively minor role contradiction plays in the changes that occur in nature (level seven), this may also help account for the mistaken belief that dialectical laws are found only in society.

What stands out from the above is that the laws of the dialectic do not in themselves explain, prove, or predict anything or cause anything to happen. Rather, they are ways of organizing the most common forms of change and interaction that exist on any level of generality both for purposes of study and intervention into the world of which they are part. With their help, Marx was able to uncover many other tendencies and patterns, also often referred to as laws, that are peculiar to the levels of generality with which he was concerned. Such laws have no more force than what comes out of the processes from which they are derived, balanced by whatever countertendencies there are within the system. And like all the other movements Marx investigates, the laws of the dialectic and the level-specific laws they help him uncover are provided with extensions that are large enough to encompass the relevant interactions during the entire period of their unfolding.

Two major questions relating to this mode of abstraction remain. How do the qualities located on each level of generality affect those on the others? And what is the influence of the decision made regarding abstraction of extension on the level of generality that is abstracted, and vice-versa? The effect of qualities from each level on those from others, moving from the most general (level seven) to the most specific (level one), is that of a context on what it contains. That is, each level, beginning with seven, establishes a range of possibilities for what can occur on the more specific levels that follow. The actualization of some of these possibilities on each level limits in turn what can come about on the levels next in line, all the way up to level one, that of the unique.

Each more general level, in virtue of what it is and contains, also makes one or a few of the many (though not infinite) alternative developments that it makes possible on less general levels more likely of actualization. Capitalism, in other words, was not only a possible development out of class society, but it was made likely by the character of the latter, by the very dynamics inherent in the division of labor once it got under way. The same might be said of the relation between capitalism as such and the "modern" English capitalism in which Marx lived and the relation between the latter and the unique character of the events Marx experienced.

It is within this framework, too, that the relation Marx sees between freedom and determinism can best be understood. Whatever the level of abstraction— whether we are talking about what is unique to any individual, a group in modern capitalism, workers throughout the capitalist era, any class, or human beings as such—there is always a choice to be made and some ability to make it. Hence, there is always some kind and some degree of freedom. On each level of generality, however, the alternatives between which people must choose are severely limited by the nature of their overlapping contexts, which also make one or another set of alternatives more feasible and/or attractive, just as these contexts condition the very personal, class, and human qualities brought into play in making any choice. Hence, there is also a considerable degree of determinism. It is this relationship between freedom and determinism that Marx wishes to bring out when he says that it is people who make history but not in conditions of their own choosing (Marx and Engels 1951a, 225). What seems like a relatively straightforward claim is complicated by the fact that both the people and the conditions referred to exist on various levels of generality, and depending on the level that is brought into focus, the sense of this claim—though true in each instance—will vary.

The view of determinism offered here is different from but not in contradiction with the view presented in our discussion of the philosophy of internal relations, where determinism was equated first with the reciprocal effect found in any organic system and then with the greater or special influence of any one process on the others. To this we can now add a third, complementary sense of determinism that comes from the limiting and prescribing effects of overlapping contexts on all the phenomena that fall within them. Marx's success in displaying how the latter two kinds of determinism operate in the capitalist mode of production accounts for most of the explanatory power that one finds (and feels) in his writings.

Effects of events on their larger contexts, that is, of qualities found on more specific levels on those that fall on more general ones, can also be discerned. Whenever Marx speaks of people reproducing the conditions of their existence, the reference is to how activities whose main qualities fall on one level of generality help to construct the various contexts, including those on other levels of generality, that make the continuation of these same activities both possible and highly likely. Such effects, however, can also be detrimental. In our time, for example, the unregulated growth of harmful features associated with modern capitalist production (level two) have begun to threaten the ecological balance necessary not only for the continuation of capitalism (level three) but for the life of our species (level five).

As for the relation between the choice of extension and that of level of generality, there would seem to be a rough correspondence between narrow abstractions of extension and abstracting very low and very high levels of generality. Once the complex social relations in which a particular phenomenon is situated are put aside through a narrow abstraction of extension, there is little reason to bring these relations into better focus by abstracting the level of generality on which they fall. Thus, abstracting an extension that sets individuals apart from their social conditions is usually accompanied by an abstraction of level of generality that focuses on what is unique about each (level one). With the social qualities that were abstracted from individuals in extension now attached to the groups to which they belong (viewed as externally related to their members), efforts at generalizing tend to bypass the levels on which these social qualities would be brought into focus (modern capitalism, capitalism, and class society) and move directly to the level of the human condition (level five). So it is that for bourgeois ideology people are either all different (level one) or all the same (level five). While for Marx, whose abstractions of extension usually include a significant number of social relations, choosing the levels of generality of capitalism, modern capitalism, and class society was both easy and obvious, just as privileging these levels led to abstractions of extension that enabled him to take in at one sweep most of the connections that attention to these levels brings into focus.

And Vantage Point

The third mode in which Marx's abstractions occur is that of vantage point. Capitalists, as we have seen, are referred to as "embodiments of capital"; but capital is also said to function as it does because it is in the hands of people who use it to make profit (Marx 1959a, 794, 857–58; 1959b, 79). The state is said to be an instrument of the ruling economic class; but Marx also treats it as a set of objective structures that respond to the requirements of the economy, as an aspect of the mode of production itself (Marx and Engels 1945, 15; Marx 1959b, 103). There are many similar, apparently contradictory positions taken in Marx's writings. They are the result of different abstractions but not of extension or level of generality. They are due to different abstractions of vantage point. The same relation is being viewed from different sides, or the same process from its different moments.

In the same mental act in which Marx's units of thought obtain an extension and a level of generality they acquire a vantage point or place from which to view the elements of any particular Relation and, given its then extension, from which to reconstruct the larger system to which this Relation belongs. A vantage point sets up a perspective that colors everything that falls into it, establishing order, hierarchy, and priorities, distributing values, meanings, and degrees of relevance, and asserting a distinctive coherence between the parts. Within a given perspective, some processes and connections will appear large, some obvious, some important; others will appear small, insignificant, and irrelevant; and some will even be invisible.

In discussing Marx's conception of Relation, we saw that it was more than a simple connection. It was always a connection contained in its parts *as seen* from one or another side. So capital and labor, for example, were quoted as being "expressions of the same Relation, only seen from the opposite pole" (Marx 1971, 491). Or again, Marx says, capital has one "organizational differentiation or composition" (that of fixed and circulating capital) from the point of view of circulation and another (that of constant and variable capital) from the point of view of production (1968, 579). Both circulation and production are part of the extended capital Relation. A criticism of the political economists is that they try to understand capital only from the point of view of circulation, but to grasp the nature of wealth in capitalism, Marx believes, the decisive vantage point is that of production (1968, 578).

It is clear that the decisions Marx makes regarding extension and levels of generality greatly affect the kind of vantage points he abstracts, and vice-versa. The amount of mutual dependence and process that is included in an abstraction of extension largely determines what can be seen and studied from this same abstraction taken as a vantage point. Giving production the extension of reproduction or capital the extension of capital accumulation, for example, enables Marx to bring into view and organize the system of which they are part in ways that would not be possible with narrower (or shorter) abstractions. Likewise, in abstracting a level of generality, Marx brings into focus an entire range of qualities that can now serve individually or collectively (depending on the abstraction of extension) as vantage points, just as other possible vantage points, organized around qualities from other levels of generality, are excluded. Conversely, any commitment to a particular vantage point predisposes Marx to abstract the extension and level of generality that correspond to it and enables him to make the most of it as a vantage point. In practice, these three decisions (really, three aspects of the same decision) as to extension, level of generality, and vantage point are usually made together, and their effects are immediate, though on any given occasion one or another of them may appear to dominate.

In the social sciences, the notion of vantage point is most closely associated with the work of Karl Mannheim (1936, pt. 5). But for Mannheim, a point of view is something that belongs to people, particularly as organized into classes. The conditions in which each class lives and works provides its members with a distinctive range of experiences and a distinctive point of view. Because of their separate points of view, even the few experiences that are shared by people of opposing classes are not only understood but actually perceived in quite different ways. As far as it goes, this view—which Mannheim takes over from Marx—is correct. Marx's conception of point of view goes further, however, by grounding each class's perceptions in the nature of its habitual abstractions in order to show how starting out to make sense of society from just these mental units, within the perspectives that they establish, leads to different perceptual outcomes. In uncovering the cognitive link between class conditions and class perceptions, Marx helps us understand not only *why* Mannheim is right but *how* what he describes actually works. As part of this, point of view becomes an attribute of the abstraction as such (Marx speaks of the point of view or vantage point of accumulation, relations of production, money, etc.) and only secondarily of the person or class that adopts it (Marx 1963, 303; 1971, 156; 1973, 201).

We can now explain why Marx believes workers have a far better chance to understand the workings of capitalism than do capitalists. Their advantage does not come from the quality of their lives and only in small part from their class interests (since the capitalists have an interest in misleading even themselves about how their system works). More important, given what constitutes the lives of workers, the abstractions with which they start out to make sense of their society are likely to include "labor," "factory," and "machine," especially "labor," which puts the activity that is chiefly responsible for social change at the front and center of their thinking. Within the perspective set up by this abstraction, most of what occurs in capitalism gets arranged as part of the necessary conditions and results of this activity. There is no more enlightening vantage point for making sense of what is, both as the outcome of what was and as the origins of what is coming into being. This is not to say, of course, that all workers will make these connections (there are plenty of reasons coming from their alienated lives and from the ideological barrage directed at them that militate against it), but the predisposition to do so that is rooted in the initial abstraction of vantage point is there.

For capitalists, just the opposite is the case. Their lives and work incline them to start making sense of their situation with the aid of "price," "competition," "profit," and other abstractions drawn from the marketplace. Trying to put together how capitalism functions within perspectives that place labor near the end of the line rather than at the start simply turns capitalist dynamics around. According to Marx, in competition, "everything always appears in inverted form, always standing on its head" (1968, 217). What are predominantly the effects of productive activity appear here as its cause. It is demands coming from the market, itself the product of alienated labor, for example, that seem to determine what gets produced, as in the theory of "consumer sovereignty."

As with thinking in terms of processes and relations, common sense is not wholly devoid of perspectival thinking. People occasionally use expressions such as "point of view," "vantage point," and "perspective" to refer to some part of what we have been discussing, but they are generally unaware of how much their points of view affect everything they see and know and of the role played by abstractions in arriving at this result. As with their abstractions of extension and level of generality, most people simply accept as given the abstractions of vantage point that are handed down to them by their culture and particularly by their class. They examine their world again and again from the same one or few angles, while their ability to abstract new vantage points becomes atrophied. The one-sided views that result are treated as not only correct but as natural, indeed as the only possible view.

Earlier we saw that one major variety of bourgeois ideology arises from using too narrow abstractions of extension (dismissing parts of both processes and relationships that are essential for accurately comprehending even what is included) and that a second comes from abstracting an inappropriate level of generality (inappropriate in that it leaves out of focus the main level[s] on which the qualities we need to understand are located). There is a third major form of bourgeois ideology that is associated with the abstraction of vantage point. Here, ideology results from abstracting a vantage point that either hides or seriously distorts the relations and movements that pertain to the particular problem that concerns us. Not everything we need or want to know emerges with equal clarity, or even emerges at all, from every possible vantage point.

A related form of ideology results from examining a phenomenon from only one side, no matter how crucial, when several are needed—all the while being unaware of the limits on what can be learned from this side alone. This is what Hegel has in mind when he claims that to think abstractly (in the ideological sense of the term) is "to cling to one predicate" (1966, 118). Murderers, servants, and soldiers, who serve as Hegel's examples, are all much more than what is conveyed by viewing them from the single vantage point associated with the labels we have given them. Marx is even more explicit when, for example, he berates the economist Ramsay for bringing out all the factors but "one-sidedly" and "therefore incorrectly" (1971, 351) or equates "wrong" with "one-sided" in a criticism of Ricardo (1968, 470).

What needs to be stressed is that Marx never criticizes ideology as a simple lie or claims that what it asserts is completely false. Instead, ideology is generally described as overly narrow, partial, out of focus, and/or one-sided, all of which are attributable to faulty or otherwise inappropriate abstractions of extension, level of generality, and vantage point, where neither these abstractions nor their implications are grasped for what they are. While correctly pointing to the material roots of ideology in capitalist conditions and in the conscious manipulations of capitalists and bringing out how it functions to serve capitalist interests, most discussions of ideology completely ignore the misapplication of the process of abstraction that is responsible for its distinctive forms.

Among the major vantage points associated with bourgeois ideology, where the error is not simply one of restricting analysis to a single perspective but where the one or few that are chosen either hide or distort the essential features of capitalism, are the following: the vantage point of the isolated individual, the subjective side of any situation (what is believed, wanted, intended, etc.), the results of almost any process, anything connected with the market, and all of what falls on level five of generality, particularly human nature.

The isolated individual, man separated from both natural and social conditions, is not only the preferred abstraction of extension in which bourgeois ideology treats human beings; it also serves as its preferred vantage point for studying society. Society becomes what social relations look like when viewed from this angle. When one adds that within each person it is such subjective qualities as beliefs, wants, or intentions that are bourgeois ideology's preferred vantage points for viewing the rest of the person, it should be no surprise that the objective features of any situation of which people are a part are so undervalued. In this perspective, an individual is chiefly what he or she believes him- or herself to be, and society itself is what many individuals operating one at a time in the absence of strong social pressures or significant material restraints have made it.

There is also an obvious link between abstracting human beings narrowly in extension, abstracting this extension on levels one and five of generality, and abstracting this extension on these levels of generality as preferred vantage points. By abstracting the isolated individual in extension, one omits the various social and other connections that would incline one to bring levels two, three, and four of generality into focus in order to learn how these connections have acquired the specific characteristics that make them important. And because the contexts associated with modern capitalism, capitalism, and class society are seldom if ever brought into focus, the qualities that fall on these levels can hardly serve as useful vantage points. To the limited extent that anything from these contexts does get examined from the vantage points associated with bourgeois ideology, the result is usually a hodgepodge of mismatched qualities from different levels of generality, with some more and some less in focus, all loosely held together by the language of external relations. Whatever integration is achieved by such studies only succeeds in breaking up and dissembling

the organic unity that exists on each of these levels, making a systematic understanding of any kind that much more difficult.

Other than the isolated individual and his or her subjective qualities, another
family of vantage points that is well represented in bourgeois ideology are the
results of various social processes, especially those found in the market. Already
narrowly abstracted in extension as finished products, the processes by which
these results have emerged are no longer visible. Thus, capital is simply the
means of production; a commodity is any good that is bought and sold; profit
is something earned by capitalists; and the market itself is an over-the-counter
exchange of goods and services that follows its own extra social laws. When used
as vantage points for viewing the capitalist system, these dead building blocks
can only construct a dead building, an unchanging system whose emergence at
a certain point in history is as much a mystery as its eventual demise. The ultimate distortion occurs in what Marx calls the fetishism of commodities (or
capital, or value, or money), when these results take on a life of their own and
are viewed as self-generating. Whenever any static and narrowly conceived of
set of results are used as a vantage point for examining origins, there is a danger of substituting the end for the beginning in this way.

Still other vantage points put to heavy use in bourgeois ideology are whatever is taken to be part of the human condition, the whole of level five and especially human nature as such, or rather what is taken to be human nature. Starting out from these vantage points, phenomena whose most important qualities
fall on levels one to four lose their historical specificity and are made to appear
as obvious and inevitable as the flat abstractions that introduce them. In this
way, approaching capitalist distribution, as the political economists are accused
of doing, from the vantage point of a level five notion of production—that is,
production in so far as it partakes of the human condition—makes it appear
that the existing capitalist division of wealth is equally "natural."

Marx, who on occasion makes use of all these vantage points, favors vantage
points connected with production, the objective side of any situation, historical
processes generally, and social class, particularly at the level of generality of capitalist society. The reason he privileges such vantage points varies, as does the extension he gives them, with the level of generality on which he is operating. Beyond this, Marx's abstraction of vantage point—as indeed of extension and level
of generality—can usually be traced to his theories and what they indicate is necessary to uncover some part of the organic or historical movement of the capitalist mode of production. One must be careful, here as elsewhere, not to place
within Marx's method many of the judgments and decisions regarding priorities that could only come from the theories he developed with its help.

Equally characteristic of Marx's practice in abstracting vantage points is the
easy facility he shows in moving from one to the other. Aware of the limitations
inherent in any single vantage point, even that of production, Marx frequently
alters the angle from which he examines his chosen subject matter. While whole

works and sections of works can be distinguished on the basis of the vantage point that predominates, changes of vantage point can also be found on virtually every page of Marx's writings. Within the same sentence, he can move from viewing wages from the vantage point of the worker to the vantage point of society as a whole (1963, 108). Marx's analysis of the complex relations between production, distribution, exchange, and consumption, which has already come into this work on several occasions, also provides what is perhaps the best example of how often he changes his abstractions of both extension and vantage point and how important this practice and his facility in it was for obtaining his results (1904, 274–92).

As with his abstractions of extension and level of generality, Marx's abstractions of vantage point play a crucial role in the construction of all his theories. It is Marx's abstractions of vantage point that enable him to find identity in difference (and vice-versa), to actually catch sight of the organic and historical movements made possible by his abstractions of extension, and to classify and reclassify the world of his perceptions into the explanatory structures bound up in what we call Marxism.

Earlier, in discussing Marx's theory of identity, we saw that abstracting an extension that is large enough to contain both identical and different qualities of two or more phenomena is what makes the coexistence of identity and difference possible, but one's ability to actually see and therefore to examine either set of qualities depends on the vantage point adopted for viewing them. Sticking with one vantage point will restrict understanding any relation to its identical or different aspects when, in fact, it contains both. Marx, however, can approach the relation of profit, rent, and interest from the vantage point of surplus-value, of their identity or what they have in common as the portion of value that is not returned to the workers who produced it, as well as from any of the vantage points located in differences arising from who holds these forms of surplus-value and how each functions in the economic system.

Abstracting vantage points that bring out the differences between two or more aspects of an interactive system also highlights the asymmetry in their reciprocal effect. Granted such a reciprocal effect, production was said to play the dominant role on all five levels of generality on which Marx operates. But it is only by abstracting production as a vantage point that its special influence on other economic processes and on society as a whole on each level can be seen for what it is. As Marx says, with the level of class societies in mind, the existence of the ruling class and their functions "can only be understood *from* the specific historical structure of their production relations" (1963, 285 [emphasis added]).

Along with his abstractions of extension, Marx's abstractions of vantage point play an equally important role in establishing the flexible boundaries that characterize all his theories. In Marx's division of reality into objective and subjective conditions, it is by abstracting a vantage point first in one and then in the other that he uncovers the more objective aspects of what is ordinarily taken to be subjective (extending the territory of the objective accordingly), and vice-versa. Together with the aforementioned theory of identity, changes in the abstraction of vantage point enable Marx to actually see objective and subjective conditions as "two distinct forms of the same conditions" (1973, 832). Likewise, it is by abstracting a particular vantage point that Marx can see aspects of nature in society, or the forces of production in the relations of production, or economic in typically noneconomic structures, or the base in the superstructure, and then vice-versa, adjusting the abstraction of extension for each pairing accordingly. Looking at the relations of production from the vantage point of the forces of production, for example, even the cooperative power of workers can appear as a productive force (Marx and Engels 1964, 46).

Marx's various class divisions of society, based as we have seen on different abstractions of extension for class, are also discernible only from the vantage point of the qualities (functions, opposition to other classes, consciousness, etc.) that serve as the criteria for constructing a given classification. That is, if class is a complex Relation made up of a number of different aspects, and if the composition of any particular class depends on which ones Marx includes in his abstraction of extension and brings into focus through his abstraction of level of generality, then his ability to actually distinguish people as members of this class depends on which aspect(s) he abstracts as his vantage points for viewing them. It also follows that as Marx's vantage point changes, so does his operative division of society into classes. In this way, too, the same people viewed from the vantage points of qualities associated with different classes may actually fall into different classes. The landowner, for example, is said to be a capitalist in so far as he confronts labor as the owner of commodities, or functions as a capitalist vis-à-vis labor (rather than as a landowner vis-à-vis capitalists), whenever he is viewed from this traditional capitalist vantage point (Marx 1963, 51).

Viewed from the vantage point of any one of his qualities, the individual's identity is limited to what can be seen from this angle. The qualities that emerge from the use of other vantage points are ignored because for all practical purposes, at *this* moment in the analysis and for treating *this* particular problem, they simply don't exist. Hence, people abstracted as workers, for example—that is, viewed from one or more of the qualities associated with membership in this class—where the object of study is capitalist political economy, are presented as not having any gender or nation or race. People, of course, possess all these characteristics and more, and Marx—when dealing with other problems—can abstract vantage points (usually as part of noncapitalist levels of generality) that bring out these other identities.

Given his flexibility in abstracting extension, Marx can also consider people from vantage points that play down their human qualities altogether in order to highlight some special relation. Such is the case when he refers to the buyer as a "representative of money confronting commodities"—that is, views him from the vantage point of money inside an abstraction of extension that includes money, commodities, and people (1963, 404). The outstanding example of this practice is Marx's frequent reference to capitalists as "embodiments" or "personifications" of capital, where living human beings are considered from the vantage point of their economic function (1958, 10, 85, and 592). The school of structuralist Marxism has performed an important service in recovering such claims from the memory hole to which an older, more class-struggle-oriented Marxism had consigned them. However useful decentering human nature in this manner is for grasping some of the role-determined behavior that Marx wanted to stress, there is much that is volunteerist in his theories that requires the adoption of distinctively human vantage points, and only a dialectical Marxism that possesses sufficient flexibility in changing abstractions—of vantage point as of extension and level of generality—can make the frequent adjustments that are called for.

If Marx's abstractions of extension are large enough to encompass how things happen as part of what they are, if such abstractions of extension also allow him to grasp the various organic and historical movements uncovered by his research as essential movements, then it is his abstractions of vantage point that make what is there—what his abstractions of extension have "placed" there—visible. The movement of the transformation of quantity into quality, for example, is made possible as an essential movement by an abstraction of extension that includes both quantitative changes and the qualitative change that eventually occurs. But this transformative process is not equally clear or even visible from each of its moments. In this case, the preferred vantage point—not the only one possible, but simply the ideal—is one that bridges the end of quantitative changes and the start of the qualitative one. Viewing the cooperation among workers, for example, from the vantage point of where its transformation into a qualitatively new productive power begins provides the clearest indication of where this change has come from as well as where the process that brought it about was heading.

The movement of metamorphosis, we will recall, is an organic movement in which qualities associated with one part of a system get transferred to its other parts. In the case of the metamorphosis of value, the main instance of this movement in Marx's writings, some of the central relationships that constitute value get taken up by commodity, capital, wage-labor, et cetera. Only an abstraction of extension that is large enough to include its different phases as internally related aspects of a single system allows us to conceive of metamorphosis as an internal movement and of its subsequent stages as forms of what it starts out as. But to observe this metamorphosis and therefore to study it in any detail we must accompany this abstraction of extension with an abstraction of vantage point in the part whose qualities are being transferred. Thus, the metamorphosis of value into and through its various forms is only observable as a metamorphosis from the vantage point of value.

As regards contradiction, Marx says, as we saw, "in capitalism everything seems and in fact is contradictory" (1963, 218). It *is* so—in reality, and with the help of Marx's broad abstractions of extension, which organize the parts as mutually dependent processes. But it *seems* so only from certain vantage points. From others, the incompatible development of the parts would be missed, or misconstrued, or, at a minimum, seriously underestimated. The vantage point from which Marx usually observes contradictions is the intersection between the two or more processes said to be in contradiction. It is a composite vantage point made up of elements from all these processes. Of course, if one has not abstracted differences as processes and such processes as mutually dependent, there is no point of intersection to serve as a vantage point.

What we've called the double movement of the capitalist mode of production can be approached—that is, viewed and studied—from any of the major contradictions that compose it, and in each case, given internal relations, the elements that are not directly involved enter into the contradiction as part of its extended conditions and results. In this way, the vantage point that is adopted organizes not only the immediate contradiction but establishes a perspective in which other parts of the system acquire their order and importance. In the contradiction between exchange and use-value, for example, the relations between capitalists and workers are part of the necessary conditions for this contradiction to take its present form and develop as it does, just as one result of this contradiction is the reproduction of the ties between capitalists and workers. Given the internal relations Marx posits between all elements in the system, this makes capitalists and workers subordinate aspects of the contradiction between exchange and use-value. The whole process can be turned around: adopting the vantage point of the contradiction between capitalists and workers transforms the relations between exchange and use-value into its subordinate aspects, again as both necessary preconditions and results. The actual links in each case, of course, need to be carefully worked out. Hence, contradictions can be said to overlap; they cover much the same ground, but this ground is broken up in various ways, along a variety of axes, based on as many different foci.

Even when the shift in vantage points appears to be slight, the difference in the perspective opened up can be considerable. For example, take the contradiction between capital and wage-labor, on the one hand, and that between capitalists and workers, on the other hand. The vantage point for viewing the former is the intersection of two objective functions, while the preferred vantage point for viewing the latter is where the activities and interests of the two classes who perform these functions intersect. Each of these contradictions contains the other as major dependent aspects (neither capital nor capitalists could appear and function as they do without the other, and the same holds for wage-labor and workers). Yet, though both contradictions can be said to cover more or less the same ground, the different perspectives established by these contrasting vantage points allows Marx to distinguish how people create their conditions from how they are created by them and to trace out the implications of each position without dismissing or undervaluing the other—all the while presenting both contradictions as undergoing similar pressures and in the process of a similar transformation.

Marx's laws offer still another illustration of the crucial role played by the abstraction of vantage point. As was pointed out earlier, all of Marx's laws are tendencies arising from the very nature of whatever it is that is said to have them. In every case, it is Marx's abstraction of extension that brings the various organic and historical movements together under the same rubric, making how things happen a part of what they are, but it is his abstraction of vantage point that enables him (and us) to actually catch sight of them as a single tendency.

The law of the falling rate of profit, for example, is a tendency inherent in the relation of profit to the "organic composition" of capital, which Marx understands as the ratio of constant to variable capital (or the investment put into the material means of production as compared to that put into buying labor power). With the proportion of investment going to constant capital because of technological development always on the rise, less and less of any given investment goes to buy variable capital. But only labor power creates value, and therefore surplus-value. With a constantly decreasing proportion of investment involved in producing surplus-value, therefore, the rate of profit as a percentage of total investment must also go down (Marx 1959a, pt. 3).

Like all tendencies in Marx's work, this one too is subject to countertendencies, both on the same and on the other levels of generality (state subsidies, inflation, devaluation of existing capital, etc.), which are often strong enough to keep the tendency for the falling rate of profit from appearing in the balance sheet of businessmen at the end of the year. To observe this tendency, therefore, and to be in a position to study the constant pressure it exerts on the concentration of capital (another law) and through it on the entire capitalist system, one must follow Marx in abstracting an extension for profit that includes its relation over time to the organic composition of capital and view this Relation from the vantage point of this composition (granted, of course, the capitalist level of generality on which both of these are found). Without such abstractions of extension, level of generality, and vantage point, one simply cannot see, let alone grasp, what Marx is talking about. With them, one can see the law despite all the sand thrown up by countertendencies. Hence, the irrelevance of various attempts by Marx's critics and followers alike to evaluate the law of the falling rate of profit based on analyses made from the vantage point of one of its possible results (the actual profits of real businessmen), or from capitalist competition, or some other vantage point located in the marketplace. All the laws in Marxism can be described, studied, and evaluated only inside the perspectives associated with the particular vantage points from which Marx both discovered and constructed them.

The Role of Abstractions in the Debates over Marxism

It will have become evident by now that it is largely differences of vantage point that lay behind many of the great debates in the history of Marxist scholarship. In a debate between Ralph Miliband and Nicos Poulantzas in the *New Left Review* on the character of the capitalist state, for example, the former viewed the state chiefly from the vantage point of the ruling economic class, while the latter viewed what are essentially the same set of relations from the vantage point of the socioeconomic structures that establish both the limits and requirements for a community's political functions (Poulantzas 1969; Miliband 1970).[4] As a result, Miliband is better able to account for the traditional role of the state in serving ruling class interests, while Poulantzas has an easier time explaining the relative autonomy of the state and why the capitalist state continues to serve the ruling class when the latter is not directly in control of state institutions.

The debate over whether capitalist economic crisis is caused by the tendency of the rate of profit to fall or arises from difficulties in the realization of value, where one side views the capitalist economy from the vantage point of the accumulation process and the other from the vantage point of market contradictions, is of the same sort (Mattick 1969; Baran and Sweezy 1966).[5] A somewhat related dispute over the centrality of the capitalist mode of production as compared to the international division of labor (the position of World System Theory) for charting the history and future of capitalism is likewise rooted in a difference of preferred vantage points (Brenner 1977; Wallerstein 1974). So, too, is the debate over whether bourgeois ideology is mainly a reflection of alienated life and reified structures or the product of the capitalist consciousness industry, where one side views the construction of ideology from the vantage point of the material and social conditions out of which it arises and the other from that of the role played by the capitalist class in promoting it (Mepham 1979; Marcuse 1965).

Earlier, in what is perhaps the most divisive dispute of all, we saw that those who argue for a strict determinism emanating from one or another version of the economic factor (whether simple or structured) and those who emphasize the role of human agency (whether individual or class) can also be distinguished on the basis of the vantage points they have chosen for investigating the necessary interaction between the two (Althusser 1965; Sartre 1963). To be sure, each of these positions, here as in the other debates, is also marked by somewhat different abstractions of extension for shared phenomena based in part on what is known and considered worth knowing, but even these distinguishing features come into prominence mainly as a result of the vantage point that is treated as privileged.

The different levels of generality on which Marx operates is also responsible for its share of debates among interpreters of his ideas, the main one being over the subject of the materialist conception of history: is it all history, or all of class history, or the period of capitalism (in which earlier times are conceived of as precapitalist) (Kautsky 1988; Korsch 1970)? Depending on the answer, the sense in which production is held to be primary will vary, as will the abstractions of extension and vantage point used to bring this out.

Finally, the various abstractions of extension of such central notions as mode of production, class, state, et cetera, have also led to serious disagreements among Marx's followers and critics alike, with most schools seeking to treat the boundaries they consider decisive as permanent. However, as evidenced by the quotations that practically every side in these disputes can draw upon, Marx is capable of pursuing his analysis not only on all social levels of generality and from various vantage points but with units of differing extension, only giving greater weight to the abstractions that his theories indicate are most useful in revealing the particular dynamic he is investigating. The many apparently contradictory claims that emerge from his study are in fact complementary, and all are required to "reflect" the complex double movement (historical—including probable future—and organic) of the capitalist mode of production. Without an adequate grasp of the role of abstraction in dialectical method, and without sufficient flexibility in making the needed abstractions of extension, level of generality, and vantage point, most interpreters of Marx (Marxists and non-Marxists alike) have constructed versions of his theories that suffer in their very form from the same rigidity, inappropriate focus, and one-sidedness that Marx saw in bourgeois ideology.

In an often quoted though little analyzed remark in the introduction to *Capital,* Marx says that value, as compared to larger, more complex notions, has proven so difficult to grasp because "the body, as an organic whole, is more easy to study than are the cells of that body." To make such a study, he adds, one must use the "force of abstraction" (1958, 8). Using the force of abstraction, as I have tried to show, is Marx's way of putting dialectics to work. It is the living dialectic, its process of becoming, the engine that sets other parts of his method into motion. In relation to this emphasis on the force of abstraction, every other approach to studying dialectics stands on the outside looking in. The relations of contradiction, identity, law, et cetera, that they study have all been constructed, made visible, ordered, and brought into focus through prior abstractions. Consequently, while other approaches may help us to understand what dialectics is and to recognize it when we see it, only an account that puts the process of abstraction at the center enables us to think adequately about change and interaction, which is to say, to think dialectically, and to do research and engage in political struggle in a thoroughly dialectical manner.[6]

Notes

1. Possible exceptions to this relative neglect of abstraction in discussions of Marx's method include E. V. Ilyenkov (1982), where the emphasis is on the relation of abstract to concrete in *Capital;* Alfred Sohn-Rethel (1978), who shows how commodity exchange produces certain ideologi-

cal abstractions; Derek Sayers (1987), who stresses the role of the process of abstraction in producing ideology; Leszek Nowack (1980), who presents a neo-Weberian reconstruction of some
aspects of this process; Roy Bhaskar (1993), who treats most of what occurs in abstraction under
conceptualization; and Paul Sweezy (1964), still the best short introduction to our subject, who
stresses the role of abstraction in isolating the essentials of any problem. Insightful, though limited, treatments of abstraction can also be found in articles by Andrew Sayers (1981), John Allen
(1983), and particularly Ronald J. Horvath and Kenneth D. Gibson (1984). An early philosophical
account of abstraction, which Marx himself had a chance to read and admire, is found in the work
of Joseph Dietzgen (1928). Dietzgen's contribution to our subject is described briefly in chapter 3.

2. The school of Critical Realism, associated with the work of Roy Bhaskar, made just the opposite assumption, particularly in its earliest publications. See, for example, Bhaskar's *A Realist
Theory of Science* (1975). In subsequent works, such as *Dialectic: The Pulse of Freedom* (1993), Bhaskar
has given the process of abstraction a much higher profile in his system. For my critical appreciation of this particular version of dialectical thinking, see chapter 10 of this volume.

3. Other important dialectical movements are mediation, interpenetration of polar opposites,
negation of the negation, precondition and result, and unity and separation. Except for "precondition and result," the main subject of the next chapter, these movements will receive fuller treatment in my next book on dialectics. For now, it is sufficient to point out that the role that abstraction plays in constructing and helping to make visible the movements of quantity/quality change,
metamorphosis, and contradiction applies equally to them.

4. Both thinkers seriously modified the views expressed in these articles in later works (Miliband 1977; Poulantzas 1978), and these revisions too can be explained in large part through changes
in their abstractions of vantage point.

5. There are still other Marxist interpretations of capitalist crises (as, indeed, of the state) that
are also largely dependent on the vantage point adopted. Here, as in the other debates mentioned,
it was enough to refer to a single major cleavage to illustrate my claim regarding the role of abstractions.

6. Not all of the important questions associated with dialectics have been dealt with in this essay. Missing or barely touched on are the place and/or role within dialectical method of reflection, perception, emotion, memory, conceptualization (language), appropriation, moral evaluation, verification, wisdom, will, and activity, particularly in production. I am painfully aware of
their absence, but my purpose here is not to provide a complete overview of dialectics but to make
it possible for people to begin to put it to work by deconstructing the much-neglected process of
abstraction, which, along with the philosophy of internal relations, I take to be at the core of this
method. My next volume on dialectics, which focuses on appropriation as Marx's preferred
abstraction for knowing, being, and doing in their interaction with one another on the level of
generality of capitalism overall, will try to make up for these lapses. It will also contain a more systematic treatment of the moments of inquiry and exposition, as forms of activity under appropriation, as well as a critical survey of some of the more important contributions to dialectical
method that have been passed over in the present work.

STEP 4

Studying History Backward: A Neglected Feature of Marx's Materialist Conception of History

1

History is the story of the past, and like any story it begins in the past and proceeds forward to the present or however near the present one wants to take it. This is how it happened. This is also the order in which this story is usually told. It doesn't follow, however, that this is the ideal order for studying the meaning of the story, especially as regards its final outcome. Marx, for one, believed that we could best approach how the past developed into the present by adopting the vantage point of the present to view the conditions that gave rise to it—in other words, if we studied history backward.[1] In his words, "the actual movement starts from existing capital—i.e., the actual movement denotes developed capitalist production, which starts from and presupposes its own basis" (1963, 513).

This is not a lesson to be gleaned from most writers on Marx's materialist conception of history, where the most popular debates deal with the nature of the "economic factor" and the effect it is presumed to have on the rest of society, with historical periodization, relative autonomy, and, above all, the paradoxical juxtaposition of freedom and determinism. Irrespective of their political views, virtually all sides in these debates examine history in the order in which it happened. Thus, whether one takes changes in the forces of production, or in the relations of production, or in economic structures, or in material existence as determining new developments in the social order (and no matter how strong or weak a sense is given to the notion of "determine"), what brings about the change is generally treated first and the change that is brought about second, with the latter being viewed from the vantage point of the former, as its "necessary" result. Basing themselves on the order in which Marx often presents his conclusions—"The hand mill gives you society with the feudal lord; the steam mill society with the industrial capitalist" (n.d., 122)—they have assumed, wrongly, that this is also the order in which Marx conducted his studies and would have us conduct ours.

Marx's unusual approach to studying history is rooted in his acceptance of the Hegelian philosophy of internal relations, the much-neglected foundation of his entire dialectical method. Based on this philosophy, each of the elements that come into Marx's analysis includes as aspects of what it is all those other elements with which it interacts and without which it could neither appear nor function as it does. In this way, labor and capital, for example, in virtue of their close interaction, are conceived of as aspects of each other. Labor-power could not be sold or get embodied in a product over which workers have no control if there were no capitalists to buy it, just as capitalists could not use labor to produce surplus-value if labor-power were not available for sale. It is in this sense that Marx calls capital and labor "expressions of the same relation, only seen from the opposite pole" (1971, 491). Likewise, the unfolding of this interaction over time, its real history, is viewed as internally related to is present forms. Things are conceived of, in Marx's words, "as they are and *happen*" (Marx and Engels 1964, 57 [emphasis added]), so that the process of their becoming is as much a part of what they are as the qualities associated with how they appear and function at this moment.

With the philosophy of internal relations, a major problem arises whenever one wants to stress a particular aspect or temporal segment of this ongoing interaction without seeming to deny or trivialize its other elements. One of the main ways Marx tried to resolve this problem is with the notion of "precondition and result." Like contradiction, metamorphosis, and quantity/quality change—though less well known than any of these—the notion of precondition and result enables Marx to pursue his studies more effectively by bringing certain aspects of change and interaction into sharper focus. Specifically, precondition and result is a double movement that processes in mutual interaction undergo in becoming both effects and makers of each other's effect simultaneously. For this, the two must be viewed dynamically (it is a matter of *becoming* a precondition and *becoming* a result) and organically (each process only takes place in and through the other).

According to Marx, capital and wage-labor are "continually presupposed" and "continuing products" of capitalist production (1971, 492). Indeed, "Every precondition of the social production process is at the same time its results, and every one of its results appears simultaneously as its preconditions. All the production relations within which the process moves are therefore just as much its product as they are its conditions" (1971, 507). Besides capital and wage-labor, Marx also treats foreign trade, the world market, money, and the supply of precious metals as both preconditions and results of capitalist production (1971, 253; 1957, 344). Of crucial importance for us is that establishing something as a precondition occurs by abstracting it from a situation that it has not only helped to bring about but of which it is itself, grasped now as a result, a fully integrated part.

Viewing precondition and result as two movements in the process of becoming and at the same time as aspects of a single movement requires, first, an abstraction of extension (of what all is included) that is large enough to encompass their interaction over time. Thus, as preconditions and results of one another, capital and wage-labor are each conceived of as including the other throughout the long course of their common evolution. Second, integrating the separate movements—in which capital serves as a precondition for wage-labor and simultaneously becomes a result of wage-labor—within a single combined movement without losing the distinctive character of each can only be done by changing vantage points for viewing them in mid-analysis. To treat labor as a precondition for capital, in other words, it is necessary to view labor from the vantage point of capital already grasped as a result, since we only know that one thing is a precondition for another when the latter has emerged in some recognizable form. It is not only that we must have the result in hand in order to examine what served it as a precondition, but it is the very occurrence of the result that transforms its major interlocking processes, its present conditions, into preconditions. Only when capital assumes the form of a result can labor take on the form of its precondition, so that the one becoming a result and the other becoming a precondition can be said to take place simultaneously.

However, as we saw, capital always includes wage-labor as one of its aspects. Thus, capital in its form as a result includes wage-labor, now also in the form of a result. And it is by adopting the vantage point of labor in this latter form that we can see that one of its major preconditions is capital. Here, too, and for similar reasons, labor's becoming a result and capital's becoming a precondition occur simultaneously. And this takes place simultaneously with the processes referred to above by which capital becomes a result and labor becomes one of its main preconditions. In both cases, investigating how something that exists came to be proceeds from its present form, the result, backward through its necessary preconditions.

As the interaction between processes in an organic system is ongoing, so too is the acquisition of qualities that makes them into preconditions and results of one another. Wage-labor has been both a precondition and result of capital (and vice-versa) throughout the long history of their relationship. Nevertheless, at any given moment, whenever either of these processes is singled out as a precondition, it is abstracted in extension as something less developed, possessing fewer of the qualities it eventually acquires in capitalism, than the result it is said to give rise to. Such is the case whenever two or more interacting processes are reabstracted, rearranged, to occur as a sequence. While interacting processes in an organic system are always mutually dependent, viewing their relations diachronically requires that they be abstracted at different phases in what has been a common evolution. This is necessary if Marx is to get at the distinctive

influence of particular aspects of that interaction over time, avoiding the opposing pitfalls of a shallow eclecticism, where everything is equally important
and hence nothing worth investigating, and causalism, where a major influence
erases all others while leaving its own progress unaccounted for. It is Marx's way
of establishing dialectical asymmetry, and with it of unraveling without distortion what might be called the double movement, systemic and historical, of the
capitalist mode of production.

2

The double movement of precondition and result occupies the central place in
most of Marx's historical studies. Searching for the preconditions of our capitalist present is the little-appreciated key with which Marx opens up the past. It
is what happened in the past that gave rise to this particular present that is of
special concern to him, but what exactly this was can only be adequately observed and examined from the vantage point of what it turned into. As Marx
says, "The anatomy of the human being is a key to the anatomy of the ape. . . .
The bourgeois economy furnishes a key to ancient economy, etc." (1904, 300).
Though frequently quoted, the full implications of this remark, especially as
regards Marx's method, have seldom been explored. It is essentially a directional
signpost intended to guide our research, and the direction in which it points is
back. And this applies to unique events and situations as well as to the processes
and relations whose level of generality places them in modern capitalism, the
capitalist era (the time frame for most of Marx's studies), the period of class
history, or the lifetime of our species.

Reading history backward in this way does not mean that Marx accepts a
cause at the end of history, a "motor force" operating in reverse, a teleology.
Instead, it is a matter of asking where the situation under hand comes from and
what had to happen for it to acquire just these qualities, that is, it is a matter of
asking what are its preconditions. In this case, the search for an answer is aided
by what we already know about the present, the result. Knowing how the "story"
came out, placing such knowledge at the start of our investigation, sets up criteria for relevance as well as research priorities.

It also provides a perspective for viewing and evaluating all that is found.
Whereas the alternative of viewing the present from some point in the past requires, first of all, that one justify the choice of just this moment with which to
begin. With the result unknown, or only vaguely known and completely
unanalyzed, there is no compelling reason to begin at one moment rather than
another. Likewise, the choice of what kind of phenomena—social, economic,
political, religious, et cetera—to emphasize at the start of such a study can only
be justified on the basis of a principle drawn from outside history, since the historical investigation that might confirm its value has yet to take place. Also associated with this approach is the tendency to offer single-track causal explanations

of the ties between what has been separated out as the beginning and what is found to come after. By viewing the past from the vantage point of the present, however, Marx can focus on what is most relevant in the past without compromising his adherence to a thoroughgoing mutual interaction throughout history.

Marx said that his approach uses both "observation and deduction" (1973, 460). He starts by examining existing society; he then deduces what it took for such complex phenomena to appear and function as they do; after which, he continues to research in the directions indicated by these deductions. By combining observation and deduction in this way—not once, but again and again— Marx can concentrate on what in the past proved to be most important and show why, while avoiding the parlor game, all too common among historians and the general public alike, of second-guessing what might have been. By ignoring the alternatives that were present at earlier stages, Marx is often misunderstood as denying that people could have chosen differently and that things might have taken another course. But this would only be true if he had begun with a cause located sometime in the past and had treated its subsequent effects as inevitable. Instead, starting with an already existing result, he is concerned to uncover what did in fact determine it, what the events themselves have transformed into its necessary preconditions. It is the necessity of the fait accompli, and only graspable retrospectively. Necessity read backward into the past is of an altogether different order than the necessity that begins in the past and follows a predetermined path into the future.

In investigating history backward, Marx makes an important distinction between preconditions that are themselves wholly results, albeit earlier forms of their own results now functioning as preconditions, and preconditions that have at least some features that come from previous social formations. It is the difference between what capitalism required to develop as compared to what it required to emerge in the first place. In the latter case, one precondition was the appearance in towns of large numbers of people who were willing and able to sell their labor-power and become a proletariat. This condition was met by the massive exodus of serfs from the estates due mainly to the various acts of enclosure that characterized late feudalism. Similarly, the accumulation of wealth that capitalism required in order to get under way could only come from sources other than the exploitation of labor that capital alone makes possible. Once in place, even minimally so, the capitalist mode of production accumulates wealth through its own distinctive means, reproducing in this way one of its major preconditions. In Marx's words, "The conditions and presuppositions of the becoming, of the arising, of capital presuppose precisely that it is not yet in being but merely in becoming; they therefore disappear as real capital arises, capital which itself, on the basis of its own reality, posits the conditions for its realization" (1973, 459).

The developments in feudalism that made the new turn toward capitalism possible were themselves, of course, internally related aspects of that mode of production, but they had no place or role in what came after. Marx refers to these developments as "suspended presuppositions [*aufgehobne Voraussetzungen*]" (1973, 461). They were necessary for the creation of capitalism, but there is no need for capitalism, once under way, to reproduce them. Examining currently existing capitalism backward through its preconditions and results leads in due course to the origins of the system. "Our method," Marx says, "indicates the points . . . where bourgeois economy as a merely historical form of the production process points beyond itself to earlier historical modes of production" (1973, 460). At this point, in order to trace the transformation of feudalism into capitalism, distinctively capitalist preconditions and results get replaced as the main objects of study by the suspended presuppositions of feudalism. The question that guides research still is what capitalism—now viewed in its earliest stage—required, and the direction in which study proceeds remains as before: backward.

What needs emphasizing is that Marx seldom treats feudalism as just another mode of production alongside capitalism. Hence, feudalism's most distinctive structures at the high point of their development receive little attention. Also, feudalism is seldom examined as the mode of production that produced capitalism—hence, the relative neglect of the former's internal dynamics. Instead, feudalism almost always comes into Marx's writings as the social formation in which the immediate origins of capitalism are to be found. "The formation of capitalism," Marx says, "*is* the dissolution process of feudalism" (1971, 491 [emphasis added]). It is as an essential part of capitalism that feudalism is studied. Thus, it is the particular ways in which the disintegration of feudalism occurs that is of prime interest to Marx, for it is here that he uncovers the preconditions of capitalism. And the same applies to earlier periods, for the roots of capitalism extend even there. They are all precapitalist and of interest primarily as such. Consequently, moving from capitalism back through its preconditions to feudalism and slavery there is no pretension of offering these three stages as a model of development through which every country must pass, as too often occurs when they are treated in reverse order. This is another example of the difference between necessity read backward from the present and necessity read forward from some point in the past. Its wide popularity notwithstanding, what's called the "Marxist periodization of history" is but another unfortunate result of standing Marx's method on its head. In sum, looking back from the vantage point of what capitalism has become to what it presupposes enables Marx to concentrate on specific features in the rubble of the past that he would otherwise miss or underplay, just as it enhances his understanding—essentially transforming the last moments of a dying system into the birthing moments of a new one—of what is found.

To be sure, Marx can also examine the relation of precondition and result from the vantage point of the former, beginning in the past and looking ahead; in which case, it is more accurate to speak of "cause" (or "condition") and "effect," and he occasionally adopts this order (and these terms) in expounding his conclusions, especially in more popular works, such as his preface to the

Critique of Political Economy (1904). What makes cause and effect less satisfactory as a way of organizing research is that before we have an effect it is difficult to know what constitutes the cause, or—once we've decided what the cause is—to know where the cause comes from, or—having determined that—to know where in its own evolution as the cause to begin our study. Consequently, the complex interaction by which the cause is itself shaped and made adequate to its task by the effect, now functioning in its turn as a cause, is easily lost or distorted, even where—as in Marx's case—causes and effects are viewed as internally related. If Marx still uses the formulation "cause" and "effect" (or "condition," "determine," and "produce" in the sense of "cause"), this is usually a shorthand and first approximation for bringing out for purposes of exposition some special feature in a conclusion whose essential connections have been uncovered by studying them as preconditions and results.

Unable to follow Marx's practice in making abstractions, lacking a conception of internal relations and a workable grasp of the often conflicting demands of inquiry and exposition, most of Marx's readers have forced his words on precondition and result into a causal framework. The components of capitalism get divided into causes (or conditions, generally understood as weak or broad causes) and effects, with the result that the former, separated from their real causes, are made to appear ahistorical, possibly natural, as something that cannot be changed or even seriously questioned. Thus, when Marx presents man as a social product, the multiple ways in which people also create society are distorted if not completely missed. While, conversely, those who emphasize Marx's comments on human beings as creators of society generally miss the full impact of what is meant in his references to people as social products. Whereas, for Marx, man is "the permanent precondition of human history, likewise its permanent product and result" (1971, 491). Unable to sustain this dialectical tension, bourgeois ideology is replete with one-sided distortions that come from causal interpretations of this and other similar remarks in Marx's writings.

3

The same double movement of precondition and result that dominates Marx's study of the past plays a decisive role in his inquiry into the future. In the philosophy of internal relations, the future is an essential moment in the present. It is not only what the present becomes, but whatever happens in the future exists in the present, within all present forms, as potential. In the same way that Marx's fuller study of the present extends back into its origins, it extends forward into its possible and likely outcomes. For him, anything less would detract from our understanding of what the present is and our ability to mold it to our purposes. Antonio Gramsci has said that for a Marxist the question "What is man?" is really a question about what man can become (1971, 351). Whether directed at human beings, a set of institutions, or a whole society, the unfolding of a potential has a privileged status in Marx's studies. But how does one go about studying the future as part of the present?

According to Marx, investigating the past as "suspended presuppositions" of the present "likewise leads at the same time to the points at which the suspension of the present form of production relations gives signs of its becoming foreshadowings of the future. Just as, on one side, the pre-bourgeois phases appear as merely historical, i.e., suspend presuppositions, so do the contemporary conditions of production likewise appear as engaged in suspending themselves and hence in posing the historical presuppositions for a new state of society" (1973, 461). Whether studying the past or the future, it is chiefly a matter of looking back, deriving presuppositions from the forms that contain them. We have seen Marx apply this to the past grasped as the presuppositions of the present, but how can he grasp the present as presuppositions of a future that has yet to occur? Whence the sense of the future that allows him to look back at the present as its presuppositions?

There would appear to be two main answers. First, and especially as regards the near future (what lies just ahead in capitalism) and the middle future (represented by the socialist revolution), what is expected is derived by projecting existing tendencies (laws) and contradictions forward. The vantage point is the present, but a present that has been abstracted in extension to include the overlapping trajectories and buildup of various pressures that emerge from the immediate past. As regards the near future, Marx frequently abstracted the processes he saw in the world as having a temporal extension large enough to include what they were becoming as part of what they are, going so far as to use the name associated with where they were heading but have not yet arrived to refer to the whole journey there. In this way, all labor that produces or is on the verge of producing commodities in capitalism is called "wage-labor"; money that is about to buy means of production is called "capital"; small businessmen who are going bankrupt and peasants who are losing their land are referred to as "working class," et cetera (1963, 409–10 and 396; Marx and Engels 1945, 16). Marx frequently signals the futuristic bias in his naming practice with such phrases as "in itself," "in its intention," "in its destiny," "in essence," and "potentially."

As regards the middle future, the moment of qualitative change not in one or a few processes but in the whole social formation of which they are part, Marx's chief point of departure is the knot of major contradictions that he found in investigating capitalism. "The fact," he says, "that bourgeois production is compelled by its own immanent laws, on the one hand, to develop the productive forces as if production did not take place on a narrow restricted social foundation, while, on the other hand, it can develop these forces only within these narrow limits, is the deepest and most hidden cause of crises, of the crying contradictions within which bourgeois production is carried on and which even at a cursory glance reveal it as only a transitional, historical form" (1971, 84). "Even at a cursory glance," Marx believes, it is clear that capitalism cannot go on much longer. All we have to see is that it builds upon and requires a social foundation—essentially, private appropriation of an expanding social product—that cannot support its growing weight.

Projecting capitalism's major contradictions forward in this manner involves subjective as well as objective conditions—in Marxist terms, class struggle as well as the accumulation of capital—in their distinctive interaction. Marx never doubts that it is people who make history, but, as he is quick to add, "not in circumstances of their own choosing" (Marx and Engels 1951a, 225). Most of Marx's own work is devoted to uncovering these circumstances for the capitalist era, but always in connection with how they affect and are likely to affect the classes (the relevant abstraction for people) operating in them. Responding to pressures from their social and economic situation and to the results of their own socialization, these classes are further predisposed to choose and act as they do by the range of alternatives available to them. But all the circumstances pertaining to capitalism and modern capitalism that are mainly responsible for how people behave are changing. Projecting the sum of such changes forward, organizing the narrowing options that they provide as contradictions, Marx can foresee a time when a renewed burst of class struggle will bring the capitalist era to a close. There is nothing in any of these unfolding and overlapping tendencies and contradictions that allows Marx to predict with absolute certainty what will happen, and especially not when and how it will happen. The future so conceived does not fit together neatly like the pieces of a puzzle but is itself a set of alternative outcomes, no one of which is more than highly probable. Such is the dialectical form of the future within the present, the sense of "determined" contained in the notion of "potential."

The second main way in which Marx constructs a future from which to look back at the present applies chiefly, though not solely, to the far future or socialist/communist society that he believes will follow the revolution. In studying the presuppositions of the present in the past, Marx's focus is on the capitalist character of the present and its origins in a precapitalist past. Unlike those of our qualities that partake of the human condition, the qualities that have arisen as part of capitalism can be expected to change drastically or even disappear altogether when capitalism does. Having been posited as a historically specific result, capitalist forms of life can now be posited as the historical premise for what they in turn make possible. We have simply replaced the relations these present forms were found to have to their real past with a similar set of relations to their likely future, except that the position and therefore the role of the present has been reversed. The point is that if the forms of life associated with capitalism belong to the order of things that have historical presuppositions—which is to say, if they emerged in real historical time—they are also capable of serving as presuppositions for what follows. And for Marx, as we saw, it is the very analysis that reveals them as the one (as results) that reveals them "at the same time" as the other (as presuppositions) and in the process gives us "foreshadowings of the future."

Marx constructs his vision of the far future by abstracting out the historically specific conditions of capitalism (treating as preconditions what have proven to be historical results) as well as by projecting existing tendencies and contradictions forward, taking full account of changes in standards and priorities that would occur under a socialist government. We learn, for example, that "workmen, if they were dominant, if they were allowed to produce for themselves, would very soon, and without great exertion, bring the capital (to use a phrase of the vulgar economists) up to the standard of their needs." Here, the "workers, as subjects, employ the means of production—in the accusative case—in order to produce wealth for themselves. It is of course assumed here that capitalist production has already developed the productive forces of labor in general to a sufficiently high level for this revolution to take place" (1963, 580). Marx begins by removing the historically specific conditions of capitalist production that have made workers into a means for producing surplus-value (itself the result of earlier history) and then projects forward what these workers would be able to do with the instruments of production once left on their own. Having constructed some part of the socialist future from the vantage point of the present, he then reverses himself and looks back at the present from the vantage point of this future to specify one of its major preconditions, which is highly developed productive forces.

In projecting existing tendencies and contradictions into the future (whether near, middle, or far), the eventual outcome is viewed as the further extension of a result that has its central core in the present. With the shift of vantage point to the future, however, the future becomes the result, and what exists now becomes part of its extended preconditions, along with what had formerly been set off as the present's own preconditions. By having its status changed from that of a result to that of a precondition, the way the present instructs us about the future also changes. Taken as a result, present forms are used as a basis for projecting the tendencies and contradictions that constitute its own real history forward, while viewing present forms together with their origins as preconditions of the future allows Marx to use the present to help clarify the future in much the same way that he uses the past to help clarify the present. By examining the conditions of earlier times from the vantage point of capitalism, as its presuppositions, Marx could learn not only what led to our present but obtain a fuller understanding of capitalism as a later development and transformation of just these presuppositions. Chiefly, it was a way of singling out what had proven to be the most important parts of our history and embedding them, now suitably altered, as essential features in a dialectically arranged present.

Similarly, our image of the future acquires clearer definition to the extent that important elements in present-day society can be treated as its preconditions. Criteria of relevance and research priorities for studying what is coming into being are also affected. Naturally, there are severe limits that this approach places on the amount of detail Marx can offer about the future. Unlike the free flights of fancy with which utopian socialists constructed their future societies, Marx never severs the internal relations that connect the future to its past and therefore to the variety of possibilities as well as to the dominant tendencies inherent in that past. Marx gives no detailed blueprints of the future, it appears, because his method does not permit him to have any.[2]

The sequence presented above deserves to be restated: Marx begins by viewing the past from the vantage point of the present (moving from result to precondition). Again, from the vantage point of the present but including now the ties that have been uncovered with the past, he projects this present forward to some stage of the future (moving from one part of the result to another). Finally, adopting the vantage point of what has been established in the future, he examines the present taken together with its ties to the past (moving from result to preconditions). Marx could not construct any part of the future without treating it as a development out of the present. The present would not exhibit any development unless it was first constituted as a system of interacting processes arising out of its past. And the future would not emerge even to the minimal degree it does in Marx's writings if he had not taken the final step of adopting the vantage point of the future to look back on the present. Paradoxically, it is this last move that also rounds out Marx's analysis of the capitalist present.

The main effect of casting the relation between past, present, and future as part of the interaction of precondition and result is that it enables Marx to bring into focus for purposes of study the historical movement of the capitalist mode of production without either dismissing or trivializing its organic movement. He can now fix upon the present in a way that throws into the sharpest possible relief the changes (already made) that tie it to its real past and those (in the process of taking place) that connect it to its probable future, pointing to major influences where they exist while holding fast to the mutual interaction that characterizes each stage in the development.

Further, viewing the present from the vantage point of its as yet unrealized potential gives to our capitalist present the value of a stepping-stone. From a sense of having arrived, we become newly aware and highly sensitized to the fact of going somewhere, of constructing here and now—from somewhere in the middle of the historical process—the foundations for a totally different future. With this, the project and our intentions as part of it assume a greater place in our consciousness, and in class consciousness, with a corresponding impact on our actions. Marx's future-oriented study of the present becomes increasingly relevant, therefore, just as this future, as indicated by this same study, becomes more and more of a realistic possibility.[3]

Notes

1. This chapter makes heavy use of the three modes of abstraction, especially that of vantage point, described in chapter five. Those who experience difficulty following how Marx used the

process of abstraction to study history will benefit from rereading the relevant sections on abstraction above.

2. This being said, there is a considerable amount of information on what communism will look like scattered throughout Marx's writings. For a reconstruction of the way of life that emerges from these comments, see Ollman 1979, 48–98.

3. A more detailed account of how Marx investigated the future inside the present can be found in chapter 9 in this work and in my forthcoming book, "Communism: Ours, Not Theirs."

CHAPTER 7

Dialectic as Inquiry and Exposition

1

Besides a way of viewing the world, the dialectic also serves Marx as a method of inquiry and as a type of organization and set of forms in which to present his findings. Marx points to the difference between these latter two roles (he assumes here the function of the dialectic as a way of seeing things) when he says, "of course the method of presentation must differ in form from that of inquiry. The latter has to appropriate the material in detail, to analyze its different forms of development, to trace out their *inner connections*" (1958, 19 [emphasis added]). Nothing that was said above regarding the philosophy of internal relations was meant to deny the empirical character of Marx's method of inquiry. Marx does not deduce his knowledge about capitalism from the meanings of terms but, like a good social scientist, does research to discover what is the case. Marx even delayed finishing *Capital* II, in part because he wanted to see how the crisis about to break out in England would develop (Rubel 1950, 5).[1]

The dialectical method of inquiry is best described as research into the manifold ways in which entities are internally related. It is a voyage of exploration that has the whole world for its object, but a world that is conceived of as relationally contained in each of its parts. The first question this raises is how to decide on the parts in which and between which one will seek for relations. The need to divide up reality into what are, in effect, instrumental units is a common problem for all thinkers who ascribe to a philosophy of internal relations. This is the problem Marx tries to solve by what he calls the "force of abstraction" (1958, 7–8).

An "abstraction," as the term is ordinarily used, is a part of the whole whose ties with the rest are not apparent; it is a part that *appears* to be a whole in itself.[2] According to Marx, to hold that the world is actually composed of such "abstractions" is evidence of alienation. However, believing otherwise does not release Marx from the requirement of operating with units (also called "abstractions"); it simply gives him more latitude in setting out what these will be and in deciding how much of what is relationally contained in them to bring forward at any one time. The results of Marx's own process of abstraction (the mental process by which he arrives at his abstractions) are not only such new factors as the relations of production and surplus-value but all the other factors that come into his investigation as well. They have all been individuated or abstracted out of the whole that is relationally contained in each. And again, which group of qualities Marx chooses to treat as a unit is determined by the real similarities and differences that exist in the world together with what he sees of them and the particular problem under consideration.

But if Marx may be said to abstract all the units with which he deals in order to be able to deal with them at all, he does not refer to every one as an "abstraction." Instead, this term is usually used to refer to those units whose ties with reality are fully obscured, where the particular society in which they exist has been completely lost sight of. Thus, labor—which, as labor in general, Marx takes to be a special product of capitalism—is spoken of as an "abstraction" because most people believe that it has existed in all social systems. In contrast, whenever productive activity is particularized as slave labor, indentured labor, wage-labor, et cetera, the conditions in and through which labor exists are brought into the open, and labor in these instances ceases to be an abstraction.

Once a decision was made on his units, Marx's next task was to examine the manifold ways in which these units are related, either as mutually dependent wholes or as components in some larger whole—usually both. In examining their interaction, he begins with each part in turn, frequently altering the perspective in which their union is viewed. Thus, capital (generally the core notion of "capital") serves as one vantage point from which to work out the intricacies of capitalism; labor serves as another, value as another, et cetera. In each case, while the interaction studied is the same, the angle and approach to it differ. Marx's ability to treat apparently distinct elements in a relation as aspects of each in turn is evident when, referring to "politics, art, literature, etc.," he says that industry "can be conceived as a part of that general movement, just as that movement can be conceived of as a particular part of industry" (1959b, 110).

Marx assumes that the patterns of change embodied in the laws of the dialectic are universal, and they serve him as the broad framework in which to look for particular developments. However, the real crisscrossing influences at work in any situation are his proper subject matter. The enormous difficulties involved in extricating himself from such a maze required the kind of genius for grasping connections that Marx is reputed to have had in great abundance.[3] The maze itself is revealed in all its complexity in an early appraisal Marx made of his task: "We have to grasp the essential connections between private property, avarice, and the separation of labor, capital, and landed property; between exchange and competition, value and the devaluation of man, monopoly and competition, etc.; the connection between this whole estrangement and the money system" (1959b, 68).[4]

The task Marx pursues of grasping the "essential connections" of capitalism is what makes Marxism a science. It is the relations that Marx considers crucial for understanding any system or factor that are convened in "essence" (*Wesen*).[5] Marx often contrasts "essence" with "appearance," or what we can observe directly. Actually, essence includes appearance but transcends it in every direction in which what is apparent acquires its importance. Since what Marx takes to be crucial in understanding anything, however, depends in part on the problem under consideration, what he considers its essence will also vary. What is the essence of man? Some of Marx's comments indicate that it is his activity, others that it is his social relations, and still others that it is the part of nature he appropriates.[6] The compromise, that it is all these in their interrelations, misses the point that it is through this category that Marx has chosen to emphasize one or the other. This is the chief difficulty in the way of adopting the commonsense translation of *Wesen* as "core" or "structure," with their connotation of unchanging stability, and makes the popular equation of the term "essential" with "economic conditions" impractical.[7]

As the work of uncovering essences, science then is primarily concerned with those major relations that are not open to direct observation; it is a matter of extending the ties between entities, conceived of as internally related to one another, further than we do in ordinary life. If to know anything is to know its relations or, in Engels's words, "to allocate to each its place in the interconnection of nature" (1954, 308), to know anything scientifically is to grasp its place in nature more fully than is possible without specialized research. As Marx says, the "hidden substratum" of phenomena "must first be discovered by science" (1958, 542).

In a letter to Kugelmann, Marx goes so far as to maintain that such relations are the entire subject matter of science (1941, 74). This extreme view is staked out again in *Capital* III: "all science would be superfluous if the outward appearance and the essence of things directly coincided" (1959a, 797). If fundamental relationships could be understood for the looking, we would not have to ferret them out. Afterward, it is often found that the truth about an entity runs counter to appearances: "It is paradox that the earth moves around the sun, and that water consists of two highly inflammable gases." For Marx, "Scientific truth is always paradox, if judged by everyday experience of things" (Marx and Engels 1951a, 384). The job of the scientist, then, is to learn the relevant information and piece it together so as to reconstruct in his or her mind the intricate relations, most of them not directly observable, that exist in reality.[8]

Marx's comments should indicate why most discussions on the theme "Is Marxism a Science?" are carried on at cross purposes. On Marx's definition, Marxism's claim to be a science is clearly justified, and he would not have been interested to debate the question using any other definition; nor, with my purpose of getting at what he is saying, am I. It is also worth noting in this connection that the German term *Wissenschaft* has never been so closely identified with the physical sciences—and hence with the criteria operating in the physical sciences—as its English equivalent. Marx's use of "science" and our own use of this term to refer to his ideas must also be understood with this in mind.

2

If the dialectic as inquiry is the search for internal relations within and between abstracted units, the dialectic as exposition is Marx's means of expounding these relations to his readers. We will recall that Marx specifically condemns explanations in economics and theology that attempt to go back to first causes and claims that they assume what still has to be accounted for, namely, the relations existing in the first cause (Marx 1959b, 68–69). Explanation for Marx always has to do with clarifying relationships; it is helping others to discover the "hidden substratum" that one has discovered through science. But how does one report on relations when what one sees is not relations between things but things as Relations? Marx's solution is to try to present his readers with a "mirrored" version of reality. He says that success in exposition is achieved "if the life of the subject-matter is ideally reflected as in a mirror." When this occurs, "it may appear as if we had before us a mere *a priori* construction" (1958, 19).

Marx's self-proclaimed goal, then, is to produce works whose parts are so interlocked they seem to belong to a deductive system. This is also the sense in which he asserts that all his theoretical writings are an "artistic whole" (Marx and Engels 1941, 204). But, as Lafargue tells us, Marx was constantly dissatisfied with his efforts "to disclose the whole of that world in its manifold and continually varying action and reaction" (*Reminiscences* n.d., 78).[9] He felt that he was never able to say just what he wanted. Marx's correspondence during the time he was writing his major work in political economy is full of allusions to his efforts at perfecting his exposition. The approach adopted in *Contributions to a Critique of Political Economy* (1859) was soon left behind. Just months before *Capital* I was published, he once more altered his exposition, in this instance to meet his friend Kugelmann's request for a more didactic account. The second German edition of *Capital* I was again significantly revised, and so too the French edition that followed a few years later. And at the time of Marx's death in 1883, Engels tells us that Marx was again planning to revise his major work (Marx 1958, 23). It appears, therefore, that this mirrored presentation of reality remained a goal that Marx was forever approaching but on the basis of his own evidence never actually attained.

The chief means at Marx's disposal for creating a reflection of the reality he uncovered were the organization of his material and his choice of terms. Marx presents his subject matter both historically, laying stress on factors he considers most important, and dialectically, which for him meant elucidating their internal relations in the period—class history, capitalism, or modern capitalism—under examination. *Capital* offers many examples of material organized along each of these lines: capital, labor, and interest, for example, are examined in terms of origin and also as component parts of each other and of still other factors. In their correspondence, Marx and Engels frequently discuss the problems involved in harmonizing these two types of organization (Marx and Engels 1941, 108, 110, and 220–23).

What appears here as a clear dichotomy, however, like all such "polar opposites" in Marxism, is really not one. Engels tells us that the dialectical method "is nothing else but the historical method only divested of its historical form and disturbing fortuities" (Marx and Engels 1951a, 339). We have already seen that for Marx any factor is a product of historical development. The dialectical tie that binds value, labor, capital, and interest in *Capital* only holds good for a single period in world history. Thus, by uncovering the connection between these and other social factors Marx is also displaying a moment in their unfolding historical relations. And, conversely, in writing history all developments are conceived of as temporal aspects of the mutually dependent conditions he is dealing with.

The two outstanding features of Marx's use of the dialectic for presentation are, first, that each subject is dealt with from many different vantage points, and second, that each subject is followed out of and into the particular forms it assumes at different times and in different contexts. Engels notes the presence of this first feature in his preface to *Capital* III, where he lists some of the difficulties he encountered in editing the unfinished volumes of *Capital* (Marx 1959a, 3). This tactic of presentation led Marx to treat production, for example, when he was really dealing with consumption (how production affects consumption and vice-versa), or distribution (the same) or exchange (the same) (Marx 1904, 274ff.). Again, the capitalist acquires his full character in Marx's writings only through being discussed in studies on factory work, the role of the state, the demands of the market, et cetera, aside from examinations in which he is the principal. And whenever the capitalist is the principal, we are certain to find insights on the proletariat, the state, the market, et cetera, viewed now from this angle. One result is that Marx's works can often appear very repetitious.

As for tracing things through their development into various forms, the outstanding example of this in Marxism is the metamorphoses of value from labor, where it originates, to commodity, money, capital, profit, interest, rent, and wages. This is a neat, no doubt too neat, outline of *Capital*, where each of these factors is treated as another form of what is essentially the same thing. In presenting the same thing from different angles and apparently disparate ones as "identical," Marx is trying to mirror a reality where entities are connected as essential elements in each other's Relations.

Not able to unfold all the relations in a factor immediately, Marx is forced to deal with any problem in stages, using what Paul Sweezy calls the method of "successive approximations" (1964, 11). In any one place and even, as Sweezy rightly points out, in any one book, Marx treats his material in a very partial manner. His conclusions, therefore, are generally of a provisional nature, since the introduction of new information or a new vantage point will often require that a conclusion be reworked and expanded (Sweezy 1964, 18).

Consequently, in exposition, Marx generally assumes the greater part of what he grasps in a Relation in order to get on with his task and in so doing subsumes what is unexpressed in the part expressed. Thus, on any given occasion, Marx's concepts convey only part of what they could convey and may, on another occasion, actually convey for him. We follow him—if we do—only by paying attention to the context, but even this has proven very difficult for readers who are unaware of the philosophical commitments that underlie his unusual use of language. When Marx says, "no equation can be solved unless the elements of its solution are involved in its terms," therefore, this has a literal application to Marxism (Marx and Engels 1941, 386). An experience that many people have as they continue to study Marx's writings is that terms they think they know take on new and broader meanings. In fact this may be taken as one of the surest signs that one is making progress in understanding Marx.

Besides forcing him to make assumptions in order to treat a Relation one-sidedly, Marx's conception of reality also requires some shorthand method to point out the connections he sees without having to go into them in detail. The specialized vocabulary that serves this purpose for Marx has been the bane of critics from his time to our own. Some of its main terms and expressions are as follows: "reflection" (Spiegelbild), "corresponding case" (Entsprechung), "manifestation" (Ausserung), "confirmation" (Bestatigung), "another expression" (andrer Ausdruk), "in the same measure" (in dem selben Grade), "in one of its aspects" (nach der einen Seite), and "another form" (andrer Art). Clearly, these expressions do not all mean the same thing, but they perform the common function for Marx of drawing attention to the internal relations he sees between apparently different entities; in every case, the elements referred to are held to be aspects of one another.

This is the only way to understand such otherwise confusing claims as, "Value in general is a form of social labor" (1951, 52), or when Marx calls money "the commodity in its continually exchangeable form" (1959a, 378) or private property "the material summary expression of alienated labor" (1959b, 83); and this list, of what are not peripheral but central theses in Marxism, could be extended much further. Lacking the relational framework to make sense of such "equations," critics generally misinterpret them along causal lines, setting apart horse and cart where Marx meant each conception to convey both.[10]

Perhaps the most difficult of these shorthand usages to comprehend is the term "identical." When Marx says, "division of labor and private property are . . . identical expressions," he is not offering an empty tautology but directing us to the internal ties he sees between these two in real life. This assertion is followed by the explanation that "in the one the same thing is affirmed with reference to activity as is affirmed in the other with reference to the product of activity" (Marx and Engels 1964, 44). Leaving aside the specific nature of the connection Marx sees between the division of labor and private property, what is clear is that each is said to be a necessary condition of the other and is conceived of as part of the other.

The English philosopher F. H. Bradley, who also subscribes to a philosophy of internal relations, distinguishes between "identity" and "similarity" by stating that the latter can only apply to objects that "remain at least partly undistinguished and unspecified" (Bradley 1920, 593). And whenever such objects are fully analyzed, that is, when their internal relations to each other are uncovered, they are seen to be identical.[11] Identity, for Marx as for Bradley, is the relation between entities whose role as necessary elements in one another is appreciated for what it is. Consequently, a full account of any one requires an account of the other (or others).[12]

Two corollaries of Marx's unusual view of identity, which have already been briefly alluded to, are that he feels he can use the same word to refer to heterogeneous entities and several words to refer to what we would take to be the same one. The different things expressed by a single term are the varied aspects of the relationships bound up in it. In wanting to exhibit connections that cross into separate fields, Marx sometimes feels constrained to borrow terms from their commonsense homes and apply them elsewhere. In so doing, he is merely tracing out their component relations further than he usually does. Sometimes he goes as far as to use the same expression for all as well as each of the main elements in the interrelated reality that it depicts. His much-misunderstood use of "man's essential powers" and "society" are examples of this. Using more than one word to convey the same thing is again a way of emphasizing a particular tie. In this case, the entity viewed from diverse angles is given names corresponding to how it appears or functions from each. The whole of Marxism supplies us with examples of these two practices, although they are more noticeable in the early works.[13]

Notes

1. Marx says, " 'it is necessary to observe the actual development up to the point when things are completely ripe, and it is only after that that we can "consume productively," that is to say theoretically' " (qtd. in Rubel 1950, 5).

2. Marx sometimes opposes "abstractions" to "concretes," where the whole is more apparent (1904, 293). A similar use of these two expressions is to be found in Hegel, who holds that to leave some aspects (for him "determinations") aside when representing an object is to be "abstract"; whereas a "concrete" is said to be the object "conserved in the plentitude of its determinations" (1927, 29).

3. Engels claims that without Marx the understanding of capitalism would have occurred, but more slowly and piecemeal, because Marx "alone was capable of following all the economic categories in their dialectical motion, to link the phases of their development with the causes determining it, and to reconstruct the edifice of the whole of economics in a monument of science, the individual parts of which mutually supported and determined one another" (*Reminiscences* n.d., 91).

4. As a statement of Marx's problem, this is a statement already imbued with the solution. By referring to these entities as "estrangement," Marx shows that the major relations in capitalist society have already been understood; it is his understanding of these relations that is expressed in the term "estrangement."

5. The German term *Wesen* has no exact equivalent in the English language. Besides "essence," it is also translated on occasion as "nature," "being," and "entity." The fact that *Wesen*, which always suggests certain internal ties, can be rendered by "entity" may indicate that the relational sense Marx gives to social entities has some basis in the German language, which readers of the English version of his work necessarily miss.

6. Marx equates man's "life-activity" with his "essential being" (1959b, 75); elsewhere, he calls the "essence of man" the "ensemble (aggregate) of social relations" (Marx and Engels 1964, 646). And of communism, Marx says, "Man appropriates his total essence in a total manner" (1959b, 106).

7. For an example of the latter error, see Popper 1962, 107. Together with its synonyms, "hidden substratum" (*verborgen Hintergrund*), "inner connections" (*innere Bande*), and "intrinsic movements" (*innerliche Bewegungen*)—the list is not complete—"essence" bears a large responsibility for charges that Marxism is a metaphysical system.

8. Engels takes a slightly different tack, pointing out that our senses give us access to different qualities or types of relations, and says, "to explain these different properties, accessible only to different senses, to bring them into connection with one another, is precisely the task of science" (Engels 1954, 309).

9. Marx once compared his condition with that of the hero in Balzac's *Unknown Masterpiece*, who, by painting and retouching, tried to reproduce on canvas what he saw in his mind's eye (Berlin 1960, 3).

10. John Plamenatz, for example, writes: "We know that, according to Marx, the 'relations of production' find 'legal expression' in the system of property. Just what is meant by 'finding legal expression' I do not pretend to know. Nevertheless, two inferences are, I think, permissible: that the system of property is very closely connected with the 'relations of production,' and that it is the latter which determines the former and not the other way about" (1961, 30).

11. Mao Tse-tung offers another relevant insight when he says that identity is the relation of two elements in an entity where each finds "the presuppositions of its existence in the other" (1968, 60).

12. It is in this sense that Marx declares, "the social reality of nature, and human natural science, or natural science about man, are identical terms" (1959b, 111). Marx sometimes makes the same kind of equation without using the concept "identity," as when he says, "the relation of the productive forces to the form of the intercourse *is* the relation of the form of the intercourse to the occupation or activity of the individuals" (Marx and Engels 1964, 87 [emphasis added]). Another way of doing this is seen in the example, "bourgeois, i.e., capital" (Marx and Engels 1945, 21).

13. Our account of the moments of inquiry and exposition in Marx's method is further elaborated in chapters 6, 8, 9, and 11.

CHAPTER 8

Marxism and Political Science: Prolegomenon to a Debate on Marx's Method

1

The debates between Marxists and non-Marxists that have been raging for a half-century and more in the disciplines of sociology, history, economics, and philosophy are strikingly absent in political science. This is true not only in Anglo-Saxon countries, where Marxists particularly in academia have always been a rare breed, but even on the continent, where Marxists and Marxist ideas have traditionally played an important role in every sector of social life.

What makes this absence especially difficult to explain is the fact that a large number of political scientists have long accepted such essentials of the Marxist critique of their discipline as that it deals with superficialities and is generally biased on behalf of the status quo. An in-house survey of political scientists, for example, showed that two out of three "agreed" or "strongly agreed" that much scholarship in the profession is "superficial and trivial" and that concept formation and development is "little more than hair splitting and jargon" (Sommit and Tannenhouse 1964, 14). The belief that most studies in political science are more useful to those who have power than to those who are trying to attain it is not as widespread, but it, too, is gaining ground. These biases are present not only in the theories that are offered to explain empirical findings but in the choice of problems to research and in the very concepts (themselves rooted in theory) by which the project and its product are thought about and communicated. The distortions introduced into political science, for example, by the standard assumption of the legitimacy and longevity of the present political system have yet to be adequately explored. In many ways, the least important biases (or parts of bias, since they always belong to a system of thought) are the values that an increasing number of scholars admit to at the start of their studies. This is the part of the iceberg that shows, and at least here readers stand warned.

Charges of bias, as is well known, are easier to voice than to argue, and when

laid to bad faith they are generally unconvincing. Few of our colleagues actually take themselves for civil servants. The same political scientists who perceive the pervading bias in the field often feel uneasy about their inability to
analyze it. Similarly, most political scientists (whether the same ones or not)
who condemn the profession for triviality are reduced to contributing more
of the same, since they do not know what else to study or how (with what theories, concepts, techniques) to study it. What is missing is a theory that would
provide the necessary perspective to study and explain, to research and criticize both political life and accepted modes of describing it, that is, political
science. Marxism is that theory.

The reasons why a Marxist school of political scientists has not yet emerged,
despite what appear to be favorable conditions, are rooted chiefly in the historical peculiarities of both Marxism and political science. Marx concentrated most
of his mature efforts on the capitalist economy, but even aside from essays on
French and English politics and the early critique of Hegel there is a lot more
on the state in his writings than is generally recognized. In particular, *Capital*
contains a theory of the state that, unlike Marx's related economic theories, is
never fully worked out. This is a subject Marx hoped to develop if and when
his work in economics permitted. An outline of his overall project gives the state
a much more important role in his explanation of capitalism than would appear to be the case from a glance at what he completed.

After Marx died, most of his followers erroneously attributed an influence
to the different social spheres in proportion to the treatment accorded them in
his published writings. This error was facilitated by the standard interpretation
of Marx's well-known claims on the relationship between the economic base
and the social-political-cultural superstructure. If the economic life of society
is wholly responsible for the character and development of other spheres, the
activities that go on in the latter can be safely ignored or, if need be, deduced.
Engels's end-of-life correspondence is full of warnings against this interpretation, but they seem to have had little effect. Among Marx's more prominent early
followers, only Lukács, Korsch, and Gramsci wholly reject such economic determinism as the framework in which to understand the state. The ever more
active role of the state in directing the capitalist economy, however, has led a later
generation of Marxists to make the state a prime object of study. Among the
most important fruits of this effort are Ralph Miliband's *The State in Capitalist
Society* (1969) and *Marxism and Politics* (1977), Nicos Poulantzas's *State, Power,
Socialism* (1978), James O'Connor's *The Fiscal Crisis of the State* (1973), Jürgen
Habermas's *Legitimation Crisis* (1976), Martin Carnoy's *The State and Political
Theory* (1984), Bob Jessop's *The Capitalist State* (1982), John Ehrenberg's *The
Dictatorship of the Proletariat* (1992), Paul Thomas's *Alien Politics* (1994), Ellen
Meiksins Wood's *Retreat from Class* (1986), Alan Gilbert's *Marx's Politics* (1981),
Eric Olin Wright's *Class, Crisis, and the State* (1978), August H. Nimtz Jr.'s *Marx
and Engels: Their Contribution to the Democratic Breakthrough* (2000), Philip

Corrigan's edited *Capitalism, State Formation, and Marxist Theory* (1980), and (though he might deny it) Gabriel Kolko's *The Triumph of Conservatism* (1963).

Given the minor role of the state in Marxism, as interpreted by most Marxists, it is little wonder that academics who chose to study politics were not attracted to this theory. The history of political science as a distinct discipline, however, has also contributed to this disinterest. Unlike economics and sociology, which began as attempts to understand whole societies, the origins of political science lay in jurisprudence and statescraft. Instead of investigating the workings of the political process in its connection with other social processes, political science has seldom strayed beyond the borders of the political process as such. Aims have generally revolved around making existing political institutions more efficient. There is no radical tradition, no group of major radical thinkers, and no body of consistent radical thought in political science such as one finds—at least to some degree—in sociology, economics, and history. From Machiavelli to Kissinger, political science has been the domain of those who—believing they understood the realities of power—have sought their reforms and advancement within the system, and it has attracted equally practical-minded students.

Can political science open itself to Marxist studies despite all these handicaps? I believe Marxism makes an essential contribution to our understanding of politics, but to grasp it we have to know something about the dialectical method with which Marx's theories are developed. Only then, too, will many of the dissatisfied political scientists referred to above be able to see *what* else they could study and *how* else they might study it. I believe it is necessary, therefore, that Marxists in political science today give priority to questions of method over questions of theory, insofar, of course, as the two can be distinguished. For it is only upon grasping Marx's assumptions and the means, forms, and techniques with which he constructs his explanations of capitalism that we can effectively use, develop, and revise, where necessary, what he said. And perhaps as important for Marxists teaching in universities, only by making this method explicit can we communicate with non- (and not yet) Marxist colleagues and students whose shared language masks the real distance that separates our different approaches.

Given these priorities, this attempt to relate Marxism to political science will focus on Marx's method. It may be useful, however, to review briefly those elements in Marx's theory of the state that were developed with the help of his method. Whether dealing with politics or any other social sector, it must be stressed, Marx is concerned with all of capitalism—with its birth, development, and decay as a social system. More specifically, he wants to understand (and explain) where the present state of affairs comes from, how it coheres, what are the main forces producing change, how all these facts are dissimulated, where the present is tending (including possible alternatives), and how we can affect this process. Marx's theory of the state seeks to answer these questions for the political sphere, but in such a way as to illuminate the character and development of capitalism as a whole (which is no different than what could be said of his theories about other areas of capitalist life).

The main subjects treated in Marx's theory of the state, taken in the above manner, are as follows: (1) the character of the state as a social power, embodying the kind of cooperation required by the existing division of labor, that has become independent of the individual producers; (2) the effect of social-economic relations pertaining to class rule on state forms and activities and the state's function in helping to reproduce these relations; (3) the effect of state forms and activities on the production and realization of value; (4) the control, both direct and indirect, over the state exercised by the dominant economic class combined with the informal control over the state exercised by the imperatives of the economic system; (5) the state's role in the class struggle, especially through legitimating existing institutions and practices and repressing those who dissent from them; (6) the conditions in which the state acquires a degree of autonomy from the dominant economic class; (7) the ways in which politics is ordinarily understood, the social origins of this political ideology, and the role it plays in helping the state perform its distinctive functions, particularly those of repression and legitimation; and (8) the possibility inherent in the foregoing, taken as historical tendencies, for the emergence of a form of state that embodies communal control over social power, which is to say, that seeks to abolish the basis of the state itself.

What Marx has to say on each of these subjects (the actual contents of his theory of the state) cannot be given at this time; but even listing what it covers should indicate some of the methodological problems involved. In practically every instance, Marx's theory of the state is concerned with locating relations inside a system and depicting the effect of that system on its relational parts. Without some grasp of what is happening here, many of his particular claims will appear confused and contradictory. The apparent contradiction between statements that seem to treat the state as an "effect" of economic "causes" and those that present a "reciprocal interaction" between all social factors offers one such difficulty. Another is the way Marx treats past and possible future developments in the state as somehow part of its present forms. A third, suggested by the first two, is that the concepts that express such ties have at least partly different meanings from those found in ordinary speech. Only resort to Marx's method can clear up these and related problems.[1]

2

Most discussions of Marx's method have focused either on his philosophy, particularly on the laws of the dialectic as outlined by Engels, or on the strategy of exposition used in *Capital* I. Such accounts, even when accurate, are very lopsided and, what is worse, useless for the scholar interested in adopting this method for his or her work. Numerous assumptions and procedures are left out, and their place in the construction and elaboration of Marx's theories is vague at best. In attempting to make up for these lapses, I may have fallen victim to the opposite error of overschematization, and this is a danger that readers of the following pages should bear in mind.

Two further qualifications are required before I begin. First, I don't accord much importance to the different periods in Marx's career. This is not because there were no changes in his method, but because such changes as did occur between 1844, the year he wrote *The Economic and Philosophic Manuscripts,* and the end of his life are relatively minor. I have chosen, nevertheless, to empha-size his later so-called mature writings, and the few examples drawn from early works involve aspects of his method that remained the same throughout his career. Second, the method outlined below is that used in Marx's systematic study of capitalism. Consequently, all of its elements can be found in *Capital,* that is, in the work he did for *Capital* and in the finished product, while only some of them are used in his shorter, more occasional pieces. How many of these elements appear in a given work also depends on Marx's skill in using his method, and neither his skill nor his style (another subject frequently confused with method) enter into our discussion.

What, then, is Marx's method? Broadly speaking, it is his way of grasping real-ity and of explaining it, and it includes all that he does in organizing and manipu-lating reality for purposes of inquiry and exposition. This method exists on five levels, representing successive stages in its practice: (1) ontology; (2) epistemol-ogy; (3) inquiry; (4) intellectual reconstruction; and (5) exposition. Other social science methods could probably be broken down in this way. What is distinctive about Marx's method, then, is not that it has such stages but that Marx is con-scious of having them and, of course, the peculiar character he gives to each one.

Ontology is the study of "being." As an answer to the question "What is re-ality?" it involves Marx's most fundamental assumptions regarding the nature and organization of the world. As a materialist, Marx believes, of course, that the world is real and exists apart from us and whether we experience it or not. But that leaves open the question of its parts and how they are related to each other and the whole to which they all belong. What is most distinctive about Marx's ontology is his conception of reality as a totality composed of internally related parts and his conception of these parts as expandable, such that each one in the fullness of its relations can represent the totality.

Few people would deny that everything in the world is related to everything else—directly or indirectly—as causes, conditions, and results; and many insist that the world is unintelligible save in terms of such relations. Marx goes a step further in interiorizing this interdependence within each element, so that the conditions of its existence are taken to be part of what it is. Capital, for example, is not simply the physical means of production but includes the whole pattern of social and economic relations that enables these means to appear and func-tion as they do. While Durkheim, standing at the other extreme, asks that we grasp social facts as things, Marx grasps things as social facts or Relations and is capable of mentally expanding these Relations through their necessary conditions and results to the point of totality. This is a version of what historically has been called the *philosophy of internal relations*.

There are basically three different notions of totality in philosophy:

1. The atomistic conception, which goes from Descartes to Wittgenstein, that views the whole as the sum of simple parts, whether things or facts.
2. The formalist conception, apparent in Schelling, *probably* Hegel, and most modern structuralists, that attributes an identity to the whole independent of its parts and asserts the absolute predominance of this whole over the parts. The real historical subjects in this case are the preexisting, autonomous tendencies and structures of the whole. Research is undertaken mainly to provide illustrations, and facts that don't "fit" are either ignored or treated as unimportant residue.
3. The dialectical and materialist conception of Marx (often confused with the formalist notion) that views the whole as the structured interdependence of its parts—the interacting events, processes, and conditions of the real world—as observed from any major part.[2]

Through the constant interaction and development of these parts, the whole on this latter view also changes, realizing possibilities that were inherent in earlier stages. Flux and interaction, projected back into the origins of the present and forward into its possible futures, are the chief distinguishing characteristics of this world and are taken for granted in any inquiry. However, since this interdependence is structured—that is, rooted in relatively stable connections—the same interaction accords the whole a relative autonomy, enabling it to have relations as a whole with the parts whose order and unity it represents.

These relations are of four sorts: (1) the whole shapes the parts to make them more functional within this particular whole (so it is that capitalism, for example, generally and over time gets the laws it requires); (2) the whole gives meaning and relative importance to each part in terms of this function (laws in capitalism are only comprehensible as elements in a structure that maintains capitalist society and are as important as the contribution they make to this structure); (3) the whole expresses itself through the part, so that the part can also be taken as a form of the whole. Given internal relations, we get a view of the whole, albeit a one-sided view, when examining any of its parts. It is like looking out at a courtyard from one of the many windows that surround it (a study of any major capitalist law that includes its necessary conditions and results, therefore, will be a study of capitalism); and (4) the relations of the parts with each other, as suggested above, forge the contours and meaning of the whole, transform it into an ongoing system with a history, an outcome, and an impact. It is the presence of these last two relations that sets the first two apart from the formalist conception of the totality to which they also apply.

Also deserving mention are the relations Marx sees between two or more parts within the whole and the relations between a part and itself (a form of itself in the past or in the future). What are called laws of the dialectic are meant to indicate the more important of these relations. Engels considers the most important of these laws, "the transformation of quantity to quality—mutual penetration of polar opposites and their transformation into each other when carried to extremes—development through contradiction or negation—spiral form of development" (n.d., 26–27). Explaining these laws now would prove too long a detour. For the present, it is sufficient to note their character as generalizations about the kind of change and interaction that occur in a world understood in terms of internal relations. These generalizations are particularly important for the lines of inquiry that they open up and will be discussed later in connection with that stage in Marx's method.

3

Based on Marx's ontology is his epistemology, or how he comes to know and arrange in thought what is known. If Marx's ontology provides him with a view of what the world consists of, his epistemology is how he learns about this world. This stage of his method is in turn composed of four interlocking processes (or aspects of a single process): perception; abstraction (how Marx separates what is perceived into distinct units); conceptualization (the translation of what is abstracted into concepts with which to think and communicate); and orientation (the effects abstractions have on his beliefs, judgments, and action—including future perceptions and abstractions).

Perception, for Marx, covers all the ways in which people become aware of the world. It goes beyond the activity of the five senses to include a variety of mental and emotional states that bring us into contact with qualities (feelings and ideas as well as physical substance) that would otherwise elude us.

In actual fact, we always perceive somewhat more (or less) and differently from what is seen or heard directly, having to do with our knowledge, experience, mood, the problem at hand, et cetera. This difference is attributable to the process of abstraction (sometimes called individuation) that transforms the innumerable qualities present to our senses into meaningful particulars. Abstraction sets boundaries not only for problems but for the very units in which they are studied, determining how far into their interdependence with other qualities they extend. If everything is interrelated, as I have said, such that each is a part of what everything else is, it is necessary to decide where one thing ends and another begins. Given Marx's ontology, the abstracted unit remains a Relation in the sense described above. Its relative autonomy and distinctness result from his having made it so for the present, in order to serve certain ends. A change in ends often leads to individuating a somewhat altered unit out of the same totality. Capital, for example, can be grasped as the means of production used to produce surplus-value; the relations between capitalists and workers are sometimes added; and sometimes this abstraction is enlarged to include various conditions and results of these core activities and relations—all in keeping with Marx's concern of the moment.

Marx's main criticism of bourgeois ideologists is that, while they deal with abstractions, they are neither concerned with or even aware of the relations that link these abstractions to the whole, and which make them both relative and historically specific. Thus, "freedom," in their minds, is separated from the conditions that make it possible for some people to do what they want and others not. Having fallen out of view in this way, the larger context is easy to ignore or, if noted, to dismiss as irrelevant. Marx, of course, also thinks with abstractions—of necessity. All thought and study of the totality begins by breaking it down into manageable parts. But, as Lukács points out, "What is decisive is whether this process of isolation is a means towards understanding the whole and whether it is integrated within the context it presupposes and requires, or whether the abstract knowledge of an isolated fragment retains its 'autonomy' and becomes an end in itself" (1971, 28). Marx, unlike the bourgeois ideologists he criticizes, is fully conscious that he abstracts the units he then proceeds to study (rather than finding them ready-made) and is aware of their necessary links with the whole.

The advantages of Marx's procedure are, first, he can manipulate—as we saw above—the size of any unit in keeping with his particular problem (though the many common experiences and problems of anyone living in capitalist society means that there is greater similarity between Marx's and other people's abstractions than this point would suggest); second, he can more easily abstract different qualities or groups of qualities, providing himself in this way with a "new" subject for research and study (surplus-value and relations of production are examples of this); and, third, because the abstractions people carve out are the result of real historical conditions, particularly of their knowledge and interests as members of social classes, the study of their abstractions becomes for Marx an important means of learning about the rest of society.

The process of conceptualization that comes next is more than simply labeling the units that are abstracted. Naming the abstraction also enables it to draw upon the understanding in the language system to which this name belongs. In Marx's case, this means to extend its sense through the senses—albeit shifting and provisional—already attributed to related concepts. Likewise, given internal relations, the real-world structures reflected in the meaning of any concept immediately become part of what can be thought or expressed by other concepts. The work of separating out a part from an internally related whole is done by the process of abstraction and not—as many would have it—by conceptualization (though the former is often abstracted as a moment in the latter). The specific contribution of conceptualization is that by giving abstractions a linguistic form it allows them to be more easily understood and remembered but also communicated. If concepts without abstractions are hollow, abstractions without concepts are mute.

Marx's own achievement is sometimes characterized in terms of the fuller understanding made possible through the introduction of new concepts, such as "surplus-value." Engels compares Marx's contribution in economics, for example, to Lavoisier's in chemistry. Priestly and Scheele had already produced oxygen but didn't know that it was a new element. Calling it "dephlogisticated air" and "fire air," respectively, they remained bound within the categories of phlogistic chemistry, which understood fire as something *leaving* the burning body. Lavoisier gave the name "oxygen" to the new kind of air, which enabled him to grasp combustion as oxygen *combining* with the burning body. Abstracted as something outside the burning body and distinct from fire, it could join with the body during fire.

In much the same way, Marx was not the first, according to Engels, to recognize the existence of that part of the product that is now called "surplus-value." Others saw that profit, rent, and interest come from labor. Classical political economy investigated the proportions of the product that went to workers and capitalists. Socialists condemned this distribution as unjust, but "all remained prisoners of the economic categories as they have come down to them" (Marx 1957, 14–16). The statement of fact, which was widely regarded as the solution, Marx took as the problem, and he solved this problem essentially by reabstracting its main elements and calling them "surplus-value." In giving a name to the origins and ongoing relations to workers of profit, rent, and interest, "surplus-value" allows us to perceive the common thread that runs through these apparently distinct economic forms. With this new concept Marx was able to rethink all the main categories in political economy, just as Lavoisier, proceeding from the new concept of "oxygen," had done with the categories of phlogistic chemistry.

The tie between the process of conception and the process of abstraction makes it clear that the elasticity that characterizes Marx's abstractions will apply equally to the meanings of his concepts. Thus, "capital" in Marx's writings means more or less along a continuum consisting of its necessary conditions and results depending on the size and composition of the corresponding unit in Marx's abstraction of capital. The elastic definitions that some critics have noted in Marx's works can only be grasped by returning to his process of abstraction and the ontology of internal relations that underlies it.

Inextricably linked with perception, abstraction, and conception as a part of Marx's epistemology is the process of orientation. Marx believes that judgments, attitudes, and action cannot be severed from the social context in which they occur (including the interests of the people operating in it) and the real alternatives it allows. It is not simply a matter of what is taken as true and false but of the structure of explanation inherent in the categories used in thinking. With the aid of the philosophy of internal relations, this structure is extended by Marx into the very lives of the people involved. Consequently, what any group believes and does is inextricably linked to the ways, including categories, in which it grasps and defends both. The sum of all this constitutes their distinctive orientation to the world. Marx's own judgments and efforts as a revolutionary are likewise part of how he understands capitalism, an understanding also reflected in the categories that he uses. Aware of this, Marx—unlike utopian socialists past and present—never engages in moral exhortation based on adherence to some external principle but tries to win people to socialism by getting them to accept the structure of his explanation.[3]

4

After ontology and epistemology, the next stage in Marx's method is that of inquiry. What Marx is looking for and how he understands what he finds exercise a decisive influence over his inquiry. And what he is looking for is essentially the internal structure and coherence of the capitalist system, its existence as a historically specific totality. No matter what Marx's immediate subject, his greater subject is capitalist society, and, whenever and however he proceeds in his research, this society is always kept in mind.

Marx's method as inquiry is his attempt to trace out relations between units, themselves conceived of as Relations, in order to uncover the broad contours of their interdependence. Given their logical character as internal relations, these ties may be sought in each Relation in turn or between them, conceived of now as separate parts within some larger whole. In practice, this means that Marx frequently changes both the vantage point (and hence perspective) from which he sets out and the breadth of the units (together with the meanings of their covering concepts) that come into his analysis. Thus, for example, capital (generally the core notion of "capital") serves as one vantage point from which to investigate the intricacies of capitalism; labor serves as another, value as another, et cetera. In each case, while the interaction studied is largely the same, the angle and approach to it (and with it the emphasis in definitions) differ.

More directly of concern to political scientists and wholly in keeping with Marx's example, Gramsci in *The Prison Notebooks* investigates the intersecting social Relations, class, civil society, political party, bureaucracy, and state to uncover as many one-sided versions of the society of his time. The chief advantage of Marx's approach is that it enables him (and Gramsci) to discover major influences without losing sight of interaction and change throughout the complex, as tends to happen when looking for relations between narrowly defined static factors. Likewise, the transformation of one social form into another (indicated by a change in the operative concept) is best captured when tracing development within each social Relation. Note Gramsci's sensitivity to how social classes and bureaucracies become political parties and how political parties can become a state (1971, 146–49, 155, 157–58, 191, 227–28, and 264).

In keeping with the internal relations he posits between past, present, and future, Marx's inquiry into the world in which he lived spends a good deal of time looking backward into origins and forward into possibilities. For him, they are essential parts of the present and are necessary for a full understanding of how anything in the present works.[4] Also in keeping with Marx's preferred focus on capitalism and, to a lesser extent, on the periods of class society and modern capitalism, his study of people is usually restricted to the classes to which they belong. It is when people act in society as members of a class, Marx believed, that they have their greatest effect on what that society is, does, and becomes, particularly as regards the "big" questions and at the most crucial moments of its development. Without denying (or even completely ignoring) people's identity as individuals and as members of groups other than class, including the human species, it is what they do as classes and the interaction of opposing classes in the class struggle that mainly concerns him and allows some to refer to his method as "class analysis." When it is not used to minimize the role of material conditions in Marx's analysis and if it is understood dialectically, this otherwise partial and one-sided label can be quite useful.

Marx also assumed that the patterns of change and interaction embodied in the laws of the dialectic are universal, and they often served as the broad framework in which to look for particular developments. The law of the transformation of quantity to quality made him sensitive to how social factors change their appearance and/or function through the growth or diminution of one or more of their elements. Thus, money, for example, is said to function as capital only when it reaches a certain amount. The law of the interpenetration of polar opposites encouraged him to examine each social Relation for its opposite and, when faced with apparent opposites, to look for what unites them. In this way, wealth and poverty in capitalism are found to be opposite though mutually dependent aspects of the same Relation.

The law of development through contradictions is undoubtedly the most important of these dialectical laws. The processes that compose any complex organism change at different speeds and often in incompatible ways. Viewed as internally related tendencies (i.e., as elements in each other and in a common whole) whose forward progress requires that one or the other give way, they become contradictions. The resolution of these contradictions can significantly alter the totality. Examining totalities for their contradictions is a way of looking for the sources of conflict, sources that may be apparent even before a conflict fully materializes. Contradictions frequently come in clusters, and their unity and order of importance are equally subjects of Marx's research.

Research of any kind, Marx's included, is a matter of seeking for enough pieces to make sense of a puzzle that is destined to remain incomplete. In trying to trace the inner workings of capitalist society, Marx adopted a strategy and set of priorities to aid him in this task. He began, for example, by investigating social Relations like capital, commodity, and value, which are rich in evident connections with the concrete totality. He also chose to concentrate on England, using the most advanced capitalist society of his time as the laboratory in which to study capitalism as a system.

According to Marxist theory, it is mainly material production that reproduces the conditions of existence of the totality, and in the mutual interaction between all social factors it is mainly economic factors that exercise the greatest influence. Consequently, Marx generally begins his study of any problem or period by examining economic conditions and practices, particularly in production. The economic interests of the classes involved are also placed front and center, and the contradictions he takes most care to uncover are economic ones. If we originally abstracted Marx's method from his theories in order to focus on certain aspects of this method, it is necessary to return to these theories again and again to see how he uses this method and for what.

Special attention is also given to the interaction between real processes and the ways in which they are understood. On one occasion, Marx describes *Capital* as a " 'critique of economic categories or, if you like, the system of bourgeois economics exposed in a critical manner' " (qtd. in Rubel 1957, 129). *Capital*, then, is equally a work about how capitalism works and how it is understood by the "experts." As indicated, Marx's main criticism of bourgeois ideology in any field is that bourgeois thinkers are unaware of the larger context that surrounds and is expressed in their particular descriptions and explanations. Generally, they err in taking immediate appearances for the whole truth, treating what is directly perceptible as logically independent of the structured interdependence of elements that give it meaning. In tracing the internal connections of this interdependence, Marx is uncovering the essence of these ideas, an essence that frequently contradicts the truth reflected in appearances. In bourgeois political economy, for example, the fact that workers get paid by the hour is taken to mean that wages based on the sum of hours worked represents full payment for labor. By uncovering the relations between labor and the social conditions in which it occurs, including notions like wages in which these conditions are ordinarily understood, Marx is able to show that workers receive back only part of the wealth that they have produced.

Marx's reputation as a scholar has seldom been questioned, even by his foes. He believed that to criticize any subject one should know it and what others have written about it in some detail. He went so far as to learn Russian in the last years of his life in order to read what had been written in Russian on ground rent. All sources of information and techniques for gathering information available in his day were respected and made use of—government reports, surveys, questionnaires, fiction, newspapers—and there is no reason to believe that he would be less open to the many advances in these areas made by modern social science.

Once this is admitted, however, it is clear that Marx would be particularly concerned with what kind of information is worth collecting, the assumptions underlying various techniques for gathering it, how studying a subject can affect it, and especially with the influence of the concepts used (explanatory structures) on whatever is learned with their help. Presented with the typical attitude survey, for example, Marx would undoubtedly focus on the biases in what is asked, how it is asked, the sample to whom it is asked (the indifference generally shown to social class divisions), and the conditions reflected in the favored response (such that changes in these conditions ordinarily bring another response). He would probably specify, too, that no amount of questioning, given prevailing false consciousness, could possibly reveal how our society really works. It does not follow that Marx would ignore attitude surveys—as so many of his followers unfortunately do—but that his use of them would be highly qualified and critical.[5]

5

Marx's ontology declares the world an internally related whole; his epistemology breaks down this whole into relational units whose structured interdependence is reflected in the meanings of his concepts; his inquiry, by tracing the links between these units, fills in the details of this whole. Intellectual reconstruction, the fourth stage in Marx's method, comes with the completion of these processes. In intellectual reconstruction, the whole with which Marx began, real but featureless because unknown, is transformed into the rich, concrete totality of his understanding. By inserting a moment of intellectual reconstruction between inquiry and exposition, I am suggesting, of course, that the self-clarification Marx achieves upon putting together the results of his research and initial deductions is not quite the same as the analysis found in his published writings. This raises at least three crucial questions: (1) Where do we find this earlier "understanding" if not in his published writings? (2) How does it differ from what appears there? and (3) What is its status in what we call "Marxism"?

Marx kept voluminous notes on what he was reading and thinking, most of which falls between simply taking down what he found in his sources and writing first drafts of works he intended to publish. This was Marx thinking something through to make sense of it for himself, and possibly for Engels reading over his shoulder. Given the great quantity and variety of materials Marx needed to sift and connect, he obviously felt that this was a step he could not ignore. He made no attempt to publish these notebooks, but a half-century after he died two of the most important of them appeared as *The Economic and Philosophic Manuscripts of 1844* (1959b)—first published in 1931—and *Grundrisse* (foundations; 1973)—first published in 1939. The evidence for what I call Marx's "intellectual reconstruction" comes mainly from these two works, one from 1844, when he was twenty-six years old, and the other from 1858, when he was forty. I do not include the *German Ideology* here, which was written in 1846 and first published in 1929, since this is a work Marx wanted to publish but didn't because he couldn't find a publisher.

While a lot has been written about the alleged differences between early and late Marx, there has been no serious effort to probe the differences between what is, in effect, published and unpublished Marx (whether early or late). Yet, everyone who has read the *1844 Manuscripts* and the *Grundrisse* recognizes that there is something very special at work here. For example, it is clear that both contain much more on Marx's theory of alienation and his vision of communism than one finds in any of his published writings. Marx also makes much greater use of the vocabulary associated with the dialectic when he knows he is going to be the only reader than when he is writing for others. It would appear that, at least in these respects, what Marx required (or found helpful) in order to make sense of the world for himself was not quite the same as what he thought others required to make sense of and be convinced by what he had come to understand.

Given these not insignificant differences, the status of these unpublished writings in Marxism becomes an important question. Where do we find the fullest and most accurate statement of Marx's views on capitalism and history: in what he wrote for himself, or in what he wrote for workers and the general public? Before answering, it is worth noting, too, that Marx was very aware of the difficulty of some of his writings, especially for workers, and that he not only wanted his analysis to be understood but accepted and acted upon. And far from being dry academic exercises, his works were meant to have a powerful emotional impact on his readers. All this had an influence on how he organized his presentation, what he stressed and played down, and the examples, arguments, and even vocabulary he used. At a minimum, as we saw, it led to understating (not removing) in his published works the contribution that the theory of alienation, his vision of communism, and the dialectical method made to his own understanding of the world.

One could say that Marx's published writings represent a marriage between what he really understood of the world (and the forms in which he understood it) and the strategy of representation he adopted to simplify and clarify his views and to convince others, most of whom knew little political economy and less dialectics, of their truth and importance. While not ready to declare Marx of the *1844 Manuscripts* and the *Grundrisse* the "essential Marx," I hope this discussion demonstrates how indispensable these two works are for arriving at an accurate understanding of "what Marx really meant." It should also put us on guard against using any brief comment from his published writings—a tactic used by all sides (particularly with regard to the preface to the *Critique of Political Economy*)—to ascribe an unambiguous sense to Marx's claims in any area. What does he really believe? What is part of his strategy for presenting it?

Two more aspects of Marx's intellectual reconstruction deserve mention here. First, what makes his reconstruction a success is not only that all the main parts have been connected but that he is able to catch a glimpse of the overall system at work in each of them. If Marx had studied the American Congress, for example, he would not have been satisfied—as most political scientists are—with

knowing "how laws are made." Marx's intellectual reconstruction would necessarily include the history of Congress as a social-political phenomenon interacting with other institutions and practices in society (responding to them all
but to none more than to the economic structure), its role in the class struggle,
its relation to alienation, and the ways in which these functions and relations
are disguised from the people whose daily activity as citizens help to reproduce
them. For orthodox political scientists who understand Congress independently
of the totality (or place it in the somewhat larger abstraction, politics), the role
of this law-making body in securing capitalist interests and its character in light
of this role can never be adequately appreciated. In the Marxian intellectual
reconstruction, on the other hand, Congress would be understood as capitalism incarnated within the legislative body, as the political rule-making form of
capitalist society, and the presence of other aspects of this totality within this
form is never lost sight of.

Second, within Marx's reconstruction of the totality, as much "superstructure" as "base," as much people's activities as their products, the central place
is held by contradictions. The overarching contradiction that Marx sees in capitalism, the contradiction that includes in its folds all other capitalist contradictions in their peculiar interaction, is that between social production and private appropriation. This has been reformulated by some as the contradiction
between "capitalism's ever more social character and its enduringly private
purpose" (Miliband 1969, 34), or between how production is organized and how
it could be organized now given existing technology and culture (Williams 1968,
26); but each of these restatements brings out only part of its meaning. As the
contradiction embodying the unity of all of capitalism's major contradictions,
the relation between social production and private appropriation registers
Marx's complex understanding of this system as a concrete totality. It is the most
general as well as the most sophisticated result of his research, capitalism understood in its inner workings, and it is present in one form or another in every part of his intellectual reconstruction.

A first approximation of the intellectual reconstruction achieved by Marx
occurs whenever anyone observes that there is a pattern in the facts of capitalist life. What is the connection between sending people to jail for years for petty
thefts while permitting major thefts in the form of oil depletion allowances,
burning potatoes at a time when people are going hungry, allowing apartments
to remain vacant in the midst of a housing shortage, letting machines rust while
growing numbers of workers are unemployed, or forcing city dwellers to die
from suffocation and to drink from sewers when technology does not require
it? The decisive distinction between "radicals" and "liberals" is that the latter
understand most social problems as relatively independent and haphazard hap-
penings and try to solve them one at a time. Not aware of their shared identity
as interrelated parts of the capitalist system, they cannot deal with these ills at
the only level on which a successful solution is possible, on the level of the whole

society, and are reduced in the last analysis to alternating between the extremes of condemnation and despair.

Those who accept the label "radical," on the other hand, generally recognize that what liberals take to be the loose ends of a hundred unconnected ropes are knotted together as so many necessary (or at least highly probable) aspects of capitalist life. Too often missing in their understanding, however, are the structures (essences, laws, contradictions) that mediate the particular events and the capitalist system as a whole. To grasp how capitalism is responsible for a given fact, one must know the interrelated functions that bring the requirements of the system (with the imperative of capital to accumulate at its core) to bear on the people and processes involved. Otherwise, capitalism, as an answer to our dilemma, is itself an abstraction that brings little enlightenment. Learning these mediations necessarily takes place in a spiral fashion: each success in intellectual reconstruction advances the processes that occur in ontology, epistemology, and inquiry, which in turn permit a fuller concretization of the totality, et cetera. The interaction between the different moments of Marx's method that is suggested here, the need for repetition and their progress as an integral approach, should also put readers on guard against possible distortions introduced by my own strategy of exposition, which treats them one at a time.

6

The problem posed for Marx's exposition—the fifth and last step in his method—is how to explain capitalism as a system of structured interdependence relationally contained in each of its parts. If the questions that guide Marx's inquiry deal with how particular capitalist practices have come about and how their very forms reflect the workings of the capitalist system, the answers that guide his exposition seek to reestablish this system (now incorporated in his intellectual reconstruction) in an account of these forms. Though often confused, and never more so than in works on Marxism, comprehension and explanation are distinct functions and involve different techniques. From Marx's intellectual reconstruction of capitalism, it is clear that he would reject explanations that concentrate on prior conditions, or that reduce reality to a few empirical generalizations, or that establish ideal models, or that are satisfied with simply classifying the facts. In each of these cases, the explanation takes the form of relating two or more abstractions; the fuller context remains untouched. For Marx, capitalism is the only adequate explanation for whatever goes on inside it, but this is capitalism understood as a concrete totality.

The metaphor Marx uses to refer to his goal in exposition is a "mirrored" version of reality. He believes success is achieved if "the life of the subject matter is ideally reflected as in a mirror" and adds that when this happens, "it may appear as if we had before us a mere a priori construction" (1958, 19). Marx's goal then is to bring together the elements uncovered by his research in such a manner that they seem to belong to a deductive system. From comments by Engels and Paul Lafargue and from Marx's own frequent revisions of *Capital* (each draft and each edition contained major changes), it would appear that the mirrored presentation of reality remained a goal that continually eluded him. Just before his death, Marx was again planning to revise *Capital.*

Marx sought to reproduce the concrete totality present in his understanding chiefly in two ways: by tracing the interaction of social relations in the present, and by displaying their historical development as parts of a system through changes in their forms. In presenting their interaction, Marx frequently changes vantage points, making the ties he uncovers appear as part of each Relation in turn. The dulling effect of repetition is partly offset by the changes in vocabulary that usually accompany shifts in perspective. The predominant role of economic factors is brought out by presenting this interaction within economic Relations more often and in greater detail than within other Relations. Likewise, the unique role accorded contradictions in structuring the totality is reflected in the amount of attention that he gives them.

Contradictions and economic factors also occupy privileged positions in Marx's account of the development of social Relations through their different forms. With many others, Marx believes that explaining anything is, in large measure, explaining how it came to be. Where Marx stands apart is in believing that how it came to be is also part of what it is. This underlies his use of history to present current events and institutions as manifestations of a process: development is growth through internally related forms, and tendencies—which emerge from the past and arch toward the future—are considered as much a part of present-day social relations as their appearances.

Given the internal relations Marx sees between practice and ideas, the development that occurs in the one will—through their interaction—be reflected in the other. Marx's account, therefore, of the history of capitalism deals with changes in capitalist ideology as well as in the forms of capitalist life. The numerous quotations from the history of political economy found in *Capital*, therefore, are as much the object of Marx's critique as the system whose self-understanding they embody. This also enables Marx to present his own understanding of capitalism, which emerges from this same totality, as the critical culmination—however unfinished—of this development.

Marx's exposition of social interaction and development—like the inquiry through which he uncovered it and the intellectual reconstruction in which he grasps it—proceeds through a combination of analysis and synthesis. The central, most distinctive social Relations of capitalism are analyzed and shown to contain within themselves the structured interdependence and movement of the concrete totality. Marx insists that the importance of a Relation for the functioning of the capitalist system and not its historical appearance should determine the order of exposition. The analysis of capital, for example, precedes that of rent. This advice was easier given than followed, for Marx's own outlines and many revisions of *Capital* begin with different social Relations—capital, money, value, and finally commodity (which may only show that these four social Relations share top billing in his understanding of capitalism).

While Marx tries to unravel capitalism from each major social Relation, he simultaneously reconstructs the system by synthesizing the one-sided views of the whole obtainable from these different vantage points. The inner workings of capitalism that emerge from the social Relation, capital, have another emphasis and appearance than the same interdependence that emerges as part of value, et cetera. In presenting each of these one-sided views of the whole, Marx also makes certain assumptions regarding the functioning of aspects at its periphery, assumptions that are later made good when these same aspects emerge as central features of other Relations. The role of the market, for example, is assumed in the treatment of value in *Capital* I, but surfaces in the discussion of circulation in *Capital* II and is integrated into the value Relation in *Capital* III. The structured interdependence of capitalism, therefore, an interdependence present in his understanding of each major social Relation, is approached by "successive approximations" in his exposition (Sweezy 1964, 11). The explanation of capitalism offered in any one work (even when that work is the three volumes of *Capital*) is incomplete to the extent that major social Relations remain unanalyzed. Studies of capitalist politics, culture, and ethics, as well as of capitalist economics, are required to bring this work of synthesis to a conclusion, and—as I noted earlier—Marx did have such ambitious projects, but *Capital* simply grew to occupy all his time.

The process of synthesis can also be seen in the manner in which Marx's concepts acquire their fuller meanings. Given the requirements of communicability, terms used at the start of a work convey everyday notions, or something very close. The more general abstractions, expressed by concepts that refer to the more evident qualities of the human condition, or what Marx calls "simple categories," play this role best and are used to help explain the more historically concrete abstractions, the "complex categories" whose meanings involve us directly and immediately in capitalist structures. In this way, the concept "labor," for example, taken as a synonym of simple productive activity of a kind that is found everywhere, is used to help explain concepts like "commodity," "value," and "capital."

In general, and particularly at the start of a work, the social relations analyzed are the more historically concrete abstractions, and the work of unraveling them proceeds with the aid of more limited, general abstractions. But in the course of exposition, what began as simple categories with evident meanings will begin to look like concrete categories themselves, their meanings developing as the conditions in which they are embedded are uncovered. Labor, which appears as a general abstraction at the start of *Capital*, is gradually shown to be a historically specific form of productive activity, that is, wholly abstract, alienated productive activity of a kind that exists only in capitalism. Thus, while simple categories help make possible the analysis of complex ones, they are themselves being synthesized into complex categories (capable of undergoing their own analysis, of serving in their turn as windows through which to view the concrete totality).

Unable to provide adequate definitions for the complex categories whose meanings stretch to the limits of the system or for the simple categories that will soon grow into complex ones, Marx can only provide "indications" (or one-sided descriptions) and images that expand a Relation with the aid of the reader's own imagination, making Marx's striking metaphors a part of his method as well as of his style of writing. Treating what I've called indications as full definitions is a serious error, since the introduction of new indications will often appear to contradict what was said earlier. Does "capital," for example, mean "that kind of property which exploits wage labor" (Marx and Engels 1945, 33), "the means of production monopolized by a certain section of society" (Marx 1958, 10), or "the objective conditions of labor as separate from him" (Marx 1953, 488–89)? The answer, of course, is that the full meaning of "capital" incorporates all of these indications together with the dozen more found in *Capital* grasped in their peculiar interrelations. In such cases, striving for closure too soon can only be self-defeating.

Of all the stages of Marx's method, it is the dialectic as exposition that stands most in need of rethinking by modern-day Marxists. After all, the problems involved in communicating Marx's intellectual reconstruction of the capitalist totality were never more than partially solved. And the misunderstanding about which Marx complained and that he tried to combat with successive revisions of his major work has, if anything, grown worse. In this situation, I am tempted to view many well-known distortions of Marxism—such as economic determinism and various structuralist interpretations—as useful first approximations to a full explanation of Marxism to positivist-minded audiences (meaning most educated people in Western societies). Making the transition between factoral and process thinking, between operating with external and internal relations, while learning about the special effect of the capitalist mode of production on social and political phenomena may in fact require explanatory strategies of this type. The danger, of course, is to allow such misshapen and/or one-sided versions of Marxism to stand in for the full cloth in exposition or to pose as the truth of Marx's intellectual reconstruction.[6]

7

Once we understand that Marx is trying to present us with a mirror image of capitalism as a concrete totality and the logical character of this totality, the techniques he adopted in exposition (including his use of language) become less opaque. We are also ready to take as much from Marx's theoretical statements as he puts into them. Regarding his theory of the state, which is where we began, we can now grasp the logical character of the relations Marx posits between the forms of political institutions and practices and the dominant economic class, between the state and the mode of production, between the actual operations of the state and the ideology in which they are rationalized, et cetera. We are also in a position to grasp the connection between the sum of these relations taken as ongoing processes and the capitalist system in which they are found. A detailed restatement of the theory of the state that brings out the role played by Marx's methodology must be left for another time. Here, I have limited myself to outlining this method and simply clarifying its role.

From what has been said, it should also be evident that Marx's method is not only a means of understanding his theoretical statements but of amending them to take account of developments that have occurred since his time. The workings of the major processes that make up life in capitalism must be reassessed, and whatever changes found incorporated into the meanings of their covering concepts. What is required (and has been for some time) is a new intellectual reconstruction of the concrete totality, one that balances its respect for Marx's writings with an equally healthy respect for the research of modern scholars, including non-Marxists. As with Marx's own efforts, its practical effects will depend chiefly on how well we manage to capture the structured interdependence of capitalism within its varied parts. Marx said that he wanted to force "the frozen circumstances to dance by singing to them their own melody" (1967, 253). We should not aim for anything less.

Notes

1. For my further views on the Marxist theory of the state, politics, and political science, see especially *Alienation* (1976), chaps. 29–30; *Social and Sexual Revolution* (1979), chaps. 2 and 8 (sec. 4); *Dialectical Investigations* (1993), chaps. 3–6; "What Is Political Science? What Should It Be?" (2000); and chap. 12 of this volume.

2. This schema for distinguishing different notions of totality was first suggested by Karel Kosik in *Dialectic of the Concrete* (1976). There are important differences, however, in what Kosik and I understand of the second and third notions of totality presented here.

3. For further discussion of this process of orientation see chaps. 4 and 10–11 of my book *Alienation* (1976).

4. See chapters 5 and 9 in this volume for more detailed accounts of how Marx studied the past and the future.

5. See my essay "How to Study Class Consciousness . . . and Why We Should" in *Dialectical Investigations* (1993) for an attempt to construct a dialectical questionnaire but also for its discussion of how to conduct a dialectical study of class consciousness.

6. For a critique of Systematic Dialectics, a new interpretation of Marx's method that overemphasizes the moment of exposition and *Capital* I as the place to see it at work, see chapter 11.

CHAPTER 9

Why Dialectics? Why Now?
or, How to Study the Communist
Future Inside the Capitalist
Present

The law locks up the man or woman
Who steals a goose from off the common,
But leaves the greater villain loose
Who steals the common from under the goose.

—Anonymous, fifteenth century, English

1

The commons, of course, was the land owned by everyone in the village. By the late Middle Ages, feudal lords were claiming this land as their own private property. In universities today we can discern two opposing kinds of scholarship: that which studies the people who steal a goose from off the commons ("Goose from Off the Commons Studies," or GFOC for short) and that which studies those who steal the commons from under the goose ("Commons from Under the Goose Studies," or CFUG for short). If the "mainstream" in practically every discipline consists almost entirely of the former, Marxism is our leading example of the latter.

But whereas seeing someone steal a goose from off the commons is a relatively simple matter—you only have to be there, to open your eyes, and to look—seeing someone steal the commons from under the goose is not, neither then nor now (Russia today is a possible exception). Here, the theft is accomplished only gradually; the person acting is often an agent for someone else; force is used, but so are laws and ideology. In short, to recognize a case of CFUG, one has to grasp the bigger picture and the longer time that it takes for it to come together. It's not easy, but nothing that we study is more important. Hence—and no matter what happened in the Soviet Union and in China—Marxism will continue to be relevant until we reclaim the commons from those who stole it from us and who go on helping themselves to it with impunity right up to this moment.

Just how difficult it is to grasp the bigger picture was recently brought home to us when a group of astronomers announced that they had discovered what they called the "Great Attractor." This is a huge structure composed of many galaxies that is exerting a strong attraction on our galaxy and therefore on our solar system and on the planet on which we live. When questioned as to why something so big was not discovered earlier, one of the astronomers replied that its very size was responsible for the delay. These scientists had focused so intently on its parts that they couldn't see what they were parts of.

Capitalism is a huge structure very similar to the Great Attractor. It, too, has a major effect on everything going on inside it, but it is so big and so omnipresent that few see it. In capitalism, the system consists of a complex set of relations between all people, their activities (particularly material production), and products. But this interaction is also evolving, so the system includes the development of this interaction over time, stretching back to its origins and forward to whatever it is becoming. The problem people have in seeing capitalism, then— and recognizing instances of GFOC Studies when they occur—comes from the difficulty of grasping such a complex set of relations that are developing in this way and on this scale.

No one will deny, of course, that everything in society is related in some way and that the whole of this is changing, again in some way and at some pace. Yet most people try to make sense of what is going on by viewing one part of society at a time, isolating and separating it from the rest and treating it as static. The connections between such parts, like their real history and potential for further development, are considered external to what each one really is and therefore not essential to a full or even adequate understanding of any of them. As a result, looking for these connections and their history becomes more difficult than it has to be. They are left for last or left out completely, and important aspects of them are missed, distorted, or trivialized. It's what might be called the Humpty Dumpty problem. After the fall, it was not only extremely hard to put the pieces of poor Humpty together again but even to see where they fit. This is what happens whenever the pieces of our everyday experience are taken as existing separate from their spatial and historical contexts, whenever the part is given an ontological status independent of the whole.

2

The alternative, the dialectical alternative, is to start by taking the whole as given, so that the interconnections and changes that make up the whole are viewed as inseparable from what anything is, internal to its being, and therefore essential to a full understanding of it. In the history of ideas, this has been called the "philosophy of internal relations." No new facts have been introduced. We have only recognized the complex relations and changes that everyone admits to being in the world in a way that highlights rather than dismisses or minimizes them in investigating any problem. The world of independent and essentially dead "things" has been replaced in our thinking by a world of "processes in relations of mutual dependence." This is the first step in thinking dialectically. But we still don't know anything specific about these relations.

In order to draw closer to the subject of study, the next step is to abstract out the patterns in which most change and interaction occur. A lot of the specialized vocabulary associated with dialectics—"contradiction," "quantity-quality change," "interpenetration of polar opposites," "negation of the negation"—is concerned with this task. Reflecting actual patterns in the way things change and interact, these categories also serve as ways of organizing for purposes of thought and inquiry whatever it is they embrace. With their help, we can study the particular conditions, events, and problems that concern us in a way that never loses sight of how the whole is present in the part, how it helps to structure the part, supplying it with a location, a sense, and a direction. Later, what is learned about the part(s) is used to deepen our understanding of the whole, how it functions, how it has developed, and where it is tending. Both analysis and synthesis display this dialectical relation.

What's called "dialectical method" might be broken down into six successive moments. There is an ontological one, having to do with what the world really is (an infinite number of mutually dependent processes—with no clear or fixed boundaries—that coalesce to form a loosely structured whole or totality). There is the epistemological moment that deals with how to organize our thinking to understand such a world (as indicated, this involves opting for a philosophy of internal relations and abstracting out the chief patterns in which change and interaction occur as well as the main parts in and between which they are seen to occur). There is the moment of inquiry (where, based on an assumption of internal relations between all parts, one uses the categories that convey these patterns along with a set of priorities derived from Marx's theories as aids to investigation). There is the moment of intellectual reconstruction or self-clarification (where one puts together the results of such research for oneself). This is followed by the moment of exposition (where, using a strategy that takes account of how others think as well as what they know, one tries to explain this dialectical grasp of the "facts" to a particular audience). And, finally, there is the moment of praxis (where, based on whatever clarification has been reached, one consciously acts in the world, changing it and testing it and deepening one's understanding of it all at the same time).

These six moments are not traversed once and for all but again and again, as every attempt to understand and expound dialectical truths and to act upon them improves one's ability to organize one's thinking dialectically and to inquire further and deeper into the mutually dependent processes to which we also belong. In writing about dialectics, therefore, one must be very careful not to single out any one moment—as so many thinkers do—at the expense of the others. Only in their internal relations do these six moments constitute a workable and immensely valuable dialectical method.

So—why dialectics? Because that's the only sensible way to study a world composed of mutually dependent processes in constant evolution and also to interpret Marx, who is our leading investigator into this world. Dialectics is necessary just to see capitalism, given its vastness and complexity, and Marxism to help us understand it, to instruct us in how to do Commons from Under the Goose Studies, and to help us develop a political strategy to reclaim the commons. Capitalism is always and completely dialectical, so that Marxism will always be necessary to make sense of it, and dialectics to make correct sense of Marxism.

3

Why now? The current stage of capitalism is characterized by far greater complexity and much faster change and interaction than existed earlier. But if society has never been so imbued with dialectics, the efforts to keep us from grasping what is taking place have never been so systematic or so effective—all of which makes a dialectical understanding more indispensable now than ever before.

Socialism's sudden loss of credibility as a viable alternative to capitalism, however, a loss largely due to the collapse of the Soviet Union, has given Marxists still another important reason to devote more attention to dialectics, for many socialists, even some who had always been critical of the Soviet Union, have reacted to this recent turn of history by questioning whether any form of socialism is possible. Perhaps unsurprisingly, one result has been a kind of "future shyness" that has afflicted the writings of many on the Left today. What does a critical analysis of capitalism without any accompanying conception of socialism look like? It describes how capitalism works, shows who gets "screwed" and by how much, offers a moral condemnation of same, prescribes—*faute de mieux*—reformist solutions, and, because these no longer work, lapses into emotional despair and cynicism. Sound familiar?

Marx would not have been pleased, for, despite the absence of any single work on socialism/communism, there are no writings of his, no matter how small, where we are not given some indication of what such a future would be like. If Hegel's Owl of Minerva comes out and also goes back in at dusk, Marx's Owl stays around to herald the new dawn. This imaginative reconstruction of the future has been sharply attacked not only by his opponents but by many of Marx's followers, such as Edward Bernstein (1961, 204–5 and 209–11) and, more recently, Eric Olin Wright (1995), who view it as a lapse into utopianism that contaminates his otherwise scientific enterprise. But do all discussions of the future have to be "utopian"? With Rosa Luxemburg (1966, 40) and others, I do not think it is utopian to believe that a qualitatively better society is possible or to hope that it comes about. What is utopian is to construct this society out of such hopes, to believe, in other words, that such a society is possible without any other reason or evidence but that you desire it.

As opposed to this utopian approach, Marx insists that communism lies "concealed" inside capitalism and that he is able to uncover it by means of his analysis (1973, 159). And elsewhere he says, "we wish to find the new world through the critique of the old" (1967, 212). Rather than a moral condemnation, Marx's "critique of the old" shows that capitalism is having increasing difficulty in reproducing the conditions necessary for its own existence, that it is becoming impossible, while at the same time—and through the same developments—creating the conditions for the new society that will follow. The new world exists within the old in the form of a vast and untapped potential. Marx analyzes capitalism in a way that makes this unfolding potential for turning into its opposite (communism) stand out. As part of this, he is not averse to describing, if only in a general way, what the realization of this potential would look like.[1]

The central place of potential in dialectical thinking has been noted by a variety of thinkers. C. L. R. James refers to the internal relation between actuality and potentiality as "the entire secret" of Hegel's dialectics (meaning Marx's as well) (1992, 129). Marcuse claims to find an insoluble bond between the present and the future in the very meanings of the concepts with which Marx analyzes the present (1964, 295–96). Maximilien Rubel makes a similar point when he suggests, half seriously, that Marx invented a new grammatical form, the "anticipative-indicative," where every effort to point at something in front of him foreshadows something else that is not yet there (1987, 25). But this still doesn't explain how Marx does it. Where exactly is the future concealed in the present? And how does Marx's dialectical method help him to uncover it?

In brief: most of the evidence for the possibility of socialism/communism surrounds us on all sides and can be seen by everyone. It lies in conditions that already have a socialist edge to them, such as workers' and consumers' cooperatives, public education, municipal hospitals, political democracy, and—in our day—nationalized enterprises. However, it also lies in conditions that don't seem to have anything particularly socialist about them, such as our developed industries, enormous material wealth, high levels of science, occupational skills, organizational structures, education, and culture. Evidence for socialism can also be found in some of capitalism's worst problems, such as unemployment and worsening inequality. For Marx and his followers, it is clear that it is the capitalist context in which all these conditions are embedded that keeps them from fulfilling their potential and contributing to a truly human existence. Abstracting from this context, Marxists have no difficulty in looking at our enormous wealth and ability to produce more and seeing an end to material want, or looking at our limited and malfunctioning political democracy and seeing everyone democratically running all of society, or looking at rising unemployment and seeing the possibility of people sharing whatever work is to be done, working fewer hours and enjoying more free time, et cetera. Unfortunately, most others who encounter the same evidence don't see this potential, not even in the parts that have a socialist edge to them. And it is important to consider why they can't.

Investigating potential is taking the longer view, not only forward to what something can develop into but also backward to how it has developed up to now. This longer view, however, must be preceded by taking a broader view, since nothing and no one changes on its, his, or her own but only in close relationship with other people and things, that is, as part of an interactive system. Hence, however limited the immediate object of interest, investigating its potential requires that we project the evolution of the complex and integrated whole to which it belongs. The notion of potential is mystified whenever it is applied to a part that is separated from its encompassing system or that system is separated from its origins. When that happens, "potential" can only refer to possibility in the sense of chance, for all the necessity derived from the relational and processual character of reality has been removed, and there is no more reason to expect one outcome rather than another.

The crux of the problem most people have in seeing evidence for socialism inside capitalism, then, is that they operate with a conception of the present that is effectively sealed off from the future, at least any notion of the future that grows organically out of the present. There is no sense of the present as a moment through which life, and the rest of reality as the conditions of life, passes from somewhere on its way to somewhere. When someone is completely lost in the past or the future, we have little difficulty recognizing this as a mental illness. Yet, the present completely walled off from either the past or the future (or both) can also serve as a prison for thinking, though "alienation" is a more accurate label for this condition than "neurosis." Those persons affected by this condition simply take how something appears now for what it really is, what it is in full, and what it could only be. Hence, with the exception of the gadgetry found in science fiction, what most people call the "future" is occupied by all the usual social features only slightly modified from how they appear and function in the present.

With this mindset, there is no felt need to trace the relations any thing has with other things as part of a system—even while admitting that such a system exists—for, supposedly, there is nothing essential to be learned about it by doing so. Likewise, operating with narrow, independent parts that are also static, there is no difficulty in admitting that there was a past and will be a future while ignoring both when trying to understand anything in the present. If people can't see the evidence for socialism that exists all around them, therefore, it is not mainly because of an inability to abstract elements from capitalism and imaginatively project how they might function elsewhere. Rather, and more fundamentally, the conditions they see about them do not seem to belong to any social system at all, so there is no system to take them out of and, equally, no system to insert them into. The systemic and historical characters of both capitalism and socialism that would allow for such projections are simply missing.

4

The dialectic enters this picture as Marx's way of systematizing and historicizing all the conditions of capitalism so that they become internally related elements of an organic whole, which is itself but the most visible moment in how its components got that way and what they may yet become. With this move, the present ceases to be a prison for thinking and, like the past and the future, becomes a stage in a temporal process with necessary and discoverable relations to the rest of the process. It is by analyzing a present conceived in this way that Marx believes he can discern the broad outlines of the socialist and communist societies that lie ahead.

The dialectical method with which Marx studies this future inside the capitalist present consists of four main steps. (1) He looks for relations between the main capitalist features of our society at this moment in time. (2) He tries to find the necessary preconditions of just these relations—viewing them now as mutually dependent processes—in the past, treating the preconditions he uncovers as the start of an unfolding movement that led to the present. (3) He then projects these interrelated processes, reformulated as contradictions, from the past, through the present, and into the future. These projections move from the immediate future, to the probable resolution of these contradictions in an intermediate future, and on to the type of society that is likely to follow in the more distant future. (4) Marx then reverses himself and uses the socialist and communist stages of the future at which he has arrived as vantage points for reexamining the present, extended back in time to include its own past, now viewed as the sum of the necessary preconditions for such a future.

Before elaborating on these steps, there are two qualifications and one clarification that need to be made. First, it should be clear that explaining how to study the future is not the same as actually making such a study. In the former, which is the case here, the details brought forward are meant to illustrate the approach and should not be taken as the results of an already completed study, though I have taken care to use only realistic examples. The second qualification has to do with Aristotle's warning that in undertaking any study we should not expect more precision than the nature of our subject permits. The potential within capitalism for socialism is real enough, but it is often unclear and always imprecise, both as regards the exact forms that will develop and as regards timing or the moment at which the expected changes will occur. In short, in investigating the future within the present, we must be careful not to insist on a standard for knowledge that can never be met.

The clarification has to do with the fact that the future that Marx uncovers by projecting the outcome of society's contradictions is not all of one piece.

Marx's varied projections make it necessary to divide the future into four different stages, communism being but the last. Through his analysis of capitalism as a system in the present that emerges out of its preconditions in the past, Marx also projects its immediate future (or its development over the next few years), the near future (or the coming of the crisis that results in a socialist revolution), a middle future or transition between capitalism and communism that we call "socialism," and, finally, the far future or communism. How Marx uses his dialectical method for inquiring into what lies ahead varies somewhat depending on the stage of the future he is concerned with. While our interest here is limited to what I've called the "middle" and "far" futures, Marx's treatment of the "immediate" and especially the "near" futures cannot be wholly ignored, since the outcomes he projects for them enter into his expectations for socialism and communism.

5

Keeping these qualifications and this clarification clearly in mind, we can return to the four steps by which Marx sought to steal the secret of the future from its hiding place in the present. The first step, as I said, was to trace the main lines of the organic interaction that charactizes capitalist society—particularly as regards the accumulation of capital and the class struggle—at this moment of time. In order to focus on what is distinctively capitalist in our situation, Marx has to abstract out (omit) those qualities—equally real, and, for different kinds of problems, equally important—that belong to our society as part of other systems, such as human society (which takes in the whole history of the species), or class society (which takes in the entire period of class history), or modern capitalist society (which only takes in the most recent stage of capitalism), or the unique society that exists at this time in this place (which only takes in what is here and now). Every society and everything in them are composed of qualities that fall on these different levels of generality. Taken together—which is how most people approach them—they constitute a confusing patchwork of ill-fitting pieces that makes the systemic connections that exist on any single level very difficult to perceive. By starting with the decision to exclude all noncapitalist levels of generality from his awareness, to focus provisionally on the capitalist character of the people, activities, and products before him, Marx avoids tripping on what human society or class history or the other levels mentioned have placed in his way in carrying out his work as our leading systematizer of capitalism.

The widespread view of capitalism as the sum of everything in our society rather than the capitalist "slice" of it has been responsible for repeated complaints, most recently from postmodernists and social movement theorists, that Marx ignores the role of race, gender, nation, and religion. He ignores them, at least in his systematic writings, because they all predate capitalism and consequently cannot be part of what is distinctive about capitalism. Though all of these conditions take on capitalist forms to go along with their forms as part of class society or the life of the species, their most important qualities fall on the latter levels of generality, and it is there (and on us, in so far as we are subject to these levels) that they have their greatest impact. Uncovering the laws of motion of the capitalist mode of production, however, which was the major goal of Marx's investigative effort, simply required a more restricted focus.

With the distinctive qualities of capitalism in focus, Marx proceeds to examine the most important interactions in the present from different vantage points, though economic processes, particularly in production, are privileged both as vantage points and as material to be studied. To avoid the overemphasis and trivialization that marks most one-sided studies, the relation between labor and capital is examined from each side in turn, and the same applies to all the major relations that Marx treats. Of equal significance is the fact that internal relations are taken to exist between all objective and subjective factors, so that conditions never come into Marx's study without umbilical ties to the people who affect and are affected by them, and the same applies to people—they are always grasped in context, with the essentials of this context taken as part of who and what they are. Capital, as Marx says, "is at the same time the capitalist" (1973, 412).

After reconstituting the capitalist present in this manner, the second step Marx takes in his quest to unlock the future is to examine the preconditions of this present in the past. If the dialectical study of the present treats its subject matter as so many Relations, a dialectical study of the past requires that we view these Relations as also processes. History comes to mean the constant, if uneven, evolution of mutually dependent conditions. The past, of course, takes place before the present, and in retelling the story one usually begins at the beginning and moves forward. But the correct order in inquiry is present first, and it is what Marx uncovers in his reconstruction of the present that guides him in his search into the past, helping him decide what to look for as well as how far back to go in looking for it. The question posed is: What had to happen in the past for the present to become what it did? This is not to suggest that what occurred was preordained (though there may have been good reasons for it), only that it did in fact take place and that it had these results. It is in following this approach that Marx is led to late feudalism as the period when most of the important preconditions for capitalism are first laid down.

6

After reconstructing the organic interaction of the capitalist present and establishing its origins in the past, Marx is ready to project the main tendencies that he finds there into one or another stage of the future. As part of this third step in his method, Marx reabstracts (reorganizes, rethinks) these tendencies as "contradictions," which emphasizes their interaction as processes that are simultaneously mutually supporting and mutually undermining one another. Over time, it is the undermining aspects that prevail. The fundamental assumption that underlies Marx's practice here is that reality is an internally related whole with temporal as well as spatial dimensions. Things that are separate and independent (if this is how one conceives them) cannot be in contradiction, since contradiction implies that an important change in any part will produce changes of a comparable magnitude throughout the system, just as things that are static (again, if this is how one conceives them) cannot be in a contradiction, since contradiction implies there is a collision up ahead. The use of "contradiction" in formal logic and to refer to some relations between the categories of capitalist political economy (the province of Systematic Dialectics; see chapter 11), rather than a true exception, offers instances of Marx's willingness—evident throughout his writings—to use a concept to convey only part of all that it can mean for him. Finally, based on what has already been achieved in examining the present and the past, Marx's contradictions also contain both objective and subjective aspects as well as a high degree of economic content.

Marx's contradictions organize the present state of affairs in capitalism, including the people involved in them, in a way that brings out how this cluster of relations has developed, the pressures that are undermining their existing equilibrium, and the likely changes up ahead. With contradictions, the present comes to contain both its real past and likely future in a manner that allows each historical stage to cast a helpful light upon the others. Early in his career, Marx compared problems in society with those in algebra, where the solution is given once a problem receives its proper formulation (1967, 106). The solution to capitalism's problems, he believed, would also become clear once they were reformulated in terms of contradictions. It is chiefly by projecting such contradictions forward to the point of their resolution and beyond, where the character of the resolution gives shape to the elements of what follows, that Marx is able to catch a glimpse of both socialism and communism. The resolution of a contradiction can be partial and temporary or complete and permanent. In the former, as exemplified in the typical capitalist crisis, the elements involved are simply reordered in a way that puts off the arrival of the latter. Our concern here is with the kind of resolution that completely and permanently transforms all of capitalism's major contradictions.

Marx sees capitalism as full of intersecting and overlapping contradictions (1963, 218). Among the more important of these are the contradictions between use-value and exchange-value, between capital and labor in the production process (and between capitalists and workers in the class struggle), between capitalist forces and capitalist relations of production, between competition and cooperation, between science and ideology, between political democracy and economic servitude, and—perhaps most decisively—between social production and private appropriation (or what some have recast as the "logic of production versus the logic of consumption"). In all of these contradictions, what I referred to earlier as the "evidence for socialism" inside capitalism can be found reorganized as so many mutually dependent tendencies evolving over time. Viewed as parts of capitalism's major contradictions, their current forms can only represent a passing moment in the unfolding of a larger potential.

Whatever necessity (best grasped as likelihood) is found in Marx's projection of a socialist revolution in what I referred to as the near future is the result of his demonstrating that the conditions underlying capitalism have become more and more difficult to reproduce, while the conditions that make socialism possible have developed apace. All this is contained in capitalism's main contradictions. According to Marx's analysis, these contradictions display capitalism as becoming increasingly destructive, inefficient, irrational, and eventually impossible, while at the same time socialism is presented as becoming increasingly practical, rational, conceivable, necessary, and even obvious—notwithstanding all the alienated life conditions and the enormous consciousness industry that work to distort such facts. Consequently, for Marx, it is only a matter of time and opportunity before the organization, consciousness, and tactics of the rising class brings about the expected transformation.

7

Marx's vision of what happens after the revolution is derived mainly from projecting the forms that the resolution of capitalism's major contradictions are likely to take in the hands of a new ruling class, the workers, who have already been significantly changed by their participation in a successful revolution and who are guided primarily by their class interests in making all major decisions. And the most important of these interests is to abolish their exploitation as a class along with all the conditions that underpin it. How quickly they could accomplish this, of course, is another matter. The question, then, is not "Why would the workers do this?" but "Why—given their interests—when they come to power would they do anything else?"

For class interests to bear the weight put on them by this account of future prospects, we need to place the relations between different classes in earlier times, including their interests, inside the main contradictions that link the present with the past and the future. Only by understanding how capitalist class interests determine the forms and functions of what I called the "evidence for socialism" inside capitalism (step one), and how, in response to these same interests, all this has evolved over time (step two), can we begin to grasp how quickly these forms and functions would change in response to the demands of a new ruling class with different interests (step three). In other words, when the capitalists (and the feudal aristocracy and slave owners before them) acquired the power to shape society according to their class interests, they did so, and the workers will do likewise. If the workers' assumption of power together with the material conditions bequeathed by capitalism provide us with the *possibility* for socialism, it is the workers' peculiar class interests together with the removal of whatever interfered with the recognition of them under capitalism that supplies us with most of its *necessity*.

While Marx's vision of socialism (or the middle future) is derived mainly from the contradictions of capitalism, his vision of communism (or the far future) is derived not only from these contradictions (that is, from projecting the resolution of these contradictions beyond the attainment of socialism) but also from the contradictions Marx sees in class history and even in socialism itself, in so far as it is a distinctive class formation. After socialism has developed to a certain point—in particular, when everyone becomes a worker, all means of production are socialized, and democracy is extended to all walks of life— the contradictions that have existed since the very beginning of classes (having to do with the general form of the division of labor, private property, the state, etc.) come gradually to resolution. At the same time and through the same processes, the contradictions that socialism still possesses as a class society (having to do with its own forms of the division of labor, private property, and the state, which Marx sums up under "dictatorship of the proletariat") are also resolved. It is the resolution of the contradictions from all these overlapping periods— capitalism, class society, and socialism—together with the forms of alienation associated with them that marks the qualitative leap from socialism to communism and that makes the latter so hard for most people today to conceive.

To summarize: Marx begins to study the future by tracing the main organic interconnections in the capitalist present. He then looks for their preconditions in the past, and he concludes by projecting the chief tendencies found in both, abstracted now as contradictions, to their resolution and beyond for the stage of the future with which he is concerned. The order of the moves is present, past, and future (unlike most futurological attempts to peer ahead that move from the present directly to the future or, as in many utopian efforts, that go directly to the future, dispensing with the present altogether).

8

Marx's method for studying the future is still not complete. In a fourth and final step, Marx reverses himself and uses the socialist and communist stages of the future at which he has arrived as vantage points for reexamining the present, now viewed (together with its own past) as the necessary preconditions for such a future. This last step, though little understood, is the indispensable means by which Marx provides the "finishing touches" to his analysis of capitalism. It is also part of his method for studying the future, since the process I have described is an ongoing one. Building on what he learns from going through one series of steps, Marx begins the dance—the dance of the dialectic—all over again. For the work of reconstructing the present, finding its preconditions in the past, projecting its likely future, and seeking out the preconditions of this future in the present, now conceived of as an extension of the past, is never truly finished.

According to Marx, "The anatomy of the human being is the key to the anatomy of the ape" (1904, 300), and the same applies to the relations between later and earlier stages of society. In the same way that our present provides the key for understanding the past, the future (that is, the likely future, in so far as we can determine it) provides the key for understanding the present. It is Marx's grasp of communism, as unfinished as it is, for example, that helps him to see capitalism as the gateway to human history rather than its end and makes it easier to distinguish the capitalist-specific qualities of current society (those that serve as the preconditions of socialism) from the qualities it possesses as an instance of class and human societies. Communism also provides Marx with a standard by which the greater part of what exists today is found wanting as well as criteria for determining priorities for research and politics, distinguishing between the kind of changes capitalism can absorb from those that set transitional forces into motion.

The transparently class character of socialist society, epitomized in the notion of "the dictatorship of the proletariat," also makes it easier to grasp the more hidden class character of capitalism. We shouldn't be surprised, therefore, that insisting that the capitalist state, whatever its democratic pretensions, is a dictatorship of the capitalist class is the most effective way to innoculate people against the dangers of reformist politics (hence the theoretical loss incurred when the French and other communist parties removed all references to the dictatorship of the proletariat from their programs).

But above and beyond all this, revisiting the present from the vantage point of its likely future concretizes and hence makes visible the potential that exists throughout the present for just such a future. To William Faulkner's supposed remark, "The past is not dead—it is not even in the past," Marx could have added, "And the future is not unborn—it is not even in the future." Potential is the form in which the future exists inside the present, but until now it has been a form without a particular content just because it was open to every conceivable content. Now, everywhere one looks, one sees not only what is but what could be, what really could be, not simply because one desires it but because the aforementioned analysis has shown it to be so. Seeing the "facts" of capitalism as "evidence" of socialism becomes so many arguments for socialism. Furthermore, informing workers of and sensitizing them to the extraordinary possibilities that lie hidden inside their oppressive daily existence greatly increases their power to act politically by indicating how and with whom to act (all those who would benefit immediately from the enactment of these possibilities), just as it enhances their self-confidence that they can succeed. In sum, by enriching capitalism with the addition of communism, Marx's dialectical analysis "liberates" potential to play its indispensable role in helping to liberate us.

Taken altogether, the future proves to be as important in understanding the present and past as they are in understanding the future. And always, the return to the present from the future instigates another series of steps from the present to the past to the future, using what has just been learned to broaden and deepen the analysis at every stage.

9

Before concluding, it needs to be stressed that the projections of the future obtained through the use of the method outlined here are only highly probable, and even then the pace and exact forms through which such change occurs owes too much to the specificity of a particular place, the vagaries of class struggle, and also to accident to be fully knowable beforehand. Marx, as we know, recognized "barbarism" as a possible successor to capitalism, though he thought it very unlikely and devoted much less attention to this possibility than we need to after the blood-curdling events of the past century.

To avoid other possible misunderstandings of what I have tried to do in this chapter, I would like to add that my account of Marx's method is not meant to be either complete or final but rather—in keeping with Marx's own approach to exposition—a first approximation to its subject matter. Further, I do not believe that Marx's use of contradiction to project existing potential is the only means he uses to uncover the socialist/communist future inside the capitalist present; it is simply the main one. Also, this approach to studying the future is not to be confused with Marx's strategies for presenting what he found, and hence with what he actually published, which always involved a certain amount of reordering that took the character of his audience into account. Nor am I maintaining that this is how Marx became a communist. That is a complex story in which Hegel's dialectic and Marx's unique appropriation of it are but part.

Once Marx constructed the chief elements of what came to be called "Marxism," however, projecting capitalism's main contradictions forward became his preferred approach for studying the future, providing that future with just the degree of clarity and necessity needed for him to use it in elaborating his analysis of the present (in doing his version of Commons from Under the Goose Studies). It is also the best way that we today can learn about a socialist future that is more than wishful thinking. Only then, too, can the vision of socialism, which has been so battered by recent events, fulfill its own potential as one of our most effective weapons in the class struggle. Putting this weapon in the hands of workers and other oppressed peoples, teaching them how to use it—to do this against all the pressures of the age—is largely why we need dialectics and, with the world that capitalism has made teetering on the brink, why we need dialectics now more than ever.

Note

1. For an attempt to reconstruct Marx's vision of socialism and communism from his scattered comments on this subject, see my book *Social and Sexual Revolution* (1979), chap. 3.

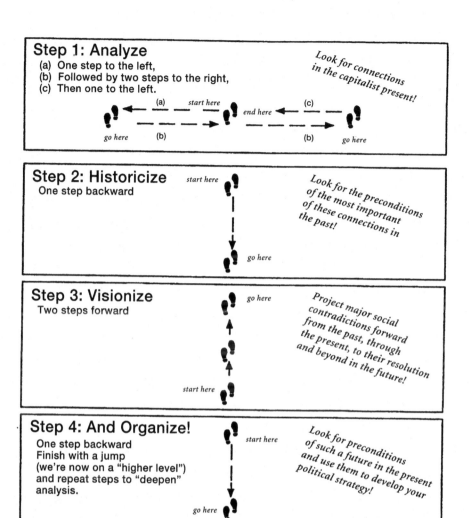

Dance of the Dialectic. (Text and choreography by Bertell Ollman; layout by Fran Moran.)

STEP 5

CHAPTER 10

Critical Realism in Light of Marx's Process of Abstraction

1

How did Odysseus make it through the rough passage between Scylla and Charybdis? With much less difficulty than most students pass through the equally dangerous straits between positivism and postmodernism. Where positivism promises the voyager a "truth" unadulterated with messy presuppositions, postmodernism overwhelms him or her with so many points of view that truth itself disappears. And many budding intellectuals have lost their bearings, if not their bodies, by traveling too close to one or another of these twin perils.

The school of Critical Realism, led by Roy Bhaskar, has—to its enormous credit—provided a workable means of avoiding this dire fate, and it has done so by reconciling what seems irreconcilable in the claims of its two opponents. Thus, positivism is said to be correct in holding that some truths are absolute and that we can discover what they are through research. And postmodernism is said to be correct in believing that the point of view of the investigator can never be completely detached from what he or she finds. The key move that Bhaskar makes is to substitute a study of ontology, or the nature of reality as such, for that of epistemology, or how we learn about reality and what it means to know it, which he says characterizes both positivism and postmodernism. But how can we learn about anything in the world without going through the process by which we learn about it? Bhaskar bypasses this problem by asking, "What must the world be like for science to be possible?" (1997, 23). His answer is that it would have to be "structured . . . differentiated and changing" (1997, 25). On these foundations, he then constructs a method for studying both natural and social phenomena that gives equal attention to uncovering what is actually there (the real order, structures, and changes in each sphere) and to examining the various biases and limitations that come from the social context in which the study is made. His point is that socially constructed points of view qualify what is found, but they do not annul it. Thus, while the kind of topics treated in the natural and social sciences may call for different approaches to inquiry as well as to explanation, neither science nor truth need be compromised in the process.

The same approach that Bhaskar takes to what has already happened or is there in front of us is also applied to the potential that is inherent in all natural and social phenomena. It, too, has a realist core of structure, differentiation, and change that studying from different points of view can qualify but never erase. The importance that Bhaskar attaches to such potential in arriving at an adequate understanding of any phenomenon—where what "is" is always firmly attached to what "could be"—is what gives his school its critical edge (hence "Critical" Realism). In recent writings, Bhaskar has formulated his ideas more and more in the vocabulary of dialectics, so that Critical Realism today can also be viewed as a version of dialectics and even—with its increasingly anticapitalist thrust—as a version of Marxist dialectics. I very much approve of this development, and in what follows I want to explore how else Critical Realism might benefit from its close association with Marxism.

2

Critical Realism, particularly in the work of Bhaskar, is like a lush tropical garden overgrown with a rich assortment of life forms, many of which we encounter here for the first time. This is its strength, and this is its weakness. In more philosophical language, Critical Realism has broken down and reorganized reality in a variety of new and often very helpful ways in order to highlight the particular connections and developments that it finds there. However, rather than laying stress on the process of abstraction with which it accomplishes this feat, it has generally been content to present us with its end linguistic results—the concepts that allow us to communicate our new abstractions.

Whenever the work of rethinking the world—which is mostly a matter of refocusing on and reorganizing what is there—devotes too much time to redefining old terms and introducing new ones, the involvement of those who would like to share in this work is largely reduced to learning a new language. In the case of Critical Realism, with dozens of new definitions, this is no easy task. Meanwhile, the mental activity of reordering the world, which underlies the newly defined terms, is trivialized or lost sight of altogether. But it is in this mental process of ordering and reordering, what Marx calls the process of abstraction, that the limits and biases of traditional understanding, as well as the possibility for a more accurate representation of reality, stand forth most clearly. Directing attention to our own process of abstraction is also the most effective means to teach others how to abstract and to enhance their flexibility in doing so. Such skills are essential to good dialectical thinking.

In what follows, I shall sketch Marx's views on the process of abstraction and its underpinnings in the philosophy of internal relations and then indicate how Critical Realism might benefit from reformulating some of its ideas along these lines.

3

In his most explicit statement on the subject, Marx claims that his method starts from the "real concrete" (the world as it presents itself to us) and proceeds through "abstraction" (the mental activity of breaking this whole down into the mental units with which we think about it) to the "thought concrete" (the re-constituted and now understood whole present in the mind) (1904, 293–94). Nowhere else does Marx attempt such a succinct summation of his method, so that the honor accorded to the process of abstraction here in letting it stand in for the whole of his method takes on a special importance. To begin with, Marx is simply recognizing that all thinking about reality as well as every effort to communicate our understanding of it requires that we operate with manage-able parts. Thus, everyone—not only Marx—starts out to make sense of their world by setting apart certain of its features and organizing them in ways that facilitate what they want to do and grasp.

The world being what it is—the very qualities of order, difference, structure, and change that Bhaskar attributes to reality—exercises the greatest influence on our abstractions (hence, the degree of overlap in the abstractions of differ-ent people and periods), but individual experiences, group interests, cultural traditions, and the purpose that drives a particular study also play a major role (hence, the often significant differences found in these same abstractions). What stands out most sharply about Marx's abstractions, apart from their size, is the amount of change and interaction that they contain. Not only do they include much of what the commonsense view would relegate to the external context, but by abstracting things, in his words, "as they really are and happen," Marx also makes how they happen part of what they are (Marx and Engels 1964, 57). And since history, for Marx, takes in the future as well as the past, this means that what things are becoming, whatever that may be, are often abstracted as essential aspects of what they now are, along with what they once were.

Marx's process of abstraction can also be said to operate in three different modes, through which it sets up three kinds of boundaries and provides three distinct kinds of focus, all of which are terribly important for the theories Marx constructs with their help. First, boundaries are set inside the space and time occupied by a particular relation, so that we focus on only this much of its in-terconnections and on only this long of the period over which they have evolved. I call this abstraction of extension. Second, boundaries are drawn inside the continuum that stretches from the unique to the most general on which are located all our qualities as human beings together with those of our activities and their varied products. This allows us to focus, in turn, on what it is about particular people, their activities, and products that only they possess, or on the qualities they possess because of the place they occupy and the function they perform in capitalism (and therefore shared by all those who share this place and function), or on the qualities that have marked people during the whole period during which social life has been organized around classes and class struggle, or on the qualities that set us apart as a distinctive species and make our lives into something called the human condition. I call this abstraction of level of generality.

Third, and last, abstraction also draws a boundary of a kind between different perspectives. All perception, all thinking, and all feeling starts from somewhere and with something, and this starting place provides a vantage point from which all subsequent effects will be viewed, understood, and even felt. At the same time that Marx abstracts an extension and level of generality, he also secures a place within the relationship he is studying from which to view and piece together its other aspects. The sum of these ties, as determined by the abstraction of extension, also sets up a vantage point from which to view and examine the whole system of which it is part. Thus, in abstracting capital, for example, Marx not only gives it an extension and a level of generality (that of capitalism) but provides it with a vantage point (that of the material means of production) from which to view its other elements (one that gives these means of production the central role), while making capital itself a vantage point from which to view the entire capitalist system (one that gives to capital the central role).

If Marx's abstractions—especially as regards the inclusion of change and interaction—are as unusual as they seem to be, it is not enough to display them. We also need to examine the philosophical assumptions that allow him to abstract in this manner. The view held by most people, both in and out of the academy, is that there are things and there are relations, and that neither can be subsumed in the other. On this view, capital is a thing that has relations with other things, and it makes no sense to treat these relations as parts of capital. Marx rejects this logical dichotomy and views capital as itself a complex Relation composed of its ties to other . . . relations. In fact, here everything, and not only capital, is grasped as the sum of its relations. Moreover, since these relations extend backward and forward in time, this also makes what capital was as well as what it is likely to become essential parts of what it now is. This view, which Marx took over from Hegel, is known as the philosophy of internal relations.

It is the philosophy of internal relations that gives Marx both the license and opportunity to abstract as freely as he does, to decide how far into its spatial as well as its temporal relations any particular will extend. Aware that reality doesn't come with its boundaries already in place, Marx knows that it is up to him to construct them. But if he draws them, he can redraw them as suits his changing purposes. In this way, the philosophy of internal relations makes a variety of abstractions possible and even helps to develop Marx's skills and flexibility in making abstractions. Those (the great majority) who operate with a philosophy of external relations—the philosophy that underlies the commonsense approach—also need to abstract. The units in and with which thinking goes on are always abstractions, whether the people involved know it or not, except that here most of the work of abstracting occurs as part of the socialization process, particularly in the acquisition of language. Once this has been forgotten, it is easy to mistake the boundaries one has just drawn as already present in the nature of reality as such.[1]

4

Does Roy Bhaskar have a philosophy of internal relations? He has denied having such a view, maintaining instead that reality contains examples of both internal and external relations (which is a nuanced version of the philosophy of external relations, since every proponent of this view will allow for some internal relations). But some of his theoretical practice suggests otherwise. He claims, for example, that "emergent social things are existentially constituted by or contain their relations, connections and interdependencies with other social (and natural) things" (1993, 54). In an accompanying footnote, Bhaskar points out that I say something similar in my book *Dialectical Investigations*. I do indeed. For all "social things" are "emergent" on one or another time scale, so we're talking here about everything in society being internally related. And since the relations that "constitute" any social thing are said to include its ties to "natural" as well as to other social things, it would appear that everything in reality is internally related. And that's the philosophy of internal relations.

With this view, as I have argued, the necessary next step is to abstract the provisional boundaries that establish separate units and allow us to think about and interact with such a world. Bhaskar doesn't take this step, at least not explicitly and not systematically. Instead, he retreats from the exposed position found above and says that it is an open question whether any relation in historical time is an internal or external one. But this assumes—contrary to the statement just cited—that there are things that are not constituted by their ties to other social and natural things, that the conditions we encounter in history already exist there as particulars or, in Bhaskar's preferred language, separate "totalities." On this view, which seems to be the prevailing one in Bhaskar's writings, there are many totalities in the world, with internal relations existing only within a totality and not between them.

This raises three questions: how do the boundaries around those things Bhaskar recognizes as totalities get set? What is the role of the process of abstraction in setting provisional boundaries around those elements and groups of elements inside each totality? And—taking note of possible mediations—what kind of relations exist between each totality and the whole of reality in which it exists? Full answers to these questions would help clarify Bhaskar's ambiguous relation to the philosophy of internal relations. Instead, Bhaskar opts to use internal relations whenever it is convenient while refusing to offer the only philosophical defense that would justify his using it. But without such a justification, most of his readers will only be shocked (or amused) by such claims as, "The goal of universal human autonomy can be regarded as implicit in an infant's primal scream" (1993, 264). And there are many other such examples.

On one occasion, Bhaskar presents the essence of dialectics as "the art of thinking the coincidence of distinctions and connections" (1993, 190). But thinking in this way requires that we abstract parts, first, as separate and, then, as aspects of one another. So mastering the process of abstraction as well as achieving flexibility in reabstracting is the key to this art. In sketching Marx's process of abstraction my main aim has been to show the compatibility of this process with the main ideas, philosophical and political, of Critical Realism. However, taking on Marx's process of abstraction together with its foundation in the philosophy of internal relations would also carry real advantages for Critical Realism. Here I can do no more than list some of them:

1. It would make it easier for Critical Realism to focus on change and interaction by taking them as given and to be more consistent in treating stability and separateness, when they "appear," as temporary phenomena that require special explanation.
2. The philosophy of internal relations would encourage Critical Realism to look for more extended relations as the proper way of understanding anything and enable it to see why that search (and our understanding) can never be completed.
3. The emphasis on abstraction provides a more adequate framework for Critical Realism's important critique of ideology, which is already based to a certain degree on challenging what Bhaskar calls "illicit abstractions" (1993, 130–31).
4. The combination of internal relations and the process of abstraction would allow Critical Realism to admit causes when they "appear" (when the abstraction of what is said to be the "cause" includes more of the past than the abstraction of what is said to be the "effect") without losing or trivializing the ongoing interaction.
5. As regards Marxism, which Critical Realism claims to accept, only the philosophy of internal relations allows one to make consistent sense of Marx's elastic meanings (see chaps. 2 and 3 in this volume).
6. It would also enable Critical Realism to understand Marxism not as a simple search for connections between what appears separate (the limited task of most radicals and unfortunately many Marxists) but as a search for what brought about a break in the initial unity of social man (and therefore society) and nature, the ideological forms this break takes in capitalist society, and how a new and higher unity of society and nature might be established.
7. As regards Critical Realism proper, making explicit the particular abstractions of extension, level of generality, and vantage point used in any given

analysis would help greatly in circumscribing what is being said from what—superficial resemblances to the contrary—is not being said. There is no need for the works of Critical Realism to be as obscure as they often are.

8. Operating with an explicit philosophy of internal relations and a systematic use of the process of abstraction would permit Critical Realism—like Marxism—to expand and contract the meaning of ordinary-language concepts in keeping with its abstractions of the moment. Having greater flexibility in altering the sense of old terms would enable Critical Realism to present its case with fewer new terms, something that could only benefit its readers. Marx managed to convey a wholly original worldview using only two new expressions: "relations of production" and "surplus-value."

9. Making systematic use of the process of abstraction should also make thinkers in this tradition more aware of what Critical Realism, as presently constituted, does and what it doesn't and can't do, unless it introduces other kinds of abstractions. For example, Bhaskar attempts to project the communist future on the basis of an analysis done with abstractions that fall on the level of generality of the human condition—needs, wants, everyone's material interests and constraints, and the reality principle—which he then treats dialectically. However, most of what we know and can know about communism derives, as Marx shows, from an analysis of the contradictions in a historically specific social formation, capitalism. It is these contradictions, one part of which is the class struggle between workers and capitalists, that reveal not only how communism might come about but a good deal of what it might look like. Only by using abstractions appropriate to this level of generality do the dynamics and possible transformation of the capitalist mode of production come into focus. Until Critical Realism gives such abstractions a central place in its analysis, there is little it can say about communism that doesn't qualify as utopian thinking (with the accompanying danger of lapsing into mysticism).

10. Recognizing the crucial role of the capitalist level of generality for some of the questions with which it is concerned should also lead Critical Realism to make more use of the abstractions of class (and particularly of capitalist and working classes), class interests, and class struggle.

11. Rooting its analysis of communism in the real possibilities, objective and subjective, of capitalism (abstracted as a cluster of unfolding contradictions), workers' class interests would replace the unconvincing emancipatory ethic that Critical Realism currently uses to bring people to join in the struggle for a better world.

12. By giving more attention to the capitalist dimension of our social life, to its class divisions, and particularly to the class interests found there, Critical Realism would also increase its contribution to raising workers' class consciousness as distinct from trying to develop everyone's humanist consciousness. In any clash between people's class interests and their common interests as members of the species, Marx believed, it is almost always the

former that wins out. (Try convincing capitalists to sacrifice a significant portion of their profits to preserve the quality of a community's water and air, even when they live in that community.)

13. Finally—to return to dialectics—by making its process of abstraction explicit and systematic, Critical Realism would also be teaching its readers how to abstract and would help them acquire flexibility in doing so, both of which are essential to effective dialectical thinking. It would also make it easier for many of them to become coproducers and not just consumers in the research tradition that Critical Realism seeks to found.

5

After listing so many benefits that would accrue to Critical Realism if it took on board the philosophy of internal relations and Marx's process of abstraction, something needs to be said about why this hasn't been done already. I see two possible explanations. First, Bhaskar probably believes that the reformulation proposed above would threaten the "realist" dimension of Critical Realism. Admittedly, emphasis on the process of abstraction has usually gone along with various idealist attempts to deny that the world exists before and apart from people's efforts to engage with it. But as the counterexample of Marx makes abundantly clear, the connection between emphasizing the process of abstraction and ontological idealism is not a necessary one. Also, as a Marxist who gives priority of place in my dialectics to this process, it may be helpful to point out that I have no difficulty in accepting Bhaskar's description of basic reality as "stratified, differentiated and changing" (though I would also add "interacting" and "mutually dependent," which are implied in the other qualities mentioned) (1993, 206). What basic reality is *not* is already separated out into the units in which we understand and communicate it to others. That occurs through the process of abstraction, in which the qualities Bhaskar ascribes to the world exercise the major—though, as we've seen, not the sole—influence. In sum, the materialist and realist basis of Critical Realism is in no danger from the reformulation that I have been urging.

A second possible explanation for Bhaskar's hesitancy in adopting the philosophy of internal relations and a systematic use of the process of abstraction can be found in his apparent disinterest in what is required for effective exposition. Marx, as we know, made a sharp distinction in his dialectical method between the moments of inquiry and exposition. I would go further and insert another moment between the two, that of intellectual reconstruction or self-clarification, which is when one puts together the results of one's inquiry for oneself before one tries to explain it to others. The priorities, vocabulary, and organization of material that help us make sense of our world are not always best suited to bring our chosen audience to the same understanding. In Marx's case, it is the difference, if you will, between the *1844 Manuscripts* and the *Grundrisse,* on the one side, and *Capital,* on the other side.

Critical Realism makes no sharp distinction between what is required for its practitioners to understand reality and what is required to explain it to others, so that, for example, the priority given to ontology in its intellectual reconstruction is left unchanged in its exposition. Recognizing the importance of this distinction, my strategy of exposition puts epistemology in the foreground, even though my own thinking on these subjects has developed largely through an ontological approach, and even though my ontology is very similar to Critical Realism's. Hence, it is at least partly inaccurate to say, as Bhaskar has (1993, 201), that my dialectic is an epistemological one. I simply believe that the most effective way of explaining my views to a mainly nondialectical audience is to begin with their own process of learning, with special emphasis on the role played by the process of abstraction. Having been helped to grasp Marx's and my abstractions of change and interaction, readers are in a better position to substitute these dialectical abstractions for their own reified ones when they move on to (back to?) the moment of ontology and come to examine with Bhaskar what the world is really like. Otherwise, starting out with ontology, the likely result for most of the people that both Bhaskar and I are trying to reach is a nondialectical grasp (whether materialist or idealist) of the dialectical reality that is there. Critical Realism really needs to devote more attention to what is required of an effective strategy of exposition for something as uncommonsensical as its dialectical view of the world.

In conclusion, Bhaskar has sometimes suggested that Critical Realism has been developed in order to supplement Marxism. If this is so, then most of what I have offered above can be taken as an attempt to make this common-law marriage more fruitful for both sides.

Note

1. For a fuller account of the philosophy of internal relations, see chapters 2–4 in this volume. Marx's process of abstraction is examined in detail in chapter 5.

CHAPTER 11

Marx's Dialectical Method Is More Than a Mode of Exposition: A Critique of Systematic Dialectics

1

We live at a time when few people use the term "capitalism," when most don't know what it means, when an even larger number have no idea of the systemic character of capitalism or how it works, and hardly anyone grasps the role that economic categories play in this society and in our own efforts to make sense of it all. In this situation, any school of thought that puts capitalism, particularly its systemic character, and capitalist economic categories at the center of its concern can be forgiven for some of the exaggeration and one-sidedness that enters into its work. Such, anyway, is the generally favorable bias I bring to my examination of Systematic Dialectics, whether in its Japanese, North American, or European variations. All the criticisms that follow, therefore, however harsh they may appear, need to be viewed in this softening light.

For purposes of this essay, "Systematic Dialectics" refers to a particular interpretation of Marx's dialectical method that a variety of socialist thinkers have come to share. It does not cover all that these scholars have written on Marxism, or even on dialectics, but only their common—albeit often individually qualified—views on this subject. The most important of these thinkers—judging only from their contributions to Systematic Dialectics—are Tom Sekine, Robert Albritton, Christopher Arthur, and Tony Smith, and it is chiefly their writings that have provoked these remarks.

The interpretation of Marx offered by Systematic Dialectics can be summed up in three core ideas: (1) that "Marx's dialectical method" refers exclusively (or almost exclusively) to the strategy Marx used in *presenting* his understanding of capitalist political economy; (2) that the main and possibly only place he uses this strategy is in *Capital* I; and (3) that the strategy itself involves constructing a conceptual logic that Marx took over in all its essentials from Hegel.

In this logic, the transition from one concept to the next comes from unravelling a key contradiction that lies in the very meaning of the first concept. The contradiction can only be resolved by introducing a new concept whose meaning fuses the contradictory elements found in the previous one. Naturally, not all concepts are equally equipped to play this role, so this strategy also lays down a particular order in which the main categories of capitalist political economy get treated: "commodity," whose key contradiction between value and use-value is resolved by introducing "money," is followed by "money," whose key contradiction is resolved by introducing "capital," et cetera. In this manner, Marx is said to proceed from the abstract, or simple categories with limited references, to the concrete, or complex categories whose meanings reflect the full richness of capitalist society. Furthermore, the same conceptual logic that enables Marx to reconstruct the essential relations of the capitalist system enables him (if we now look back at where we've come from rather than ahead to where we are going) to supply the necessary presuppositions for each of the categories that comes into his account and eventually for the capitalist system as a whole. The underlying assumption here is that if each step in exposition can be shown to follow necessarily from the one just before, the complex social interplay that is reflected in the end result will be no less necessary than the conceptual logic with which it was constructed.

2

Before passing on to my criticisms, I would like to say that I have no doubt about Marx's use of this expositional strategy in *Capital* I. Nor do I deny its importance for what he wanted to achieve in this work, especially as regards setting capitalism apart as a relatively autonomous mode of production whose distinctive logic is reflected in the interplay of its main economic categories. But three major questions remain: (1) Is Systematic Dialectics the only strategy of presentation that Marx adopts in *Capital* I? (2) What strategies of presentation does Marx use in his other writings? and, most importantly, (3) Is it reasonable to restrict Marx's dialectical method to the moment of presentation? What, in other words, is the role of dialectics in helping Marx acquire the distinctive understanding that he expounds in *Capital* and other works?

As regards *Capital* I, it seems clear to me that Marx had other aims besides presenting the dialectical relations between the main categories of political economy. The short list would have to include unmasking bourgeois ideology (and ideologists), displaying the roots of capitalist economics in alienated social relations, showing capitalism's origins in primitive accumulation and its potential for evolving into communism, mapping the class struggle, and raising workers' class consciousness, and all of these aims required strategies of presentation that have little to do with Hegel's conceptual logic. The result is that *Capital* I contains whole sections that, according to the proponents of Sys-

tematic Dialectics (who accord great importance to both the character and order of this work), simply don't belong there or are seriously out of place.

There is no conceptual necessity, for example, calling for the discussion of
labor (as the substance of value) between the discussions of value and exchange-
value. Hence, Tom Sekine considers this an error on Marx's part (1986, 119), but
Marx thought it important enough to devote eight pages to labor, and that only
four pages into the book. Why, too—if *Capital* I is ordered by a straightforward
conceptual logic—does Marx devote so much attention to the expansion of the
working day? Where does it fit into this logic? But perhaps the biggest waste of
time, Systematic Dialectically speaking, is the sixty pages at the end of *Capital*
devoted to primitive accumulation. Systematic Dialectics dispenses with the
history of capitalism and, for that matter, its eventual replacement by communism as well as how capitalism has worked in different countries at different
stages of its development. The conceptual logic with which it operates has no
place for them. But Marx found a place for them in *Capital* and for other critical discussions of what has happened and is likely to happen in the real world
of capitalism. Their inclusion would seem to come from other strategies of presentation in the service of other aims.

There are still at least two other major features of *Capital* I that suggest strategic choices other than those acknowledged by Systematic Dialectics. The
theory of alienation, for example, which plays such a major role in the *Grundrisse* (1858), the extended essay in self-clarification with which Marx prepared
the ground for *Capital* (1867), is barely present in the finished work, and then
chiefly in the one-sided version represented by the fetishism of commodities.
Yet, labor, whenever it comes into the analysis in *Capital*, is always alienated
labor, with all that this implies, and has to be for the equation of labor and value
(and hence, too, all forms of value) to hold. This is undoubtedly why Marx introduces labor early in the discussion of value even before the mention of exchange-value. Omitting a fuller account of the theory of alienation from *Capital*, therefore, does not represent a change of mind—as Althusser and a few
others have held—but a change of strategy in expounding his systematic political economy, probably in the interest of making his analysis easier for workers to understand and act upon.

The same aim seems to lie behind the decision to use far less of the vocabulary associated with dialectics than is found, again, in the *Grundrisse*. In sum,
as important as it is, Systematic Dialectics is simply unable to account for many
of the strategic decisions that were responsible for both the form and content
of *Capital* I. In making it appear otherwise, Systematic Dialectics has simply
fallen victim to a danger that Marx himself recognized when, in finishing his
preparations for *Capital*, he noted, "It will be necessary later . . . to correct the
idealist manner of the presentation, which makes it seem as if it were merely
a matter of conceptual determinations and the dialectic of these concepts"
(1973, 151).

3

A second difficulty, as I indicated, with Systematic Dialectics is that it concerns itself exclusively, or—depending on the writer—almost exclusively, with *Capital* I, while exposition was a problem that called for strategic decisions in all of Marx's writings. Marx's subject matter was so large and complex, and the difficulty of bringing it under control and making his interpretations understandable and convincing so great, that how to present his views was an ongoing worry. In treating the Marxian corpus as a whole, it is important, of course, to distinguish occasional pieces from longer, more deliberate essays, published writings from unpublished ones, works on political economy from works on other subjects, and, to some degree, between writings from different periods. And each of these distinctions marks some corresponding effect on Marx's strategy of exposition.

As our main concern is with Marx's systemic writings in political economy, we can provisionally ignore most of these divisions. Viewing Marx's economic writings as a whole, then, what strikes us most about his exposition are the following:

1. The main effort goes into uncovering and clarifying relationships, the most important parts of which are not immediately apparent.
2. The work is unfinished, as indicated by Marx's various plans, drafts, and notes (Rubel 1981, chaps. 3–4).
3. Marx changed his mind several times on where to begin and what to emphasize, as indicated not only by these same plans but also by his different "false starts" on *Capital*—his *Contribution to a Critique of Political Economy* (1859), the unpublished introduction to this work, the *Grundrisse* (1858), "Wages, Price, and Profit" (1865), and, if we want to go further back, the *Poverty of Philosophy* (1847) and "Wage Labor and Capital" (1849). (The dates here refer to the years in which they were written; "Wage Labor and Capital" and "Wages, Price, and Profit" can be found in Marx and Engels 1951a, 66–97 and 361–405, respectively.) Marx's substantial revisions for the French and second German editions of *Capital* I together with his plans (cut short by his death) to revise *Capital* once again offer further evidence against taking any organization of his ideas as definitive.
4. Each of the main subjects that enters Marx's account is presented as it appears and functions from several different vantage points.
5. Each of these subjects is also followed through the different forms it assumes in its movement, both organic/systemic and historical.
6. Every opportunity is taken to project aspects of the communist future from capitalism's unfolding contradictions.
7. The ways in which capitalism is misunderstood and defended receive as much critical attention as the underlying conditions of capitalism and the practices of capitalists themselves.

8. The entire project proceeds through a complex mixture of presenting the conditions and events in the real world of capitalism while analyzing the concepts with which we think about them.

It is clear from all this that Marx is neither an empirical social scientist nor a Systematic Dialectician, if these are taken as exclusive designations, but once we understand how he combined the two, there is no difficulty in viewing him as both.

A brief sketch of the features that dominate Marx's exposition throughout his works on political economy is found on those pages of his unpublished introduction to *Contribution to the Critique of Political Economy* devoted to the complex interaction between production, distribution, exchange, and consumption (1904, 276ff.). We learn here that these processes are not only related to each other as necessary preconditions and results; each is also an aspect of the others, and—through their internal relations with other neighboring processes—each is also a version, albeit one-sided, of the whole that contains them all. In presenting the interaction between these processes from the vantage point of each process in turn, Marx makes use of all of these possibilities. Moreover, his flexibility in expanding and contracting the relations before him is reflected in an elasticity in the meanings of the concepts that are used. This creates serious problems for Marx in presenting his views and for us in grasping the categories with which he does so. Every serious student of Marx has encountered this difficulty, which was given its classic statement by Vilfredo Pareto when he said, "Marx's words are like bats: one can see in them both birds and mice" (1902, 332). How exactly Marx manipulates the size of the relations he is working with will be explained later. Here, I only want to make clear that this is what he does and to indicate the effect this has on the meanings of his concepts.

Marx once compared his condition to that of the hero in Balzac's *Unknown Masterpiece* who, by painting over and retouching, constantly tried to reproduce on the canvas what he saw in his mind's eye (Berlin 1960, 3). But, as Paul Lafargue, Marx's son-in-law and the only person to whom he ever dictated any work, noted, Marx was never quite satisfied with his efforts "to disclose the whole of that world in its manifold and continually varying action and reaction" (*Reminiscences* n.d., 78). Hence, all the fresh starts and revisions, the frequent changes of vantage point and in the way key elements are organized. Viewed in this light, Systematic Dialectics can only be understood as a misguided attempt to reduce Marx's varied strategies of presentation to a single one, albeit one that does play a major role in expounding the systemic nature of the capitalist mode of production in *Capital* I.

4

So far my criticisms of Systematic Dialectics have dealt with what it has to say about Marx's method of presentation. My third and far more serious criticism is that Systematic Dialectics is wrong in restricting Marx's dialectical method to but one of its several interlocking moments, that of presentation. For the thinkers in this school usually make it appear as if Marx "worked out" his understanding of capitalism in *Capital* I rather than "laid it out" there and that there is nothing problematic, or unusual, or particularly dialectical in the understanding that Marx brought to writing *Capital* I. In my view, Marx could never have written a work like *Capital* I if his own understanding of capitalism, the mode of inquiry used to acquire it, and the way of thinking that underlay his inquiry were not already thoroughly dialectical. But this requires that we expand the notion of dialectics beyond the conceptual logic that Marx used to expound some of his views in *Capital* I.[1]

For me, the problem to which all dialectics—Marx's and everyone else's—is addressed is: how to think adequately about change, all kinds of change, and interaction, all kinds of interaction. This assumes, of course, that change and interaction are a big part of what goes on in the world and that it is very easy to miss, or minimize, or distort important parts of it, with grave consequences for our understanding and even our lives. What's called "Marx's dialectical method" is his attempt to come to grips with this problem as it affected the subject matter with which he was particularly concerned. Broadly speaking, it is his way of grasping the changes and interactions in capitalism (but also in the larger world) and explaining them, and it includes all that he does in mentally manipulating this reality for purposes of inquiry and exposition.

Marx's dialectical method can be conveniently broken down into six interrelated moments, which also represent stages in its practice. These are: (1) ontology, which has to do with what the world really is, particularly as regards change and interaction; (2) epistemology, which deals with how Marx orders his thinking to take adequate account of the changes and interactions that concern him; (3) inquiry, or the concrete steps Marx takes—based on the mental manipulations undertaken in the previous moment—to learn what he wants to know; (4) intellectual reconstruction (or self-clarification), which is all that Marx does to put together the results of his research for himself (the *1844 Manuscripts* and the *Grundrisse,* neither of them meant for publication, offer us instances of this little-studied moment); (5) exposition, where, using strategies that take account of how others think as well as what they know, Marx tries to explain his dialectical grasp of the "facts" to his chosen audience and to convince them of what he is saying; and (6) praxis, where, based on whatever clarification has been reached thus far, Marx consciously acts in the world, changing it and testing it and deepening his understanding of it all at the same time.

It is not a matter, clearly, of going through these six moments once and for all, but again and again, as Marx does, since every attempt to grasp and expound dialectical truths and to act upon them improves his ability to organize his thinking dialectically and to inquire further and more deeply into the mutually dependent processes to which we also belong. In writing about dialectics, therefore, one must be very careful not to focus on any one moment at the expense of the others. The problem comes not from stressing one moment in dialectics but in neglecting the others (mistaking the part for the whole, a common undialectical error) so that even the moment that is stressed—because of all the interconnections—cannot be properly understood.

Like Systematic Dialectics, my own attempts to explain dialectics have also privileged one moment—in this case, epistemology—over the others, but I have always tried to integrate it with the rest. I chose epistemology because I believe it is pivotal both for grasping and applying all the other moments. Epistemology is also an ideal entry point for explaining Marx's overall method, since it requires fewer assumptions than if I had begun elsewhere. This is not the place, of course, to give my interpretation of Marx's epistemology, but I would like to sketch just enough of it to indicate the theoretical basis for my main objections to Systematic Dialectics.

At the core of Marx's epistemology is the process of abstraction, or the mental activity by which he brings certain qualities in the world into focus and provisionally excludes the rest. The process of abstraction would not play such a key role in Marx's method if the units into which nature (and, therefore, society too) is divided were given as such, that is, as particulars with clear boundaries separating them from each other. Operating with a philosophy of internal relations taken over from Hegel—and never criticized by Marx in all his discussions of Hegel—Marx considers all of reality as an internally related whole whose aspects can be mentally combined in a variety of ways and, therefore, into a multiplicity of different parts. To be sure, where boundaries get drawn is based, to some degree, on the real similarities and differences found in the world, but equally important in affecting these decisions are the aims, needs, and interests of the party doing the abstracting.

In a world without absolute borders, the process of abstraction provides the indispensable first step in getting the thinking process started. We can only think in parts and about parts of one sort or another. Marx believes, therefore, that everyone abstracts and that we learn how to do it "appropriately"—that is, in ways that allow us to function in the culture in which we live—during the process of socialization and particularly when acquiring language.

Once its work is done, however, most people come to treat the culturally determined units of thought that result from the process of abstraction now imbedded in language as reflecting absolute divisions in the real world. Not so Marx. Aware of the role that the process of abstraction plays in his thinking, Marx has much more flexibility in using it. It is not only that the boundaries he draws are invariably different, usually including more of the processes and interconnections involved than what is conveyed by others' concepts of the same name, but that he frequently alters them to include aspects that were previously omitted or to exclude ones that were there.

5

The boundaries Marx draws in the world with his process of abstraction are of three kinds—extension, level of generality, and vantage point—and each of them has important implications for Systematic Dialectics. Marx's abstraction of extension functions in both space and time, setting limits to how *far* a particular unit is extended in the system to which it belongs and, equally, how *long* a period of its evolution is included as part of what it now is. It is Marx's process of abstraction that allows him to view the commodity as an "abstract" (with but a few of its determinations) at the start of *Capital*, capital as a "concrete" (with a multiplicity of its determinations) later on, and to provisionally omit—as Systematic Dialectics correctly recognizes—the historical dimensions of the categories he uses in order to highlight their role in his conceptual logic.

With the abstraction of level of generality, the second mode of abstraction he employs, Marx separates out and focuses on the qualities of people, their activities, and products that come out of a particular time frame and provisionally ignores others. Here, the boundary is drawn between degrees of generality on a scale that ranges from the most general to the unique. Everyone and all that affects us and that we affect possess qualities that are part of the human condition (that is, present for the last one to two hundred thousand years), part of class society (present for the last five to ten thousand years), part of capitalism (present for the last three to five hundred years), part of modern or the current stage of capitalism (present for the last twenty to fifty years), and part of the here and now.

In order to study the systemic character of the capitalist mode of production, it was necessary for Marx to abstract society at the level of generality of capitalism and to omit qualities from other levels that would interfere with his view of what is specific to capitalism. In privileging this level of generality, Systematic Dialectics rightly underscores Marx's effort to present our society as first and foremost a capitalist society and to bring into focus the interlocking conditions and mechanisms that this involves.

The abstraction of vantage point, Marx's third mode of abstraction, sets up a vantage point or place within a relation from which to view, think about, and present its other components, one that highlights certain features and movements just as it minimizes and even misses others. Meanwhile, the sum of their ties, as determined by the abstraction of extension, also becomes a vantage point for making sense out of the larger system to which it belongs. The boundary here is drawn between competing perspectives. By starting *Capital* I with the commodity, Marx provides himself and his readers with a particular vantage point for viewing and piecing together the complex configuration that follows. On the whole, Systematic Dialectics does a good job in presenting the analysis of capitalism that derives from this vantage point.

All three modes of abstraction—extension, level of generality, and vantage point—occur together and, in their interaction, order the world that Marx sets out to study, understand, and present. But the decisions made regarding each mode often vary. Marx's abstractions of extension, for example, can include the reciprocal effects between a cluster of closely related conditions within each of these conditions in turn. By displaying these spatial relations in the absence of development or major changes, what stands out is the character of their mutual dependence or the logic of the system at a point in time.

Marx can also abstract the conditions that come into his analysis to include important parts of their real history and future potential. Here, their process of becoming, including stages through which they may have gone and whatever seems to lie ahead, are presented as essential aspects of what they are. The point, of course, is that reality is both systemic and historical, and in his abstractions Marx can omit most or all of either in order to bring the other into better focus. Thus, the abstractions favored by Systematic Dialectics are better suited to grasping how the capitalist system works, while those favored in other equally orthodox accounts are better suited to analyzing how this system developed, where it breaks down, what kind of society is likely to follow, and the role we have played and may yet play in all this.

Similarly, Marx's abstraction of level of generality doesn't only focus on capitalism in general but often on what I've called class society and modern capitalism and even, occasionally, on the level of the human condition (what is most general) and on that of what is unique in ourselves and in our situation. The interaction between the dynamics that distinguish capitalism in general (chiefly, the production and metamorphosis of value) and that which marks modern capitalism (chiefly, the most recent forms taken by capital and their effects on the class struggle) plays a particularly important role in the volumes of *Capital*, as it does in structuring the major problems and the historically specific opportunities for solving them that define our current situation. Restricting Marx's analysis to the level of capitalism in general (as Systematic Dialectics does) or to the level of modern capitalism (as some Marxist and all non-Marxist economists do with their fix on "globalization"), therefore, removes a full half of what we need to know not only to understand the world but to change it.

As regards abstraction of vantage point, here too Marx shows exemplary flexibility in adopting different vantage points in keeping with what he wants to see, grasp, present, or do at different moments of his method. Systematic Dialectics does not limit itself to the vantage point of the commodity, which opens *Capital* I, but follows Marx in using a variety of economic categories as vantage points from which to present the interlocking character of the capitalist system. However, labor, that is, alienated labor, the activity that Marx considers the substance of value, is never accorded this honor. Consequently, the origins of the capitalist market relations privileged by Systematic Dialectics are never brought clearly into view. In the words of the American playwright Amiri

Baraka, "Hunting is not those heads on the wall" (1966, 73). And as objects of study, products are no substitute for the activity that brought them into being. The overlapping processes of alienation and exploitation that are largely responsible for the capitalist character of our society can neither be perceived nor understood properly from vantage points located in their results.

Nor can we fully understand any result—and what isn't a result of something?—by ignoring what can be learned by viewing it from some vantage points located in its origins. According to Systematic Dialectics, for example, Marx's extended account of the metamorphosis of value in *Capital* provides us with the "life story" of capital; but value is a product, or result, most often referred to as a "form" of alienated labor, that is, of labor in which the workers lose some of their human powers in their products. Viewed in this light (from this vantage point), the metamorphosis of value is not only a tale about capital but also about labor, about the mystified forms assumed by the life force that has been separated from workers as it moves through the economy.

There are other important vantage points (like primitive accumulation or the relation between forces and relations of production or the unfolding of human potential in communism) that are rooted in history or on levels of generality other than capitalism that Marx uses but that Systematic Dialectics foregoes with its single-minded focus on conceptual logic. Here is the gateway to the past and the future and the unfolding contradictions that move us from the one to the other that Marx perceives (and presents) and Systematic Dialectics doesn't. But without an analysis undertaken from different spatial and temporal vantage points of the contradictions located on different levels of generality that are even now pulling our society apart and providing a rich source of evidence for what might follow, the analysis of capitalism associated with Systematic Dialectics can only offer more of the same. Unconcerned with the kind or degree of determinism Marx uncovers in history, the necessity Systematic Dialectics finds in the interplay of the categories of political economy leaves society as it finds it. Its logical necessity functions historically, whether it intends it or not, as a closed circle. From within the confines of the conceptual logic provided by Systematic Dialectics, it is hard to see how capitalism could ever change or what one might do (and even with whom one might act) to change it.

Based on this sketch of Marx's dialectical method, one might say that the proponents of Systematic Dialectics have simply abstracted an extension, level of generality, and vantage point for Marxism that leaves many of Marx's more important practices unaccounted for. And because they do not admit (or recognize) the epistemological slight of mind with which they begin, a legitimate form of emphasis turns into unacceptable one-sidedness and distortion. Something very similar happens whenever—and it is very often—Marx's multifaceted dialectic is packaged exclusively as "critique" (where the emphasis is put on the contradictions, unsupported assumptions, et cetera, in the writings of his opponents) or "class analysis" (where the class struggle occupies center stage) or "capital logic" (where the nature of capital—the real social relation, not the concept—is his privileged subject matter). In each case, the undialectical manner in which its advocates bring the favored aspect of Marx's method into focus serves to block out the rest of the method and leaves the part that remains with a task that it cannot perform on its own.

6

Conclusion: in *Capital*, Marx tries to show not only how capitalism works but why it is a transitory mode of production, what kind of society is likely to follow afterward, and how a change of this magnitude can be brought about. And all of this is contained in his dialectical analysis of how capitalism works. One might say that Marx was a unique combination of scientist, critic, visionary, and revolutionary, and it is important to grasp how these qualities fed into one another in all his theoretical work. Viewed in this light, Systematic Dialectics can be seen as an effort to reduce Marxism to a science, a science consisting of the manner in which Marx presents his understanding of the capitalist mode of production in his major work, *Capital* I. But without the critical, visionary, and revolutionary dimensions of his thinking, even this science—as I have argued—cannot be adequately understood. Yet it remains the case that a great deal of *Capital* is organized around a conceptual logic. My final conclusion, then, is that by exaggerating the role this conceptual logic plays in Marx's dialectical method—chiefly, by limiting this method to the moment of exposition and to only a few of the many abstractions of extension, level of generality, and vantage point that Marx uses in his exposition—Systematic Dialectics (with the partial exception of Tony Smith among the leading figures of this school) has kept most of its critics from recognizing and making use of the extremely valuable contribution it has made to our subject.

Note

1. What follows is a brief summary of the interpretation of Marx's method found in chapters 1–9 (particularly 5 and 8) of this book. For further detail, see these chapters.

Why Does the Emperor Need the Yakuza? Prolegomenon to a Marxist Theory of the Japanese State

1

On June 5, 1999, a junior high school principal in Osaka was stabbed and seriously injured by a member of the Yakuza (Japan's mafia) because of his refusal to have the Hinomaru (Rising Sun) flag raised and the "Kimigayo" ("Let the Emperor Rule Forever") anthem sung at a graduation ceremony. In February of the same year, another principal of a high school near Hiroshima committed suicide under conflicting pressures from the Ministry of Education, which ordered him to use the flag and the song at graduation, and his own teachers, who urged him not to. Showing such respect for the flag and the anthem was made mandatory in schools in 1989, but it has been only seriously enforced by various administrative penalties in the last couple years. What is going on here? And why has what seems like a minor cultural dispute become a major political controversy, with such dire consequences for some of the participants?

It is an odd controversy, for while those who oppose the compulsory use of the flag and anthem have shown no hesitation in giving their reasons—chief of which is these symbols' close association with Japan's imperialistic and militaristic practices before 1945—the government, though responding to most criticisms, has been strangely silent about what has led them to precipitate this crisis in the first place. What did they hope to achieve? Why is it so important to them? And why have they acted *now*? The one-sided character of this exchange together with the overheated manner in which it is conducted has led many foreign observers to put it all down to Japanese exoticism. But mysteries, even Japanese ones, generally have explanations. My attempt to unravel this political mystery will proceed through a Marxist analysis of the Japanese state, for I believe it is in the distinctive requirements of this state that we will find the reason for the government's actions.

2

The Japanese state has never been easy to understand. For example, in the thirteenth century Japan was ruled by an emperor, who was really the puppet of a retired emperor and his courtiers, who in turn responded to the orders of a military dictator, or *shogun,* who was himself completely under the control of his regent. The play of mirrors to deflect direct empirical inquiry continues to operate even today. Can the Marxist theory of the state effectively explain what one of the best books on this subject has reluctantly come to view as "the enigma of Japanese power" (Van Wolferen 1993)?

The typical Marxist critique of the state in democratic capitalist societies, however, treats the government as the chief instrument of the capitalist class and plays down the role of the bureaucracy. It generally considers only overtly political institutions as parts of the state and views democratic institutions and practices, like the Constitution and free elections, as the main sources of legitimation. For most democratic capitalist countries, including the United States, this approach serves quite well, but in the case of Japan it is grossly inadequate. What sets Japan apart from virtually all other democratic states in the capitalist world is (1) the elected government is extremely weak; (2) the higher state bureaucracy dominates both the elected government and the corporate sector; (3) a large number of top positions in government and business are held by retired bureaucrats; (4) many essential political functions are performed by what appear to be non-state bodies; and (5) the main legitimating agency for the state, for both the form it assumes and its actions, is the emperor system, a holdover from Japan's feudal past.

3

There is no dispute on the first point, though it never ceases to shock when people encounter examples of it. Shortly after assuming his post as U.S. ambassador to Japan, Walter Mondale remarked, "In the Diet, when you see bureaucrats also participating in the debates, answering questions, preparing amendments, preparing the budgets, you realize that this is a society in which the publicly elected side is very limited" (Kristof 1995, 37). When he was a U.S. senator, Mondale had a personal staff of about fifty (it is about twenty-five for members of the House of Representatives) to provide him with the information and expertise he needed to be an effective legislator. His equivalent in Japan has a staff of one or two, and cabinet ministers have only a few more. An incoming American president appoints several hundred high-ranking civil servants who, given the method of their appointment, owe their first loyalty to him. An incoming Japanese prime minister appoints a few dozen. Lacking the means to arrive at well-reasoned positions, it is not surprising that weekly cabinet meetings take only ten to fifteen minutes and consist mainly of rubber stamping what the in-house bureaucrats have already decided. Only once since 1955 has the Diet amended a budget presented to it by the civil service. The rapid turnover of prime ministers (on average one every two years) and ministers (on average one every year) also contributes to an elected government that is more shadow than substance.

When Prime Minister Keizo Obuchi became incapacitated after a stroke in early April 2000, it was his chief cabinet secretary, Mikio Aoki, a civil servant, who became acting prime minister and who seems to have played the decisive behind-the-scenes role in choosing Yoshio Mori to succeed Obuchi when he finally died. The elected government's dependence on the bureaucracy may have reached its nadir in Prime Minister Tomiichi Murayama's unsuccessful efforts in 1994 to have the bureaucrats get rid of the cockroaches in his official residence and buy him a television that worked. His successor took matters into his own hands and paid for the needed improvements himself.

In the past, when I taught courses on the Soviet Union, I devoted one month to the Communist Party and one week to the Supreme Soviet and Council of Ministers. The official government may not have deserved even that much attention. The case of Japan is not very different, except here, of course, the ultimate source of power is not, as in the former Soviet Union, a political party (or part thereof) but the higher state bureaucracy, particularly in the Ministry of Finance, the Ministry of Trade and Industry (MITI), and the State Bank. Some have questioned how this could be, given the fact that the civil service in Japan is less than half as large as its counterparts in Western capitalist countries, but this only shows that its considerable power is more concentrated and less diluted by checks and balances of various sorts. There is a shadow or separate budget (*zaito*) controlled by the Ministry of Finance, for example, that is two-thirds the size of the official governmental budget. The money, which comes from the Postal Savings System and public pension assets, is used for favored political projects wholly at the discretion of the bureaucrats in this ministry. Before Japan's defeat in World War II, of course, the short list of powerful ministries would also have included the Ministry of Defense.

A comparison might be useful: Japanese bureaucrats are not formal advisors to top politicians; they do not move freely between administration and politics or run for office while remaining bureaucrats, all of which happens in France. They do not sit in Parliament while serving as bureaucrats (as happens in Germany), or serve on presidential commissions (as happens in the United States). These are all ways in which bureaucrats in different countries influence their governments. Japan's leading bureaucrats don't have to do any of these things, because, in effect, they are the government. This is the second major feature that sets Japan apart from other capitalist democracies, and, again, there can't be many who would disagree, though few seem to be aware of the extent of the bureaucracy's power or to have worked out its full implications for the rest of Japanese society.

4

The bureaucrats' stranglehold over politicians is matched by their domination of the business community. Even mainstream scholars recognize the unusual degree of interdependence between private and governmental activities in Japan. But the bureaucracy's role goes beyond supplying helpful legislation, needed capital, and expertise to serving as the planning arm for the capitalist class as a whole, developing strategies and setting priorities for all sectors of the economy. It is the state bureaucracy and not the owners of industry or their much-touted managers and workers who are primarily responsible for what Japan, Inc. is today. Rather than simply telling businessmen what to do, Japan's ministries have perfected the old Mafia tactic of making people an offer that they can't refuse. They call it "administrative guidance." Should individual businessmen prove recalcitrant, the bureaucrats have a battery of means ranging from new laws and regulations to licenses, subsidies, loans, and tax benefits offered or refused to exact compliance; but it is usually unnecessary to carry out such threats.

In actual fact, there are probably fewer conflicts between the bureaucracy and the business world than there are between different sectors of the bureaucracy, so part of the enigma that needs to be explained is why capitalists cooperate with the state as fully as they do. Some have suggested that the higher civil service in other capitalist countries, such as France, exercise similar power over their private sectors, but this is to miss an important difference of kind as well as of degree. With the elected government effectively neutralized, Japan's leading bureaucrats, unlike their equivalents in other capitalist countries, are simply without rivals as their country's chief economic enforcers and strategists.

The easy acquiescence of Japan's businessmen to "administrative guidance" goes back to the origins of capitalism in Japan. The section of lower *samurai* who came to power with the Meiji Restoration of 1868 established profitable business monopolies and then sold them at a pittance to a privileged few, mainly from their own clans. It was privatization rather than capital accumulation that gave Japan its first *zaibatsus* (business empires). Unlike Western Europe, where—broadly speaking—capitalists came before capitalism, which in turn preceded a state dedicated to serving their interests, Japan seems to have reversed this process. Wishing to catch up with the technological and military achievements of the overbearing foreigners who had just forced them to open their ports to trade, the new Japanese state created capitalists in a manner not very different from how the feudal state in Europe had created knights and barons.[1]

From the start, the Japanese state has done whatever it could to protect its economic offspring and to ensure their growth and prosperity. How could the chief beneficiaries of these policies not "cooperate"? The hostile international business environment in which late-starting Japanese capitalists were operating along with their increasing dependence on foreign sources of raw materials further strengthened their team (national) approach to resolving business prob-lems and their reliance on the strategic leadership of the state bureaucracy. As if all this weren't enough to ensure business compliance (they prefer to call it "consensus"), the bureaucracy also plays a role in key top-level promotions in the private sector. In choosing a CEO, for example, many of the banks come to MITI with a short list from which the latter makes the final selection.

There have been sporadic attempts by a few prime ministers and major cor-porate owners to reduce their dependence on the state bureaucracy, especially in recent years, but little seems to have changed. The bureaucracy's continuing control over Japan's economic and political life raises a major theoretical prob-lem for Marxists regarding how to conceptualize the relations between the top bureaucrats, the heads of corporations and banks, and government leaders. It is not an empirical problem, for the main facts, as we have seen, are well known. Rather, it is a conceptual one. If the bureaucracy does indeed dominate the other two groups, in what sense can we speak of a ruling capitalist class? And if the capitalists don't rule, in what sense can we speak of capitalism?

5

An answer to these questions is suggested by the fact—also well known—that a large number of top bureaucrats take up leading positions in business and to a lesser extent in politics after they retire from the civil service, which usually occurs between the ages of forty-five and fifty-five. In Japan, where people re-main active until quite late in life, that gives them another twenty years or so to pursue their new careers. This practice, which is the third major feature that sets Japan apart from the rest of the capitalist world (with the possible exception of France), is so widespread that the Japanese have a word for it: *amakudari*, or "descent from heaven" (though the landing—should anyone worry—is invari-ably soft). Today, there are several thousand upper-echelon ex-bureaucrats hold-ing jobs as presidents, chairmen, directors, and managers of corporations, banks, business associations, and public corporations, usually in the same area in which they worked earlier as agents of the state.[2] This is the elite of the Japanese busi-ness community. The Department of Defense probably holds the record in our country for having its retired bureaucrats join the private sector, but the main purpose here is to win defense contracts for their new employer; hardly ever does the fledgling businessman become the CEO.

To appreciate the importance of this difference, we should add that the man-agers and directors of Japanese corporations have considerably more power in relation to their stockholders than do their counterparts in the United States. This is a result of the large amount of cross-shareholding between Japanese corporations and of their having a much lower equity-to-debt ratio—and there-fore less dependence on public offerings for their capital—than American cor-porations. Hence, the influence of state bureaucrats on corporations is less watered down by various market forces than is the case in the United States. And the person in the corporation who is most responsible for heeding "administrative guidance" from the bureaucracy is likely to be a former bureaucrat himself, often from the very ministry to which he is now responding.

The situation in politics is only slightly less incestuous, with the majority of all Japanese prime ministers and cabinet ministers since the war having come to politics by the bureaucratic route (the readjustments that followed the breakup of the once hegemonic Liberal Democratic Party (LDP) has done nothing to alter this process, though the number of exceptions has increased somewhat since 1980). Nothing like this exists—not in such numbers, and not as regards positions of this prominence (again, with the possible exception of France)—anywhere else in the world.

A major effect of *amakudari* is that most of Japan's leading bureaucrats benefit directly and personally, if not immediately, from the success of Japanese capitalism. The widespread and systematic character of this mid-life change in careers also means that they know that the decisions they make as government officials will determine their future private-sector "posting" and the fortune that comes with it. Where the transition from state functionary to capitalist is so well known beforehand, the interests of the capitalists also become the interests of the bureaucrats. As for Japan's leading businessmen, many of whom are former bureaucrats, knowing the trajectory that the current cohort of top functionaries are on, they can be confident that the decisions that are made in the state sector are in their best interests.

But if so many of Japan's leading capitalists are former civil servants and most of its leading civil servants future capitalists, it seems to make as much sense to view them all as members of the same class—separated only by a temporary division of labor—than as members of different classes. The same reasoning can also be applied to the ex-bureaucrats in the elected government, who also benefit greatly from the largess of big business. The common educational background of these three groups (in 1993, 88 percent of the top bureaucrats in the Ministry of Finance came from the University of Tokyo, chiefly from the law school), frequent intermarriage, and a high degree of formal socializing (in "friendship societies," which bring top government officials together with their retired predecessors, many of whom hold leading positions in the same area in the private sector) also argue for stressing a shared class identity over their equally apparent differences (Van Wolferen 1993, 146). If some saw the possibility for significant social mobility in the meritocratic origins of the bureaucracy, the high cost of good cram schools that start in kindergarten (without which it is virtually impossible to get into Tokyo University) has proven very successful in limiting the better bureaucratic jobs to a privileged few.

6

It is evidence such as this that allows Karel Van Wolferen, one of the most insightful writers on Japan, to claim that the top bureaucrats, businessmen, and politicians in Japan form one ruling class, which he dubs the "class of administrators" (1993, 146). While this label highlights the extraordinary role of the bureaucracy as an incubator of future capitalists and politicians, it occludes the pro-business pattern that emerges from the activities of what appear to be quite different institutions and the common interests and purposes that give rise to this pattern. When all this is taken into account, it is clear that a more apt name for these people is "capitalists."[3]

According to Marx, capitalists are those who personify or give human form to and carry out the dictates of capital, understood as self-expanding value, or wealth used with the aim of creating still more wealth. The contrast is with wealth used to satisfy need, or serve God, or expand civil or military power, or obtain glory or status. With capital, wealth becomes self-centered and concerned only with its own growth. Those who control wealth, use it in this manner, and benefit personally from the process (whether they are the legal owners of the means of production or not) belong to the same collective capitalist class. It is simply that in Japan some capitalists work in what are formally state institutions and others in what are formally private ones, though, as we have seen, most of the leading members of this class divide their lives between the two. The essential thing is that they all function as embodiments of capital, serving its (and, consequently, their own) best interests in whatever way their current positions allow. They all work to expand surplus-value and benefit materially when that happens, though *when* they are bureaucrats and politicians this is not immediately apparent.

Other countries, of course, have capitalists who become high civil servants and major politicians without ever ceasing to be capitalists. The outstanding example in the United States is Nelson Rockefeller, who was a capitalist, an ambassador, and a vice president. But most such figures, who are in any case the exceptions in their countries, start by being owners of corporate wealth. In Japan, where this career pattern is much more widespread, corporate wealth usually comes later. What appears to be the state's domination over the capitalist class, then, a view that I myself seemed to adopt at the start of this chapter and something that is often cited as a reason for the inapplicability of Marxist analysis to Japan, takes on an altogether different meaning once the boundaries between the principles are reset in this manner.

The qualities that distinguish one as a member of a class can, after all, be acquired over time. Class membership evolves, as do classes themselves; one can become part of a class in stages. And in Japan the process of becoming a capitalist for most of the leading members of that class begins with their entry into the state bureaucracy. Recognizing that Japan's top bureaucrats belong to the capitalist class does not mean that we can no longer distinguish them as that part of the class that functions (at present) in the state bureaucracy. But we now have a clearer sense of what they do there and why, and also why they receive the degree of compliance from both corporate and governmental leaders that they do. We can also better understand why capitalists in the private sector occasionally perform governmental tasks—as when Nomura Securities drafted the legislation that was meant to restrict its own behavior—without blowing a mental fuse in the way we think about public and private worlds. In Japan, the boundary between capitalists in and out of state service is simply not as clear or as rigid as their respective institutional forms of power would have us believe.[4] It is important to recognize, too, that the aim of Marxist class analysis is not to arrive at some ahistorical classificatory scheme where no one and nothing moves but to explain the workings and dynamics of whole societies, and this allows for and even requires a certain flexibility in drawing and redrawing class lines.[5] In order to capture the distinctive character of Japanese capitalism, I have thought it necessary to extend the notion of capitalist class to include the higher state bureaucrats and the leading politicians in the ruling party.

If in this situation the bureaucracy is generally allowed to take the initiative for the entire class, it is only because the other members of this class recognize that those currently working in state ministries have the best overview and clearest focus on the interests of the class as a whole. Their view is not compromised by the interests of a particular corporation or industry (as happens with managers and directors) or by those of a party or faction (as happens with government leaders). Freed from such temporary distractions, the bureaucrats are in the best position to serve the general as well as the long-term interests of Japanese capitalism and to mediate between rival factions of the ruling class whenever that is necessary. (From its work as mediator, it may appear as if the state is neutral, if one doesn't notice that it is always a faction of the same class that comes out on top.)

The capitalist state is forever tipping its hand as regards its true role on behalf of the capitalist class, and, while radicals have documented this again and again, for most people the connection is always being made as if for the first time. Chiefly, what is missing are the categories of thought to hold fast what they are learning. One of the main aims of this study is to supply such a category for the peculiar case of Japan. That category is "collective capitalist." Japan today remains a *shogunate*, but the *shogun* is not a military figure. It is the collective capitalist, which divides its time between bureaucratic, business, and governmental functions. The *samurai* who made the Meiji Revolution refused to become new feudal rulers (as happened after earlier successful revolts), opting instead to make themselves into a capitalist ruling class. But before they could do that they had to create capitalism and a capitalist class of which they could be part. Their success in establishing this new social formation with themselves as the core of its ruling class is undoubtedly one of the greatest feats of social engineering in human history. In most fundamental respects and despite all the changes brought on by World War II, Japan continues to operate inside the mold cast by these founding fathers.

7

The fourth major feature that distinguishes Japan from other democratic capitalist countries is the number of essential political functions performed by what appear to be non-state bodies. This practice, of course, can be found elsewhere. What stands out in the case of Japan are the large number of instances and their importance. To determine what these are, we must first understand what it is that states do. It is not enough to know that the state is the prime locus of political power. We also need to know how and for what this power is used. In all societies based on a social division of labor, the class or bloc of classes that controls the surplus needs society-wide help to legitimate the means by which it extracts it and to repress those who refuse to go along. Hence, in one way or another, all states engage in repression and legitimation.

Given the way that wealth is produced and distributed in the capitalist epoch, our capitalist ruling class requires two additional kinds of help from the state: in the accumulation of capital, and in the realization of value. The first involves securing the conditions that underlie the exploitation of workers—social, legal, and so forth—and the production of a surplus as well as creating profitable investment opportunities where they otherwise wouldn't exist. The second is mainly a matter of finding, establishing, and defending markets in order to make sure that what is produced gets sold. Therefore, every capitalist state has to provide these four functions: repression, legitimation, accumulation, and realization. Not to do so simply means that its ruling class would not be able to survive as the ruling class. It is not only a matter of being unable to serve their interests effectively; the capitalists would not be able to reproduce the conditions that are responsible for their very existence as a class.

Having established these functions as essential functions of the state in capitalist society, it is possible to view a body that performs any one of them as part of the state. The state here is simply the sum of these bodies, even where some of them also engage in nonpolitical activities, in which case they are both parts of the state and parts of something else at the same time.

What is crucial to Marx's theory of the state is not this or that quality of political institutions, or the power that they possess, or even the privileged position of one class, but rather the relation between all these and the requirements of the particular social and economic system in which they are situated. The procedure moves from the whole inward. The first thing to establish, then, is the nature of the whole as a class society or, in this case, as a capitalist class society. Marx calls the state "the active, conscious, and official expression" of the "present structure of society" (Marx and Engels 1975, 199) and, elsewhere, "the form of organization which the bourgeoisie necessarily adopt both for internal and external purposes, for the mutual guarantee of their property and interests" (Marx and Engels 1964, 78).

As we see from these citations, the state can be viewed as a dimension of the whole, which is capitalism, but also as an aspect of the capitalist class, as something this class does. The one takes us into the realm of "capital logic" (which relates structures to processes inside a historically specific whole), the other into the realm of capitalists' class interests (which connects people's place and function inside these structures to their activities). The two together represent the objective and subjective sides of the same complex Relation. What the state does, therefore, as well as the specific forms through which it does it, are internally related to what the ruling class is and what its interests require. It is in this sense that Marx considers the state in all class societies to be a "dictatorship" of its ruling class, whatever the degree of democratic content. This is not to be understood instrumentally, with its suggestion of arbitrariness and of an external relation between the state and its ruling class, but expressively: the state is the set of institutional forms through which a ruling class expresses its political nature (the relation is an internal one). The state is the greatest part of what it means for a ruling class to rule and is an essential feature of the class itself. Hence, all attempts to understand the state that begin in the political sphere (namely, political science) are doomed to failure.

By coming at the parts of the state from the vantage point of the ruling class, itself embedded in the mode of production that carries its name, we can also avoid getting lost in the parts and mistaking their ideological masks for reality. In the case of Japan, despite the torrents of official propaganda, we have no trouble recognizing that the elected government doesn't govern, that democracy doesn't give citizens any power, that administrators don't simply administer, and that overtly political institutions don't do all the political work. We are also given the flexibility to redraw the boundaries of what is ordinarily taken as the state to include various institutions and groups that perform essential political tasks.

Ask a practicing economist what are the boundaries of the firm and he will give one answer today and another a few days later when he is working on another problem. It is the problem that is decisive. The same is true of the state, where the problems to be solved are those of its ruling class and—by extension—of the means, institutions, and the like that are used in dealing with them. As the problems requiring immediate or greater attention vary, and as the means for solving them become more or less available, the boundaries of the state will also change. The state remains, as in the popular view, the repository of ultimate social power, but it doesn't have to comprise the same set of institutions in every society; nor do these institutions have to be fixed or restricted to their political role(s). There is simply no need for the various elements of the state to be housed under one roof, either functionally or conceptually. Indeed, there are often practical advantages for the ruling class to organize its state in another manner.

Since the elected government in Japan is so weak and the bureaucrats who have extensive power were never elected, the Japanese state has been forced to incorporate a number of other bodies to perform all the functions required of it by Japanese capitalism. Among the more important of these bodies are major business associations (often run by former bureaucrats), which participate in economic planning and coordination, helping with the accumulation of capital and the realization of value. (The chairman of one of them, Keidenren, is popularly referred to as the First Minister of Business.) Another is the United States government, particularly its military arm, which still occupies 150 bases in Japan and has the legal right to quell internal disorder. This should not be surprising when one considers that colonial governments have always been part of the state in their colonies, and for several years after World War II Japan came very close to being an American colony. Another is the emperor system, which plays, as we shall see, a crucial role in legitimation. Still others are the major media, educational institutions and foundations, religious organizations, the main trade union, Rengo, and, again as I hope to show, organized crime, the Yakuza.

If the state is not restricted to a particular geographical space or certain institutional forms but includes all bodies that perform essential political tasks for the ruling class, there should be no difficulty in viewing this strange amalgam—along with the elected government, the courts, the cops, the armed forces, and, of course, the bureaucracy—as the Japanese state. This doesn't rule out recognizing that there are major differences and disputes between these bodies (and, indeed, within each one); or that one of them, the bureaucracy, possesses by far the greatest influence; or even that subaltern classes can occasionally use this disarray to score minor victories in some of the state's more distant outposts. The fact that political power in Japan is distributed among so many bodies (and in some cases, like the bureaucracy, to different and often competing elements within them) has led to the complaint that the Japanese state is plagued by an absence of accountability. But if the state—partly through this very distribution of functions—has served its ruling class so successfully, the absence of a clear center to which representations can be made and against which pressure can be brought should perhaps be viewed as one of its major strengths.

8

What perhaps emerges most clearly from this collection of political oddities—the exceptionally weak elected government, the extraordinary power of a higher bureaucracy that is at the same time one with the capitalist class, and the distribution of essential political functions among many apparently nonpolitical bodies—is that the Japanese state is in dire need of legitimation, of a clear and compelling reason why one should obey the state even if one disagrees with its policies. Without such a reason, no amount of military and economic power can secure a state against the possibility of being overturned.

Under feudalism there was no difficulty in recognizing that the state belonged to the ruling social and economic class, but, operating under one or another version of the Divine Right of Kings/Emperors theory, people generally accepted that this was the way it was supposed to be. The capitalist class stands in a similar relation to the state under capitalism, but, unable to make the same appeal to religion, it is much more difficult to equate their interests with the general interest. For the state to serve capitalists' interests effectively under these conditions, it is necessary to have the state appear separate from and independent of the capitalist class and concerned with all citizens equally. The appearance of neutrality is usually achieved by halving political from economic functions and adopting people to perform the former who are not themselves members of the ruling economic class. But if the class that benefits most from capitalism also makes and administers the rules by which they benefit (as distinct from the state's simply being heavily influenced by capitalists or following an objective logic inherent in capital), the biased character of these rules and their administration stands out in sharp relief.

Typically, capitalists only succeeded in replacing landed aristocrats as the ruling class where the state appeared to be independent of all class ties. In Japan—where leading state bureaucrats, who are also capitalists, make the major economic decisions—this process is very incomplete. While this helps to explain the Japanese state's ability to act in such a decisive manner on behalf of the capitalist class, it also accounts for its greater vulnerability to fundamental criticism and its outsized need for effective legitimation. Some readers might find it odd that an avowedly Marxist work gives such a crucial role to the problem of legitimation, a problem usually associated with Weberian analysis, but, in the absence of effective popular rule, legitimacy becomes one of capitalism's major contradictions, and unraveling it—as we shall see—offers an unusual opportunity to expand both socialist theory and practice.

The three main sources of political legitimation in the United States are the Constitution (especially as interpreted by the Supreme Court, itself, of course, a creature of the Consitution), free elections, such as they are, and—to a lesser degree—the Office of the President, the main locus as well as symbol of national unity and power. Most Americans accept the right of our political authorities to rule over us because we have chosen them—both by adopting the Constitution and by voting, especially in presidential elections.[6] None of these sources of legitimation are available to the Japanese state, where the Constitution was drafted by nameless foreigners and forced upon the country after its defeat in World War II and where elections, though as "free" as our own, bring to office a government that practically everyone knows has very little power.[7] The Japanese state must find its legitimation elsewhere, and it does. Some of this legitimation comes from the widespread belief that the bureaucrats, who do have power, are simply the smartest people around and that they do their best to serve the national interest. Some legitimation came from the state's success in helping to build a prosperous economy, when that economy was still prosperous. Arguably, the fact that so much in the Japanese polity reflects what exists (or what people take to exist) in the United States, still popular as a model of democracy among many Japanese, contributes to the legitimacy of the political order. The media, schools, major unions, and religious institutions also add their bit by playing up the team aspects of Japanese life and pretending that there is no legitimation problem to be resolved. But even after the effect of all these means have been added up, there remains a very large legitimation deficit. Enter the emperor system (and our fifth point).

Before discussing the role of the emperor system in the Japanese state, I would like to spike a misunderstanding that may arise from my frequent comparisons between the Japanese and American political systems. I do not believe that the United States is *more* democratic than Japan, only *differently* democratic, or—more in keeping with the tenor of my remarks—*differently undemocratic.* If the United States has elections for posts that have real political power (whereas Japan does not), Japan has more than one party, including anticapitalist parties, participating in elections as serious contenders (whereas the United States does not, the Republicans and Democrats being two factions of the same capitalist party). Japan also has higher voter turnouts, which is another popular indicator used to measure degrees of democracy. As dictatorships of the capitalist class, however, American and Japanese democracies are equally biased on behalf of their ruling class and equally concerned to hide this bias. Consequently, whatever the differences in how they perform these functions, neither can be viewed as morally superior to the other.

9

Japan, though formally a democracy, is largely governed by a small group of people whom no one has elected. Their decisions benefit one class far more than others. To the extent that the Japanese people know this, and most do to one degree or another, why do they accept it? Why do they go along? The answer one hears most often is that this is what the Japanese are like, meaning either culturally or psychologically, or both. But this is to introduce as the main explanation what itself is in great need of being explained. Where does this element of Japanese culture or psyche come from? Who benefits from it? How does it work? And how do those who benefit manipulate it to help them deal with their most pressing problems? Without dismissing culture or psychology (or, it should be added, accepting a particular version of either) and without refusing them a place in the total explanation, these questions redirect our attention to the rational dimension of our inquiry, to the kind of account that people give (or could give) as to why they willingly obey the established authority.

Japan's rulers never had a popular mandate. That's why the *shoguns*, Japan's traditional military rulers, retained the more popular emperor as figurehead. After the Meiji Revolution in 1868, which was carried out by elements of the lower *samurai* from only one section of the country, the need for legitimation was especially severe. No less important at the time was the need to unite all Japanese in order to present a common front against the latest exactions coming from the West, particularly the United States. (Recall the role that divisions in India played in opening up that country to British imperialism.) Solidifying the ties between the Japanese people and the emperor must have seemed like the ideal solution to both problems.

The new rulers of Japan began by bringing the emperor from Kyoto to Tokyo, the center of government, and issuing all their decisions in his name. They reinvigorated a largely dormant Shinto religion that added divine stature to the emperor's already popular role as "father" of the Japanese people. Then, in 1873, they promulgated the Kokutai (National Essence) doctrine, which asserted that the emperor embodies in his person the will of the nation. It was said that he knew what the Japanese people needed and what was good for them, which included how they should live. The new political arrangements that the government drew up were presented as a gift from the emperor, a manifestation of his perfect wisdom and benevolence, for which people were expected to be eternally grateful and loyal. All criticism of Kokutai was made illegal, and it soon became the centerpiece of education both in schools and in the military. There is little evidence to suggest that the emperor was viewed as such a benevolent figure before the National Essence doctrine was declared or that people reacted to his supposed benevolence with the same fervent gratitude that they demonstrated subsequently. (So much for essentialist cultural or psychological explanations of Japanese exceptionalism.) With state Shintoism and Kokutai firmly in place, the legitimation of Japan's real rulers was secured for almost a century.

In 1945, with Japan's defeat in World War II, all this came to an end—or did it? Under General MacArthur's direction, Emperor Hirohito announced to the Japanese people that he was not a deity and that the war for which he was at least partly responsible was a tragic mistake. At a stroke, two mainstays of the emperor's hold on the Japanese people—his pretended divinity and his infallibility in matters of public interest—disappeared. The Allies also took great care not to give the emperor any political role in the new Constitution, where he is only mentioned as a "symbol of the Japanese state and of the unity of the people." The position itself is said to derive "from the will of the people with whom resides sovereign political power" (Hayes 1992, 282–83). Even though unnamed bureaucrats succeeded in rendering the term "will" here as "integration" in the Japanese translation—leaving the relationship between emperor and people more ambiguous than MacArthur intended—most students of Japanese postwar politics have treated the emperor as a simple anachronism, even less important than the British monarch. (Unlike his British counterpart, for example, he plays no role in appointing ambassadors, and he has no right to see state papers; nor does legislation require his seal.) I consider this to be a major misunderstanding.

In my view, the emperor remains the main source of legitimation for the Japanese state in its current form, and especially for the heavy tilt in the use of its power on behalf of the capitalist class. Despite all formal changes to his status, the emperor continues to do for Japanese capitalism what the Constitution and free elections cannot do and what the other sources of legitimation mentioned above can do only in small part. How he does this is also rather unique. As the titular head and most striking symbol of the Japanese nation, the emperor is in a position to get people to accept existing political arrangements and their biased outcomes by eliciting a transfer of sentiments and especially the loyalty people feel toward the social community, to which they belong as members of an ethnic group, to the political community, or state, to which they belong as citizens and members of different social classes.

Marx makes an important distinction between these two: the *social community*, in which the division of labor establishes a mutual dependence of all parties for the satisfaction of their needs and where the cooperation this engenders leads over time to a high degree of identification with others and an appreciation of what they contribute to one's own well-being, and the *political community*, in which one class, pursuing its narrow class interests, exercises power over everyone else. Marx also calls the latter an "illusory community," because, unlike the former, it neither belongs to everybody nor serves them equally (Marx and Engels 1964, 91–92). Yet it is of crucial importance to those who control the political community that the mass of the people believe otherwise. By presenting the emperor as standing astride both social and political communities, Japan's rulers hope to conflate the two in the popular mind, to confuse, in effect, what has constituted the Japanese as a people with the form of rule that has been constituted over them, with the aim of having people react to the latter in ways evoked by the former.

The emperor achieves this remarkable feat not by anything he says or does but simply by virtue of what he is (or is taken to be) and the importance people attach to their relation to him as members of the Japanese ethnic community. Then, once he assumes his position as head of state—the actual title used is less important than the nature of the connection that is conveyed (hence the relative unimportance of the actual wording in the Constitution)—it requires but a small shift in focus to mistake the state as the political embodiment of the social community, as the necessary means by which it acts on the world. In which case, citizenship in the state merely formalizes the rights and duties that each individual already possesses as a member of the ethnic community, and belonging to one is equated with belonging to the other. Regrettably, for all too many Japanese it also follows that non-ethnic Japanese can never become full citizens (witness the discrimination against Koreans who have lived in Japan for generations) and that ethnic Japanese who have become citizens of other countries are traitors to their "race."

The Chinese character for "state," which is used in Japan, means "family of the country," with the suggestion that the state is a natural rather than artificial construction, and puts the head of state in the position of a father in the family. To enforce this link, the father's special role in the family is even mentioned in the Japanese Constitution. An emperor, of course, is in a better position to make use of this analogy than a president would be. The American president, for example, can be fatherly, but his partisanship and impermanence makes it impossible to present him as everybody's father or to pretend that all members of the national family are of equal concern to him. The Chinese character for "bureaucracy," which is also used in Japan, also indicates the importance of the emperor's legitimizing role. It originally meant "to serve the emperor or heaven," where the emperor simply stood in for the Japanese people. Today the bureaucracy is supposed to serve the people. The total and public acquiescence to their rule by the emperor, no longer equated with the people but still viewed by many as a kind of father (with all the fairness and benevolence that this conveys), is easily mistaken as an assurance that the bureaucrats are doing a good job for everyone and not only for the privileged few.

No other royal family can point to origins as ancient as those of the Japanese emperor, and in the popular mind what is very old is often equated with what is natural. As the presumed father of the Japanese people, in a relation that is supposed to go back over two thousand years, he does not need constitutional endorsement to exercise the influence that I have attributed to him here. Since the kind of obedience he exacts can never be taken, only offered, it may even be that the lack of formal power actually aids him in the accomplishment of his task. Thus, when Lycurges, a king in ancient Sparta, wanted his people to adopt a new constitution, his first move was to abdicate, so that no one was constrained to accept what he was about to give them. Only then, he believed, would it be possible to obtain their unqualified support for the new constitution. Similarly, the emperor's influence on people's sense of who they are and how they are related to the state could only reach as deeply as it obviously does because he has no apparent means to impose his will. From his position above the political fray, standing apart from all factions, without any responsibility for particular governmental policies, and lacking the power to enforce his views (should he have any), the emperor has been distilled by his handlers into a pure concern for the well-being of the Japanese people.

This was not always the case. In the immediate aftermath of the war, the emperor's admission that he was neither divine nor infallible, together with the rise of antimilitarist, egalitarian, and republican ideas (particularly in the schools), made it very difficult for him to resume his prewar role as chief legitimator for the established order. The political turbulence that Japan experienced in the first decades after the war had many causes, but one that has not received the attention it deserves is the inability of the regime to obtain the legitimacy it required without the help traditionally supplied by the emperor system. With the formal end of the American occupation in 1952, Japan's bureaucratic rulers set about to reestablish the authority of the emperor in whatever ways they could, given the relation of class forces at the time. The main aim was to bring people to think of the emperor once again as head of state. This involved frequent attempts—in violation of the Constitution—to have the emperor act as head of state on various ceremonial occasions and pressure on the schools to introduce more traditional ideas about the imperial system into their program. It is only in this context that we can make sense of the importance Japan's nominally democratic government attaches to having students sing a national anthem that presents the country as still under the rule of the emperor.

Have I made too much of the emperor in my account of Japanese politics? Many if not most modern Japanese, after all, will say that they are indifferent to the emperor. I consider this claim suspect, however, especially if made to foreigners. Most Japanese will also say that they don't believe in Shintoism, but many of these same people will recite a Shinto prayer before building an office or a house. Religious conviction may have waned in Japan, but superstition of all kinds is alive and well. So, while very few consider the emperor divine, his status as father of the Japanese people is reasonably secure; and, given the strong sense of ethnic identity that still prevails in Japan, this is more than enough for him to perform his role as chief legitimator of the state.

10

It is not an easy task to reestablish an irrational tradition in an increasingly rational world, especially when people are still very aware of the high price their country paid for upholding this tradition in the past. The regime's first line of defense against criticisms of the emperor system is utter contumely and, when possible, refusal to acknowledge it. The ruling party's unwillingness to even hear such criticisms produced a procedural crisis recently in the Okinawa Prefectural (state) Assembly when a Communist Party deputy referred to the "brutal *tenno* [emperor] system" in a speech on Japan's role in World War II. This resulted in a five-day halt in legislative business as the conservative majority tried to get him to withdraw the "insulting remark" and apologize. He refused, and in the end, the speaker simply deleted the offensive words from the minutes.

The second and undoubtedly more effective line of defense is outright repression. It helps enormously if those inclined to criticize the imperial tradition are afraid to do so. In Japan, the task of making them afraid is performed by the Yakuza, who threaten, beat up, and even kill anyone who makes public his or her opposition to the emperor system. The Yakuza member who stabbed the junior high school principal for failing to raise the Rising Sun flag and have the "Let the Emperor Rule Forever" anthem sung at graduation was only too pleased to give his motive: "I want all the Japanese people," he said "to respect the *Hinomaru* and the *Kimigayo*. If I killed the principal, and this were reported in the mass media, it would serve as a warning to those organizations which oppose the *Hinomaru* flag being hoisted and the *Kimigayo* song being sung in the schools" (*Japan Press Weekly*, June 12, 1999, 21). Who can doubt that such warnings have had their effect?

This is not something any official governmental agency could do as systematically and therefore as efficiently—not as long as the state pretended to be a democracy, anyway. Involvement by the government would also make it appear that the emperor, as the putative head of state, had something to do with the extralegal violence, and this would detract from his presumed neutrality, to say nothing of his benevolence. But the Yakuza, with its many ties to the far Right in Japan and its well-known conception of honor, can carry out this task and in such a way that the government escapes most of the blame.[8] There is, of course, an ultranationalist Right in Japan apart from the Yakuza, but the overlap between the two is far greater than what one finds in other countries that also have a far Right and organized crime. The Japanese Yakuza is simply so much more than a bigger version of the Mafia. The great latitude that the Yakuza enjoys in repressing criticism of the emperor as well as the remarkable freedom with which it carries on its more traditional criminal enterprises could not exist without active governmental approval, all of which argues for a more functional conception of the Yakuza's role in Japanese society than is usually offered. Given the Yakuza's heavy involvement in the construction industry, the extraordinarily high government spending on public works (currently higher than the U.S. defense budget) might also be viewed as partial payment to the Yakuza for services rendered.[9] The same can be said of the ease with which many Yakusa-controlled companies received large loans (now unpaid) from state-owned or -dominated financial institutions that have contributed (to a degree yet to be determined) to the still-unfolding banking crisis that has plagued Japan for more than a decade.

The Yakuza's ties to the state go back to the late nineteenth century, when they did strong-arm work for local conservative politicians, controlled labor unrest, and served as spies and assassins for the government, going so far as to murder the queen of Korea in an incident that triggered off a war with that country in 1895. The close collaboration between the Yakuza and the new bureaucratic rulers of Japan was no doubt facilitated by the fact that both groups emerged out of the lower *samurai* of the previous period. Their cooperation continued into the twentieth century, where the list of victims—often at direct government request—broadened to include communists and radical students. In World War II, the Yakuza also helped the Japanese army pillage occupied Manchuria and China, forcing drugs on the Chinese in a replay of British policy in the 1840s.

After the war, with the introduction of a republican constitution and democratic elections, a new era had begun, but the political role of the Yakuza does

not seem to have diminished. The Liberal Democratic Party, which has dominated electoral politics since 1945, was founded largely with the money of Karoku
Tsuji, who liked to call himself the "Al Capone of Japan" (Kaplan and Dubro
1986, 67). Yoshio Kodama, the most important figure in the LDP until the late
1970s, also had wide Yakuza connections, as did several prime ministers and a
host of cabinet ministers. In 1963, in the midst of internal squabbling between
the different factions of the LDP, a coalition of Yakuza chieftans felt sufficiently
concerned with what was happening to their party to send a letter to all LDP
members of Parliament urging them to end their infighting, as this could only
benefit the Left.

But perhaps nothing reveals the Yakuza's close ties to the government better
than a speech that Bamboku Ohno, secretary general of the LDP from 1957 to
1965, gave to twenty-five hundred Yakuza at a reception for the new Godfather
of Kobe, in which he said, "'Politicians and those who go by the way of chivalry [Yakuza] follow different occupations, but they have one thing in common,
and that is their devotion to the ways of *giri* (obligation) and *minjo* (human
feeling). . . . I offer my speech of congratulations hoping that you will further
exert yourself in the ways of chivalry so as to make our society a better one'"
(qtd. in Kaplan and Dubro 1986, 82). In so far as the newly revived respect for
the emperor has something to do with the expressions of Yakuza chivalry, it appears that Ohno's congratulations were well merited.

In the United States, it is the priestly caste of lawyers that makes sure that
people show the proper deference to the Constitution and the Supreme Court.
Without this deference—aided and abetted by as much mystificatiion as that
associated with the emperor system—the Constitution and the Supreme Court
couldn't do their work of legitimation. It is only appropriate, therefore, that two-
thirds of all the lawyers in the world practice in the United States. In Japan this
role is played by the Yakuza, which, again appropriately, is four to five times the
size of the American Mafia. As far as legitimation is concerned, the Yakuza are
Japan's lawyers. And in so far as the Yakuza provides the ruling class with an
important element of the repression it requires, this also qualifies it—on the
criteria I have established—for inclusion as an integral part of the Japanese state.

11

In summary, Japan's ruling class has been very successful in transferring its rule
from one political system to another. With the exception of a handful of gener-
als, there was no postwar purge in Japan as there was in Germany and Italy. Many
figures with appalling war records continued to play leading roles in the bureaucracy, elected government, and business. A class-A war criminal even became
prime minister soon after the American military occupation came to a close. It
is no wonder—though foreigners never cease to wonder—that the Japanese
government has never been able to offer a full apology for its numerous war-

time atrocities or that it feels so attached to the flag and anthem used at that time (while both Germany and Italy have adopted new flags and anthems).[10] Similarly, it is not surprising that the leaders of the old system should try to reestablish its essentials as soon as they had a chance. But how does one put a genie back into the bottle? The American occupiers removed the emperor from politics, abolished the army, democratized the election process, broke up the Zaibatsus (economic conglomerates), gave rights to trade unions, and did away with the nationalist curricula and rituals in the schools.

The ruling class's answer was to reestablish as quickly as possible and with the indispensable help of the Yakuza the prestige of the emperor. The legitimation he offered was then used to rearrange the pieces on the board that they had inherited from the Americans. In due time, the emperor has once again become the head of state (in all but name, and, with a new Constitution in the offing, even that is likely to be corrected); the army has been renamed the "Self-Defense Force" and is among the five most powerful military forces in the world; the democratic electoral process has been bypassed by leaving most power in the hands of unelected bureaucrats; the Zaibatsus have changed their name to Kereitsu and are as economically dominant as ever; most of the trade unions have become company unions, often with company managers as their presidents, with all that this implies; and, gradually but surely, the schools have been forced to adopt a more nationalist-oriented curriculum, with all the rituals and symbols that ordinarily accompany it. With the economy currently in doldrums, however, and people's dissatisfaction with their worsening conditions on the rise, the state's need to legitimate its capitalist agenda is greater than ever. Hence, the intensification of the government's efforts to bolster the emperor's prestige in the schools and among the public generally and the backlash this has produced among those who object to where this process has already taken them and rightly fear where it is heading.

The latest salvo in the "Emperor Wars" was fired by Prime Minister Yoshiro Mori on May 15, 2000, when he said, "Japan is a country of *kami* (gods) with the *tenno* (emperor) as its core," at a meeting of the Association of Shinto Shrines (*Japanese Press Weekly,* May 20, 2000, 8). This is the organization that has been trying to get all cabinet ministers to pay official visits to the Yakasumi Shrine, the burial site of many World War II war criminals. For a prime minister, Mori's nationalist outburst was a first. All the opposition parties immediately demanded a retraction and an apology. They got neither. Another sign of what lies ahead in Japanese politics was the appearance for the first time in an LDP election platform (June 2000) of a call to revise the Japanese Constitution. Though the LDP did not specify particular reforms, no one doubts that one of the major changes they would like to introduce is making the emperor official head of state, which would then serve as a springboard for nationalist propaganda of all sorts. It appears like the battle over the emperor system is about to take center stage in Japanese political life.

The Japanese bureaucrats who negotiated Japan's terms of surrender in World War II clearly knew what they were doing when they adamanantly refused to allow the emperor to be tried as a war criminal—which the United States initially demanded—and insisted that he remain on the throne, even if deprived of all constitutional authority. In saving a mayonnaise that has failed to reach the right consistency, one works on a small bit of it until it takes. This bit is then gradually incorporated into the rest of the mixture until all the mayonnaise has reached the desired state. The bureaucrats knew that the emperor, and only the emperor, could play the role of this redeeming bit in reconstituting Japanese society, and they have proceeded accordingly.

12

If legitimation occupies as central a position in Japanese society as I have indicated, then the politics of delegitimation should be given far more attention than it has. Essentially, delegitimizing the state is to make it abundantly clear that it is run by one class for that class, that it is a class dictatorship, and that everything else it does and says is meant to hide this, or, occasionally, is a compromise forced upon one of its bodies in extremis. Delegitimation generally proceeds by two routes: (1) the actions that the state takes in serving capital, particularly as regards its four major requirements—repression, legitimation, accumulation, and realization—become so harmful to the interests of other classes and so transparent that what needs to be hidden and rationalized away simply overwhelms the means that have been set up for these purposes (economic and political crises offer many examples of this); and (2) the institutions or groups or conditions that serve as the main sources of legitimacy lose some or all of their ability to provide this service.

In the case of Japan, radicals both in and out of the Communist Party have been actively trying to unmask the class biases of the capitalist state. Relatively little attention, however, has been given to trying to undermine the authority of those forces, particularly the emperor system, that legitimate this state in the eyes of most of the general public. No doubt the reasons for this are many and complex, in which fear of retaliation from the Yakuza must figure prominently. Still, on the basis of the analysis offered here, criticism of all the sources of legitimation and particularly of the emperor system should be given a higher priority than it now has. The long and careful efforts that the state has devoted to reconstructing the emperor system is testimony not only to its importance for the ruling class but also to a brittleness in this legitimating authority that has not been exploited as effectively as it might. With the Japanese economy in serious doldrums and almost certain to get worse—with unemployment, bankruptcy, workers' suicides, many from loss of work, and death from overwork (so significant that the Japanese have a special word for it, *karoshi*) all on the rise— the capitalists' dependence on the emperor's unique contribution to maintaining the status quo has never been so great. The threat is that once people recognize that they have been repeatedly lied to and manipulated, nothing will keep large numbers of them from turning on those they worshipped just moments ago. Without the legitimation provided by the emperor system, Japan, Inc. could come apart at the seams very quickly.

While in no position to offer a full set of tactics for carrying out a politics of delegitimation, I cannot help but note that the emperor's tie to the Yakuza only succeeds in serving the purpose of legitimation if it remains implicit and appears accidental, the result of an irrational patriotic streak in these criminals, and is not recognized as an organic requirement dictated by essential state functions. But once this tie is rendered explicit and its necessity understood, what was an advantage to the system quickly becomes a major liability. There is no place in the neo-Confucian image of a wise and benevolent emperor that still exists in Japan for collusion with organized crime. The question that Japanese radicals should encourage everyone to ask, then, is, Why does the state use the Yakuza to squelch all criticisms of the emperor? Or, more sharply, Why does the emperor need the *Yakuza*? Trying to answer this question would take people a long way down the road toward delegitimizing the capitalist state in Japan.

The major debate among Japanese Marxists during the first half of the twentieth century dealt with the nature of Japanese society—is it feudal or capitalist? A great deal depended on the answer, including the kind of revolution (democratic capitalist or socialist) that one considered necessary. The fact that the Japanese state still uses a traditional feudal institution to provide such a large part of its legitimation may suggest to some that this old debate has yet to be resolved. My own position is that Japan is clearly a capitalist society, and its state a capitalist state, albeit one that for peculiar historical reasons is able to use a major precapitalist form to serve one of its essential functions. The revolution that Japan needs is not a bourgeois democratic one but a socialist one, but struggling for democratic reform of the emperor system could prove an important step in this direction.

Notes

1. Though unusual, this process was not unique. Friedrich Engels, for example, speaks of the Russian state of his day "breeding" a capitalist class (Bardhan 1984, 35).

2. The fact that the largest banks and corporations hire fewer ex-bureaucrats than their middle-size competitors, who need the extra clout to obtain parity in their relations with the ruling ministry, does not detract from our general point regarding the widespread practice of *amakudari* or the role we attribute to it. For the relevant figures, see Calder 1989, 383ff.

3. The problem of how to characterize its ruling class is, of course, only part of the larger problem of how to characterize the Japanese system as a whole. William Tabb provides a list of some of the more arresting labels that have been used in recent years: "authoritarian pluralism," "development state capitalism," "laissez-faire oriented intervention," and "planned markets" (1995, 14). Given the privileged position of capital accumulation and the exploitative relations between those who own the major means of production and those who work in them, I have no difficulty

in labeling the Japanese system a capitalist one, which doesn't keep me from recognizing its many distinctive qualities.

4. Though nowhere near as developed as in Japan, the problem—according to the *New York Times*—can even be found in the United States: "many state and local officials are becoming so deeply involved in business activities that it is difficult to tell where government ends and private business begins" (*New York Times*, Dec. 9, 1985, 7).

5. See "Marx's Use of 'Class'" in my book *Social and Sexual Revolution* (1979).

6. Given the role of presidential elections and of the Supreme Court in providing legitimation for the American system, George W. Bush's successful theft of the Florida election in 2000 brought the legitimacy of the government into question in a way that hasn't occurred since the Civil War. Only the war in Afghanistan, with the accompanying rush to support the government, kept us from learning the full extent of the danger posed by such a loss of legitimacy.

7. With its peculiar origins, it is no wonder that former Prime Minister Yasuhiro Nakasone would consider Japan's Constitution a taboo subject for a large section of Japan's political and academic communities (*Daily Yomuiri*, Dec. 5, 1994, 3).

8. The Japanese state has always backed up its efforts at legitimation with the most severe repression. The last *shogun* gave *samurai* the right to kill on the spot any commoner who acted "in a manner other than expected" (Koestler 1960, 210).

9. For the astonishing figures on the construction industry, see McCormack 1996, 33.

10. It is worth noting that the American government has not apologized for its own wartime atrocities in atomic bombing Hiroshima and Nagasaki and firebombing Tokyo. Unfortunately, most of those who have rightly criticized Japan for its moral obtuseness have given scant attention to this same fault on the part of the United States.

Bibliography

Acton, H. B. 1962. *The Illusion of the Epoch.* London: Cohen and West.

Albritton, Robert. 1999. *Dialectics and Deconstruction in Political Economy.* New York: St. Martin's Press.

Allen, John. 1983. "In Search of Method: Hegel, Marx, and Realism." *Radical Philosophy* 35:26–33.

Althusser, Louis. 1965. *Pour Marx.* Paris: Maspero.

———. 1966. "L'Objet du *Capital.*" In *Lire le Capital,* vol. 2. Ed. Louis Althusser. 9–185. Paris: Maspero.

Anderson, Kevin. 1995. *Lenin, Hegel, and Western Marxism.* Urbana: University of Illinois Press.

Arthur, Christopher. 1998. "Systematic Dialectic." *Science and Society* 62.3:447–59.

Avineri, Shlomo. 1968. *The Social and Political Thought of Karl Marx.* Cambridge: Cambridge University Press.

Ayer, A. J. 1964. *The Concept of a Person.* London: Macmillan.

Baraka, Amiri. 1966. *Home Social Essays.* New York: William Morrow.

Baran, Paul, and Paul Sweezy. 1966. *Monopoly Capital.* New York: Monthly Review Press.

Bardham, Pranab. 1984. *The Political Economy of Development in India.* Oxford: Oxford University Press.

Beamish, Rob. 1992. *Marx, Method, and the Division of Labor.* Urbana: University of Illinois Press.

Berlin, Isaiah. 1960. *Karl Marx.* London: Oxford University Press.

Bernstein, Edward. 1961. *Evolutionary Socialism.* Trans. Edith Harvey. New York: Schocken Books.

Bhaskar, Roy. 1975. *A Realist Theory of Science.* London: Verso.

———. 1993. *Dialectics.* London: Verso.

Bix, Herbert. 2000. *Hirohito and the Making of Modern Japan.* New York: Harper Collins.

Bologh, Roslyn. 1979. *Dialectical Phenomenology: Marx's Method.* Boston: Routledge and Kegan Paul.

Bradley, F. H. 1920. *Appearance and Reality.* London: George Allen and Unwin.

Brecht, Bertolt. 1968. *Me-ti livres des retournement.* Trans. Bernard Lortholary. Paris: L'Arche.

Brenner, Robert. 1977. "The Origins of Capitalist Development: A Critique of Neo-Smithian Marxism." *New Left Review* 104:25–92.

Buck-Morss, Susan. 1991. *The Dialectics of Seeing.* Cambridge, Mass.: Massuchusetts Institute of Technology Press.

Calder, Kent E. 1989. "Elites in an Equalizing Role." *Comparative Politics* 21.4 (July):379–403.

Carchedi, Guglielmo. 1987. *Class Analysis and Social Research.* Oxford: Basil Blackwell.

Carew-Hunt, R. N. 1963. *The Theory and Practice of Communism.* London: Penguin.

Carnoy, Martin. 1984. *The State and Political Theory.* Princeton, N.J.: Princeton University Press.

Cole, G. D. H. 1966. *The Meaning of Marxism.* Ann Arbor: University of Michigan Press.

Coleman, James. 1968. "The Methodological Study of Change." In *Methodology in Sociological Research.* Ed. Hubert and Ann Blalock. 105–31. New York: McGraw Hill.

Corrigan, Philip, ed. 1980. *Capitalism, State Formation, and Marxist Theory.* London: Quartet Books.

Diesing, Paul. 1999. *Hegel's Dialectical Political Economy.* Boulder, Colo.: Westview Press.

Dietzgen, Joseph. 1928. *The Positive Outcome of Philosophy.* Trans. W. W. Craik. Chicago: Charles H. Kerr.

Dunayevskaya, Raya. 1982. *Philosophy and Revolution.* Atlantic Highlands, N.J.: Humanities Press.

Dussell, Enrique. 1990. *El Ultimo Marx (1863–1882) y la Liberacion Latinamericana.* Mexico City: Siglo Veintiuno Editores.

Ehrenberg, John. 1992. *The Dictatorship of the Proletariat.* New York: Routledge.

Engels, Friedrich. 1934. *Herr Eugen Duhring's Revolution in Science [Anti-Duhring].* Trans. Emile Burns. London: Lawrence and Wishart.

———. 1954. *The Dialectics of Nature.* Trans. Clement Dutt. Moscow: Progress Publishers.

Fausto, Ruy. 1986. *Marx: Logique et politique.* Paris: Publisude.

Fisk, Milton. 1979. "Dialectic and Ontology." In *Issues in Marxist Philosophy,* vol. 1. Ed. John Mepham and David-Hillel Ruben. 117–44. Atlantic Highlands, N.J.: Humanities Press.

Fracchia, Joseph. 1999. "Dialectical Itineraries." *History and Theory* 38.2:169–97.

Freiberg, J. W. 1977. "The Dialectic in China: Maoist and Daoist." *Bulletin of Concerned Asian Scholars* 9.1:2–19.

Feuerbach, Ludwig. 1959. *Samtliche Werke,* vol. 2. Ed. Von Wilhelm Bolin and Friedrich Jodl. Stuttgart: Fromann.

Gilbert, Alan. 1981. *Marx's Politics.* New Brunswick, N.J.: Rutgers University Press.

Goldmann, Lucien. 1958. *Recherches dialectique.* Paris: Gallimard.

Gollobin, Ira. 1986. *Dialectical Materialism: Its Laws, Categories, and Practice.* New York: Petras Press.

Gould, Carol. 1980. *Marx's Social Ontology.* Cambridge, Mass.: Massachussets Institute of Technology Press.

Gramsci, Antonio. 1971. *Selections from Prison Notebooks.* Ed. and trans. Quentin Hoare and Geoffrey Nowell Smith. New York: International Publishers.

Habermas, Jürgen. 1976. *Legitimation Crisis.* Trans. Thomas McCarthy. Boston: Beacon Press.

Hampshire, Stuart. 1959. *Thought and Action.* London: Chatto and Windus.

Hartsock, Nancy. 1998. "Marxist Feminist Dialectics for the Next Century." *Science and Society* 62.3:400–13.

Harvey, David. 1996. *Justice, Nature, and the Geography of Difference.* Oxford: Blackwell.

Hayes, Louis D. 1992. *Introduction to Japanese Politics.* New York: Paragon House.

Hegel, G. W. F. 1927. *Samtliche Werke,* vol. 3. Ed. Karl Rosenkranz. Stuttgart: Fromann.

———. 1964. *The Phenomenology of Mind.* Trans. J. B. Baillie. London: George Allen and Unwin.

———. 1965. *The Logic of Hegel.* Trans. William Wallace. Oxford: Oxford University Press.

———. 1966. *Hegel: Texts and Commentary.* Ed. and trans. Walter Kaufmann. Garden City, N.Y.: Anchor Press.

Hirsch, Max. 1901. *Democracy versus Socialism.* London: Macmillan.

Hook, Sidney. 1933. *Towards the Understanding of Karl Marx.* New York: John Day.

———. 1955. *Marx and the Marxists.* Princeton, N.J.: Van Nostrand.

———. 1963. *From Hegel to Marx.* Ann Arbor: University of Michigan Press.

Horvath, Ronald J., and Kenneth D. Gibson. 1984. "Abstraction in Marx's Method." *Antipode* 16:91–136.

Hume, David. 1955. *Enquiry Concerning Human Understanding.* Indianapolis: Bobbs-Merrill.

Ilyenkov, E. V. 1982. *The Dialectics of the Abstract and the Concrete in Marx's "Capital."* Trans. S. Syrovatkin. Moscow: Progress Publishers.

Israel, Joachim. 1979. *The Language of Dialectics and the Dialectics of Language.* New York: Humanities Press.

James, C. L. R. 1992. *The C. L. R. James Reader.* Ed. Anna Grimshaw. Oxford: Basil Blackwell.

James, William. 1965. *The Will to Believe and Other Essays in Popular Philosophy.* New York: Dover.

———. 1978. *The Works of William James.* Cambridge, Mass.: Harvard University Press.

Jameson, Fredric. 1971. *Marxism and Form.* Princeton, N.J.: Princeton University Press.

Jay, Martin. 1984. *Marxism and Totality.* Berkeley: University of California Press.

Jessop, Bob. 1982. *The Capitalist State.* New York: New York University Press.

Kamenka, Eugene. 1962. *The Ethical Foundations of Marxism.* London: Routledge and Kegan Paul.

Kaplan, David, and Alec Dubro. 1986. *Yakuza: The Explosive Account of Japan's Criminal Underworld.* Reading, Mass.: Addison-Wesley.

Kautsky, Karl. 1988. *The Materialist Conception of History.* Trans. Raymond Meyer. New Haven, Conn.: Yale University Press.

Koestler, Arthur. 1961. *The Lotus and the Robot.* New York: Macmillan.

Kolko, Gabriel. 1963. *The Triumph of Conservatism.* Glencoe, Ill.: Free Press.

Korsch, Karl. 1970. *Marxism and Philosophy.* Trans. Fred Halliday. New York: Monthly Review Press.

Kosik, Karel. 1976. *Dialectic of the Concrete.* Trans. Karel Kovanda and James Schmidt. Dordrech, Holland: D. Reidel.

Kristof, Nicholas D. 1995. "Monderu-san's Last Campaign." *New York Times Magazine,* Nov. 5, 35–37.

Kuhn, Thomas. 1962. *The Structure of Scientific Revolutions.* Chicago: University of Chicago Press.

Lebowitz, Michael A. 1992. *Beyond Capital: Marx's Political Economy of the Working Class.* New York: St. Martin's Press.

Lefebvre, Henri. 1947. *Logique formelle, logique dialectique.* Paris: Editions Sociales.

Leibniz, G. W. 1952. *Monadologie.* Paris: E. Belin.

———. 1966. *Nouveaux essais sur l'entendement humain.* Paris: Garnier-Flemmarion.

Lenin, V. I. 1952. *Materialism and Empirio-Criticism.* Moscow: Foreign Languages Publishing House.

———. 1961. *Philosophical Notebooks.* In *Collected Works,* vol. 38. Moscow: Progress Publishers.

Levy, Hyman A. 1938. *Philosophy for a Modern Man.* London: Victor Gollancz.

Lewin, Richard, and Richard Lewontin. 1985. *The Dialectical Biologist.* Cambridge, Mass.: Harvard University Press.

Livant, Bill. 1998a. "The Dialectics of Walking on Two Legs." *Science and Society* 62.3:414–16.

———. 1998b. "The Hole in Hegel's Bagel." *Science and Society* 62.3:446.

———. 1998c. "I'll Make You an Offer You Can't Refuse." *Science and Society* 62.3:373–74.

———. 1998d. "Livant's Cure for Baldness." *Science and Society* 62.3:471–73.

Löwi, Michael. 1973. *Dialectique et revolution.* Paris: Anthropos.

Lukács, Georg. 1971. *History and Class Consciousness.* Trans. Rodney Livingstone. Cambridge, Mass.: Massachussets Institute of Technology Press.

Luxemburg, Rosa. 1966. *Reform and Revolution.* Trans. Integer. Columbo, Ceylon: Young Socialist Publications.

Mannheim, Karl. 1936. *Ideology and Utopia.* Trans. Louis Wirth and Edward Shils. New York: Harcourt, Brace.

Mao Tse-tung. 1968. *Four Essays on Philosophy.* Peking: Foreign Languages Press.

Marcuse, Herbert. 1964. *Reason and Revolution.* Boston: Beacon.

———. 1965. "Repressive Tolerance." In *A Critique of Pure Tolerance.* Ed. Robert W. Wolff, Barrington Moore, and Herbert Marcuse. 81–118. Boston: Beacon Press.

Marquit, Erwin. 1982. "Contradictions in Dialectics and Formal Logic." In *Dialectical Contradictions.* Ed. Erwin Marquit, Philip Moran, and Willis H. Truitt. 67–83. Minneapolis: Marxist Educational Press.

Marx, Karl. 1904. *A Contribution to the Critique of Political Economy.* Trans. N. I. Stone. Chicago: Charles H. Kerr.

———. 1910. *Theorien Über der Mehrwert,* vol. 3. Ed. Karl Kautsky. Stuttgart: Dietz.

———. 1941. *Letters to Dr. Kugelmann.* London: Lawrence and Wishart.

———. 1953. *Grundrisse der Kritik des Politischen Okonomie.* Berlin: Dietz.

———. 1957. *Capital,* vol. 2. Ed. Friedrich Engels. Moscow: Foreign Languages Publishing House.

———. 1958. *Capital,* vol. 1. Trans. Samuel Moore and Edward Aveling. Moscow: Foreign Languages Publishing House.

———. 1959a. *Capital,* vol. 3. Ed. Friedrich Engels. Moscow: Foreign Languages Publishing House.

———. 1959b. *Economic and Philosophical Manuscripts of 1844.* Trans. Martin Milligan. Moscow: Foreign Languages Publishing House.

———. 1962. *Frühe Schriften,* vol. 1. Stuttgart: Cotta.

———. 1963. *Theories of Surplus Value,* pt. 1. Trans. Emile Burns. Moscow: Progress Publishers.

———. 1967. "Toward the Critique of Hegel's Philosophy of Law: Introduction." In *Writings of the Young Marx on Philosophy and Science.* Ed. and trans. Lloyd D. Easton and Kurt H. Guddat. 249–64. Garden City, N.Y.: Anchor.

———. 1968. *Theories of Surplus Value,* pt. 2. Trans. S. Ryazanskaya. Moscow: Progress Publishers.

———. 1970. *Critique of Hegel's Philosophy of Right.* Ed. Joseph O'Malley. Trans. Annette Jolin and Joseph O'Malley. Cambridge: Cambridge University Press.

———. 1971. *Theories of Surplus Value,* pt. 3. Trans. Jack Cohen and S. W. Ryazanskaya. Moscow: Progress Publishers.

———. 1973. *Grundrisse: Foundations of the Critique of Political Economy.* Trans. Martin Nicolaus. Harmondsworth, England: Penguin.

———. 1975. *Karl Marx: Texts on Method.* Trans. and ed. Terrell Carver. Oxford: Basil Blackwell.

———. n.d. *The Poverty of Philosophy.* Moscow: Foreign Languages Publishing House.

Marx, Karl, and Friedrich Engels. 1932. *Gesamtausgabe,* vol. 1, pt. 2. Ed. V. Adoratsky. Berlin: Dietz.

———. 1941. *Selected Correspondence.* Trans. Dona Torr. London: Lawrence and Wishart.

———. 1945. *The Communist Manifesto.* Trans. Samuel Moore. Chicago: Charles H. Kerr.

———. 1949. *Briefwechsel,* vol. 9. Berlin: Dietz.

———. 1950. *Briefwechsel,* vol. 3. Berlin: Dietz.

———. 1951a. *Selected Works in Two Volumes,* vol. 1. Moscow: Foreign Languages Publishing House.

———. 1951b. *Selected Works in Two Volumes,* vol. 2. Moscow: Foreign Languages Publishing House.

———. 1952. *The Russian Menace to Europe.* Ed. Paul W. Blackstock and Bert F. Hoselitz. Glencoe, Ill.: Free Press.

———. 1961. *Werke,* vol. 4. Berlin: Dietz.

———. 1964. *The German Ideology.* Trans. S. Ryazanskaya. Moscow: Progress Publishers.

———. 1965. *The Holy Family.* Trans. R. Dixon. Moscow: Foreign Languages Publishing House.

———. 1975. *Collected Works,* vol. 3. New York: International.

———. n.d. *On Colonialism.* Moscow: Foreign Languages Publishing House.

Mattick, Paul. 1969. *Marx and Keynes.* Boston: Porter Sargent.

Mattick, Paul Jr. 1993. "Marx's Dialectic." In *Marx's Method in "Capital."* Ed. Fred Mosely. 115–34. Atlantic Highlands, N.J.: Humanities Press.

McCarney, Joseph. 1990. *Social Theory and the Crisis of Marxism.* London: Verso.

McCarthy, George E. 1990. *Marx and the Ancients.* Savage, Md.: Rowman and Littlefield.

McCormack, Gavan. 1996. *The Emptiness of Japanese Affluence.* Armonk, N.Y.: M. E. Sharpe.

———. 2001. "Japan's Houdini." *New Left Review* 7:138–44.

McLellan, David. 1969. *The Young Hegelians and Karl Marx.* London: Macmillan.

Meikle, Scott. 1985. *Essentialism in the Thought of Karl Marx.* London: Open Court.

Mepham, John. 1979. "The Theory of Ideology in *Capital*." In *Issues in Marxist Philosophy,* vol. 3. Ed. John Mepham and David-Hillel Ruben. 141–74. Atlantic Highlands, N.J.: Humanities Press.

Mészáros, István. 1986. *Philosophy, Ideology, and Social Science.* New York: St. Martin's Press.

Meyer, Alfred G. 1963. *Marxism: The Unity of Theory and Practice.* Ann Arbor: University of Michigan Press.

Miliband, Ralph. 1969. *The State in Capitalist Society.* New York: Basic Books.

———. 1970. "The Capitalist State: Reply to Nicos Poulantzas." *New Left Review* 59:53–60.

———. 1977. *Marxism and Politics.* Oxford: Oxford University Press.

Moore, G. E. 1903. *Principia Ethica.* Cambridge: Cambridge University Press.

Moseley, Fred. 1993. "Marx's Logical Method and the 'Transformation Problem.'" In *Marx's Method in "Capital."* Ed. Fred Moseley. 157–84. Atlantic Highlands, N.J.: Humanities Press.

Murray, Patrick. 1988. *Marx's Theory of Scientific Knowledge.* Atlantic Highlands, N.J.: Humanities Press.

Negri, Antonio. 1991. *Marx beyond Marx: Lessons on the Grundrisse.* Trans. Harry Cleaver, Michael Ryan, and Maurizio Viano. Ed. Jim Fleming. New York: Autonomedia.

Nicolaus, Martin. 1973. Foreword to *Grundrisse: Foundations of the Critique of Political Economy* by Karl Marx. Trans. Martin Nicolaus. Harmondsworth, England: Penguin. 7–63.

Nimtz, August H., Jr. 2000. *Marx and Engels: Their Contribution to the Democratic Breakthrough.* Albany: State University of New York Press.

Nowack, Leszek. 1980. *The Structure of Idealization: Toward a Systemic Interpretation of the Marxian Idea of Science.* Dordrecht, Holland: D. Reidel Publishers.

O'Connor, James. 1973. *The Fiscal Crisis of the State.* New York: St. Martin's.

Ollman, Bertell. 1968. "Marx's Use of 'Class.'" *American Journal of Sociology* 73 (Mar.): 573–80.

———. 1976. *Alienation: Marx's Conception of Man in Capitalist Society.* 2d ed. Cambridge: Cambridge University Press.

———. 1979. *Social and Sexual Revolution: Essays on Marx and Reich.* Boston: South End Press.

———. 1993. *Dialectical Investigations.* New York: Routledge.

———. 2000. "What Is Political Science? What Should It Be?" *New Political Science* 22.4:553–62.

———, ed. 1998. *Market Socialism: The Debate among Marxists.* New York: Routledge.

O'Malley, Joseph. 1970. "Methodology in Karl Marx." *The Review of Politics* 32.2:219–30.

Pannekoek, Anton. 1948. *Lenin as Philosopher.* London: Merlin.

Paolucci, Paul. 2000. "Questions of Method: Fundamental Problems Reading Dialectical Methodologies." *Critical Sociology* 26.2:301–28.

Pareto, Vilfredo. 1902. *Les Systèmes socialistes,* vol. 2. Paris: V. Girad and E. Brière.

Peritore, N. Patrick. 1983. "Radical Dialectics" (book-length manuscript). Copy in the author's possession.

Plamenatz, John. 1961. *German Marxism and Russian Communism.* London: Longmans.

Popitz, Heinrich. 1967. *Der Entfremdete Mensch.* Darmstadt: Wissenschaftliche Buchgesellschaft.

Popper, Karl. 1962. *The Open Society and Its Enemies,* vol. 2. London: Routledge and Kegan Paul.

Poulantzas, Nicos. 1969. "The Problem of the Capitalist State." *New Left Review* 58:67–78.

———. 1978. *State, Power, Socialism.* Trans. Patrick Camiller. London: Verso.

Priest, Graham. 1989. "Dialectics and Dialethic." *Science and Society* 53.4:388–415.

Psychopedis, Kosmas. 1992. "Dialectical Theory: Problems of Reconstruction." In *Open Marxism: Dialectics and History,* vol. 1. Ed. Werner Bonefeld, Richard Gunn, and Kosmas Psychopedis. 1–53. London: Pluto Press.

Rader, Melvin. 1979. *Marx's Interpretations of History.* Oxford: Oxford University Press.

Rees, John. 1998. *The Algebra of Revolution: The Dialectic and the Classical Marxist Tradition.* London: Routledge.

Reminiscences of Marx and Engels. n.d. Moscow: n.p.

Resnick, Stephen A., and Richard D. Wolff. 1987. *Knowledge and Class: A Marxian Critique of Political Economy.* Chicago: University of Chicago Press.

Reuten, Geert. 1997. "The Notion of Tendency in Marx's 1894 Law of Profit." In *New Investigations of Marx's Method.* Ed. Fred Mosely and Martha Campbell. 150–75. Atlantic Highlands, N.J.: Humanities Press.

Robinson, Joan. 1953. *On Re-reading Marx.* Cambridge, England: Students Bookshop.

Rosen, Menahem. 1992. *Problems of the Hegelian Dialectic.* Dordrecht, Holland: Kluwer.

Rubel, Maximilien. 1950. "La Russie dans l'oeuvre de Marx et Engels: Leur correspondance avec Danielson." *La Revue socialiste* (Apr.):327–49.

————. 1957. "Fragments sociologiques dans les inedits de Marx." *Cahiers internationaux de sociologie* 22:128–46.

————. 1959. "Les Premières lectures économiques de Karl Marx (II)." *Études de marxologie* 2:51–72.

————. 1981. *Rubel on Marx.* Ed. Joseph O'Malley and Keith Algozin. Cambridge: Cambridge University Press.

————. 1987. "Non-Market Socialism in the Twentieth Century." In *Non-Market Socialism in the Nineteenth and Twentieth Centuries.* Ed. Maximilien Rubel and John Crump. 10–34. London: Macmillan.

Ruben, David-Hillel. 1979. "Marxism and Dialectics." In *Issues in Marxist Philosophy,* vol. 1. Ed. John Mepham and David-Hillel Ruben. 37–85. Atlantic Highlands, N.J.: Humanities Press.

Sartre, Jean-Paul. 1963. *The Problem of Method.* Trans. Helen E. Barnes. London: Methuen.

————. 1976. *Critique of Dialectical Reason.* Ed. Jonathan Rée. Trans. Alan Sheridan. London: Verso.

Sayer, Derek. 1983. *Marx's Method.* Atlantic Highlands, N.J.: Harvester.

————. 1987. *The Violence of Abstraction.* Oxford: Blackwell.

Sayers, Andrew. 1981. "Abstraction: A Realist Interpretation." *Radical Philosophy* 28:6–15.

Sayers, Sean. 1985. *Reality and Reason: Dialectics and the Theory of Knowledge.* Oxford: Basil Blackwell.

Scibarra, Chris. 2000. *Total Freedom.* University Park: Penn State University Press.

Scott, Simeon. n.d. "A History of Dialectics: Thought and Social Struggle." Book-length ms.

Sekine, Tom. 1986. *The Dialectics of Capital,* vol. 1. Tokyo: Yoshindo.

Sève, Lucien. 1988. *Science et dialectique de la nature.* Paris: La Dispute.

Sherman, Howard. 1995. *Reinventing Marxism.* Baltimore: Johns Hopkins University Press.

Skillman, Peter. 1983. "Marx's Enterprise of Critique." In *Marxism.* Ed. J. Roland Pennock. New York: New York University Press. 252–76.

Smith, Tony. 1990. *The Logic of Marx's "Capital."* Albany: State University of New York Press.

Sohn-Rethel, Alfred. 1978. *Intellectual and Manual Labor.* London: Macmillan.

Sommit, Albert, and Joseph Tannenhouse. 1964. *American Political Science: Profile of a Discipline.* New York: Atherton.

Sorel, George. 1950. *Reflections on Violence.* Trans. T. E. Hulme and J. Roth. Glencoe, Ill.: Free Press.

Spinoza, Benedict de. 1925. *Ethics.* Trans. A. Boyle. London: J. M. Dent and Sons.

Strawson, Peter. 1965. *Individuals.* London: Methuen.

Sweezy, Paul. 1964. *The Theory of Capitalist Development.* New York: Monthly Review Press.

Tabb, William. 1995. *The Post-War Japanese System.* Oxford: Oxford University Press.

Taylor, Charles. 1966. "Marxism and Empiricism." In *British Analytical Philosophy.* Ed. Bernard Williams and Alan Montefiore. 227–46. London: Routledge and Kegan Paul.

Thomas, Paul. 1994. *Alien Politics.* New York: Routledge.

Trotsky, Leon. 1986. *Trotsky's Notebooks, 1933–1935: Writings on Lenin, Dialectics, and Evolutionism.* Trans. Philip Pomper. New York: Columbia University Press.

Van Wolferen, Karel. 1993. *The Enigma of Japanese Power.* Tokyo: Charles E. Tuttle.

Wallerstein, Immanuel. 1974. *The Modern World System.* London: Academic Press.

Warren, Scott. 1984. *The Emergence of Dialectical Theory.* Chicago: University of Chicago Press.

Whitehead, Alfred North. 1929. *Process and Reality.* London: Macmillan.

————. 1957. *The Concept of Nature.* Ann Arbor: University of Michigan Press.

Williams, William Appleman. 1968. *The Great Evasion.* Chicago: Quadrangle.

Wood, Ellen Meiksins. 1986. *The Retreat from Class.* London: Verso.

Wright, Erik Olin. 1978. *Class, Crisis, and the State.* London: Verso.

————. 1995. "Class Analysis and Historical Materialism." Tape-recorded talk at the New York Marxist School, Feb. 23.

Zelenỳ, Jindrich. 1980. *The Logic of Marx.* Trans. Terrell Carver. Oxford: Basil Blackwell.

Index of Names and Ideas

In line with my argument for internal relations, I have made a special effort here to bring out the connections among the ideas treated in this book by a heavy use of synonyms and cross-references and by my ordering of subsections under key concepts. The specialized vocabulary associated with dialectical method has been emphasized throughout.

abstraction: process of (general), 4, 5, 6, 7, 13, 14, 45, 46, 47, 49n, 51, 52, 59–111, 112n, 121, 128, 141, 174, 175, 177, 178, 179, 180, 181, 181n, 189, 190, 192; force of, 111, 127; concept of, 42, 60–62, 127, 128; of extension, 73–86, 90, 99, 100, 101, 102, 105, 107, 108, 109, 110, 111, 117, 121, 122, 124, 128, 141, 157, 159, 160, 163, 175, 176, 181, 189, 190; of level of generality, 74, 75, 86–99, 101, 102, 105, 109, 110, 111, 118, 162, 163, 176, 179, 189, 190, 191, 192; of vantage point, 6, 29, 32, 49n, 75, 99–111, 115, 117, 119, 122, 124, 125, 125n, 128, 131, 132, 144, 151, 152, 163, 166, 173, 176, 186, 189, 190, 191, 192; as ideational construct, 6, 24, 62, 64, 76, 127, 133n, 142, 143, 152, 174, 175, 177, 179; as ideological construct, 62, 76, 78, 102, 112n, 127, 142, 150, 178; real, 24, 62; in relation to the concrete, 24, 133n, 189. *See also* individuation; conceptualization; relation: philosophy of internal
accident. *See* chance
activity (action, practice), 46, 79, 88, 89, 90, 94, 99, 108, 112n, 125, 129, 132, 134n, 141, 143, 149, 156, 162, 175, 189, 191
Afghanistan, 215n
Albritton, Robert, 182
alienation (alienated society, estrangement), 3, 5, 48n, 49n, 62, 70, 83, 85, 91, 95, 101, 102, 110, 127, 128, 132, 134n, 149, 152, 160, 165, 166, 183, 190, 191; theory of, 77, 94, 95, 148, 184. *See also* fetishism; ideology
Allen, John, 112n
Althusser, Louis, 39, 46, 49n, 50n, 91, 110, 184
Aoki, Mikio, 182
appearance: as a dialectical category, 2, 13, 14, 17, 26, 35n, 36, 40, 41, 62, 68, 70, 75, 76, 77, 78, 79, 80, 82, 83, 86, 88, 116, 119, 129, 133, 133n, 145, 146, 151, 152, 185; in relation to essence, 79, 80. *See also* essence; abstraction; ideology
appropriate (appropriation), 80, 112n, 123, 127, 129, 134n, 149, 164, 168
approximation: first, 121, 149, 153, 168; successive, 131, 152
Aristotle, 3, 39, 161
Arthur, Chrisopher, 182
atomism, 39
attitude, 143; survey, 147, 154n
attribute. *See* quality
autonomy. *See* independence
Ayer, A. J., 52, 53, 54, 56n

Balzac, Honoré de, 134n, 186
Baraka, Amiri, 76, 191
Baran, Paul, 110
barbarism, 168
base/superstructure, 78, 79, 106, 136, 149
Bauer, Bruno, 43
becoming, 28, 65, 66, 81, 111, 116, 117, 119, 121, 165, 175, 199. *See also* process; potential
Bernstein, Edward, 158
Bhaskar, Roy, 112n, 173, 174, 177, 178, 179
bourgeois. *See* capitalism; economists

Brenner, Robert, 110

bureaucracy, 144, 194, 195, 196, 197, 198, 199, 200, 203, 204, 206, 208, 209, 210, 211, 213, 214n

Bush, George W., 215n

business (businessmen, corporations), 194, 196, 197, 199, 203, 211, 215n; small, 81, 122

Butler, Bishop, 69

Cacus, 12

capital, 14, 17, 24, 25, 26, 28, 31, 32, 34n, 36, 49n, 62, 65, 66, 67, 68, 69, 70, 75, 77, 80, 83, 85, 90, 100, 104, 107, 109, 115, 116, 117, 119, 122, 124, 128, 131, 134n, 139, 141, 143, 144, 150, 151, 152, 163, 164, 176, 183, 189, 190, 191, 192, 197, 199; concept of, 24–26, 30–31, 67, 70, 128, 143, 153; accumulation, 14, 86, 95, 100, 101, 110, 119, 122, 123, 150, 162, 196, 201, 203, 213, 214n; accumulation, primitive, 14, 183, 184, 191; variable, 24, 32, 67; logic, 194, 202, 204

capitalism (capitalist society/system/conditions/mode of production), 1, 2, 4, 6, 11, 14, 15, 16, 17, 18, 19, 20, 23, 25, 29, 32, 36, 46, 55, 62, 63, 64, 66, 68, 70, 71, 73, 75, 79, 80, 81, 82, 86, 87, 88, 89, 90, 91, 93, 94, 95, 96, 97, 98, 99, 100, 102, 103, 104, 107, 108, 109, 110, 111, 112n, 116, 118, 119, 120, 122, 123, 124, 125, 127, 128, 129, 130, 137, 138, 140, 144, 145, 146, 148, 149, 150, 153, 154, 156, 158, 159, 160, 161, 162, 163, 164, 165, 166, 167, 168, 169, 174, 178, 179, 182, 183, 184, 185, 186, 189, 190, 192, 194, 196, 197, 198, 200, 201, 202, 204, 207, 212, 213, 214, 214n, 215n (*see also* abstraction: of level of generality); modern, 23, 33, 87, 88, 90, 91, 94, 95, 96, 98, 99, 103, 118, 123, 130, 145, 162, 189, 190, 215n (*see also* abstraction: of level of generality)

capitalist (bourgeois), 1, 3, 16, 20, 24, 25, 65, 67, 70, 75, 77, 78, 81, 91, 92, 97, 99, 101, 103, 104, 106, 108, 116, 131, 142, 143, 149, 163, 164, 165, 179, 185, 194, 196, 197, 198, 199, 200, 201, 202, 203, 204, 207, 213, 214, 214n. *See also* embodiment

capitalist conditions. *See* capitalism

capitalist mode of production. *See* capitalism

capitalist society. *See* capitalism

capitalist system. *See* capitalism

Carew-Hunt, R. N., 33

category. *See* concept

cause/effect, 12, 15, 17, 18, 27, 34, 34n, 38, 47n, 71, 84, 87, 97, 102, 118, 119, 120, 121, 132, 133, 133n, 138, 139, 178. *See also* determine; condition; interaction

chance (accident), 70, 160

change (development), 3, 5, 13, 14, 17, 18, 19, 20, 27, 30, 33, 43, 48n, 59, 60, 63, 64, 65, 67, 70, 73, 76, 82, 84, 89, 90, 96, 97, 102, 107, 128, 146, 157, 158, 161, 164, 167, 168, 173, 174, 175, 176, 178, 180, 181, 185, 187, 190. *See also* becoming; process

China, 155, 210

choice, 20, 98

circulation, 85, 100

citizenship, 207, 208

civil society, 144

class, 3, 24, 30, 79, 80, 82, 89, 91, 92, 93, 95, 97, 98, 101, 102, 104, 106, 108, 110, 111, 123, 142, 144, 145, 146, 165, 166, 167, 176, 179, 198, 199, 201, 205, 207, 209, 213; analysis, 145, 191, 200; consciousness, 81, 154n, 179, 183; dictatorship (of aristocracy, capitalists, or workers), 166, 167, 202, 205, 213; interests, 18, 26, 92, 101, 103, 108, 143, 149, 165, 179, 196, 198, 199, 200, 201, 202, 204, 207, 213; ruling (dominant), 81, 93, 100, 105, 110, 138, 154, 165, 197, 199, 200, 201, 202, 203, 204, 205, 211, 212, 214n; society (division of society, history), 3, 76, 78, 80, 89, 90, 92, 94, 95, 96, 98, 99, 103, 105, 110, 118, 130, 145, 162, 163, 166, 167, 189, 190, 201, 202; struggle, 3, 12, 20, 79, 81, 90, 95, 99, 123, 138, 145, 149, 162, 164, 168, 176, 183, 190, 191. *See also* contradiction; labor: division of; alienation; history: materialist conception of

classification, 76, 79, 81, 89, 105, 106, 150, 200. *See also* abstraction

Cole, G. D. H., 91

Coleman, James, 64, 65

commodity, 16, 25, 28, 66, 67, 73, 77, 83, 85, 86, 89, 90, 94, 104, 106, 107, 122, 131, 132, 145, 152, 183, 189, 190

common sense, 14, 17, 18, 20, 25, 28, 30, 35n, 36, 38, 46, 47, 47n, 52, 53, 54, 67, 68, 69, 71, 73, 77, 91, 102, 129, 133, 175, 176. *See also* ideology; relation: external; nondialectical

communal. *See* community

communication (communicability), 51, 52, 53, 56n, 60, 63, 143, 152, 153, 174, 175. *See also* exposition

communism, as a potential within capitalism, 1, 2, 6, 55, 93, 123, 126n, 148, 158, 168, 168n, 179, 183, 184, 185, 191. *See also* potential; projection; future

community (communal), 35n, 79, 138; illusory, 207; political, 207; social, 207. *See also* alienation; ideology; state: theory of competition, 1, 94, 102, 109, 128. *See also* alienation

concept (conception, category, terminology), 4, 5, 13, 17, 23, 24, 25, 26, 30, 31, 32, 33, 35n, 38, 41, 42, 44, 45, 47, 47n, 48n, 49n, 52, 53, 54, 55, 56, 56n, 62, 65, 70, 77, 79, 132, 133, 135, 136, 142, 143, 144, 147, 152, 153, 154, 159, 164, 174, 179, 182, 183, 186, 189, 190, 192, 200. *See also* definition; language

conceptualization, process of, 31, 112n, 141, 142. *See also* abstraction; naming

concrete (living complexity), 24, 42, 60, 80, 111n, 133, 150, 151, 152, 154n, 175, 183, 189. *See also* abstraction

condition, 16, 17, 27, 34n, 67, 120, 121. *See also* cause/effect; determine; interaction

consciousness: general and individual, 45, 48n, 63, 92, 95, 97, 125, 165; false, 147; industry, 110. *See also* ideology; class consciousness

constitution, 194; Japanese, 206, 207, 208, 209, 210, 212, 215n; U.S., 204, 211

consumer sovereignty, 102. *See also* ideology

consumption, 18, 27, 29, 71, 77, 105, 131, 164, 186

context, 13, 98, 99, 103, 142, 143, 146, 163

contradiction, 4, 15, 17, 18, 41, 63, 76, 82, 84–86, 90, 93, 96, 97, 107, 108, 109, 110, 111, 112n, 116, 122, 123, 124, 138, 141, 145, 146, 149, 150, 151, 157, 161, 163, 164, 165, 166, 168, 169, 179, 183, 185, 191, 204. *See also* relation: internal; abstraction

cooperation, 17, 106, 107, 138, 159, 207

Copernicus, 12

corporations. *See* business

crisis, economic and social, 18, 85, 86, 90, 91, 110, 112n, 122, 164, 213. *See also* contradiction

critic. *See* criticism

critical. *See* criticism

Critical Criticism, 43, 48n

Critical Realism, 6, 112n, 173, 181

criticism (critique, critical, critic), 2, 4, 14, 20, 48n, 62, 76, 77, 135, 142, 146, 156, 158, 159, 191, 192, 213

dance, 154, 169

deduction (deduce, deductive system), 19, 28, 127, 130, 136, 147, 150, 151. *See also* inquiry; exposition

definition (defining, redefining), 4, 30, 31, 33, 35n, 36, 39, 75, 82, 129, 143, 144, 153, 174. *See also* language; concept; meaning

democracy, 16, 159, 164, 166, 167, 194, 195, 201, 202, 205, 209, 210, 212, 214

Descartes, René, 140

determination, as a dialectical category, 40, 48n, 67, 68, 77, 133n, 184, 189

determine (determinism), 3, 27, 34, 34n, 50n, 71, 74, 79, 90, 98, 99, 102, 107, 110, 115, 119, 121, 123, 128, 133n, 134n, 191; concept of ("bestimmen"), 34n; concept of ("bedingen"—condition or determine), 34n. *See also* cause/effect; condition; necessity; freedom

development. *See* change

dialectics/dialectical (method/approach/theory): general descriptions only, 13, 19, 49n, 86, 156, 159, 168, 174, 178, 179, 180, 184, 187, 188; Marx's, general descriptions only, 2–4, 6, 8n, 11, 14, 15, 20, 33, 47, 51, 59, 62, 104, 111, 112n, 127, 131, 137, 139, 140, 148, 154, 157, 158, 161, 166, 167, 174, 175, 180, 182, 183, 187, 191, 192; laws of, 96–98, 128, 138, 141, 145; of nature, 97

Dietzgen, Joseph, 44, 45, 46, 48n, 49n, 50n, 52, 54, 112n

distribution, 18, 26, 27, 29, 48n, 71, 90, 105, 131, 143, 186

Dunayevskaya, Raya, 35n, 63

Durkheim, Emile, 139

ecology, 92, 99

economic determinism, 27, 34, 39, 47, 110, 153. *See also* ideology; exposition

economists (bourgeois), 26, 29, 65, 94, 190, 202. *See also* political economists; science: political; science: social; ideology

economy, 23, 24, 29, 30, 31, 32, 33, 34, 34n, 37, 38, 79, 95, 96, 100, 105, 106, 110, 115, 118, 129, 130, 133n, 136, 138, 143, 146, 149, 151, 152, 163, 164, 182, 183, 190, 191, 196, 197, 201, 204, 205, 212, 213. *See also* production; distribution; exchange; consumption

embodiment (personification), of economic functions only, 80, 99, 107, 116, 199. *See also* worker; capitalist; landlords

emotion, 112n

emperor (emperor system, Hirohito), 193, 194, 203, 205, 206, 208, 209, 210, 211, 212, 213, 214

empirical (observation), 19, 52, 73, 127, 135, 150, 186. *See also* inquiry

empiricism (empiricist), 49n, 56n

Engels, Friedrich, 1, 7, 33, 44, 47n, 48n, 97, 131, 134n, 138, 141, 147, 151, 214n

England. *See* Great Britain

Epicurus, 3

epistemology, 20, 43, 46, 56n, 66, 139, 141, 147, 150, 157, 173, 181, 187, 188, 191 equality, relational, 49n

essence (essential connection): as a dialectical category, 20, 38, 41, 42, 66, 68, 70, 76, 79, 80, 128, 129, 133, 134n, 146, 150, 160, 163, 177, 183, 190, 214; concept of ("Wesen"), 134n. *See also* appearance; abstraction

estrangement. *See* alienation

ethical judgments. *See* evaluation

ethnomethodology, 20

evaluation (moral or ethical judgment), 82, 88, 112n, 152, 158, 159

evidence, of socialism only, 65, 66, 159, 160, 164, 165, 167, 191. *See also* potential; inquiry; projection

exchange, 27, 29, 65, 71, 76, 105, 111n, 128, 131, 186. *See also* market; economy; value

explanation, 4, 5, 12, 38, 43, 48n, 74, 76, 80, 88, 97, 99, 101, 135, 136, 150, 151, 152, 153, 174, 187 (*see also* intellectual reconstruction; exposition); structure of, 143, 144, 147

exploitation (exploiter), 16, 24, 26, 75, 80, 85, 91, 92, 119, 165, 201, 214n

exposition (presentation), 5, 6, 74, 75, 112n, 121, 130–34, 138, 139, 148, 150–53, 157, 168, 170, 181, 182–92. *See also* explanation; revelation

fact, 2, 52, 74, 77, 140, 143

family, 24

Faulkner, William, 167

fetishism, of commodities, value, capital, and money, 37, 80, 94, 104, 184. *See also* ideology; abstraction

feudalism (feudal), 17, 89, 90, 120, 163, 194, 196, 204, 214; lord, 116, 155, 165, 200, 204

Feuerbach, Ludwig, 42, 48n

Fichte, J. G., 49n

form, as a dialectical category, 14, 15, 19, 23, 28, 30, 33, 40, 43, 46, 62, 64, 65, 66, 67, 68, 70, 74, 77, 82, 83, 84, 86, 87, 93, 94, 96, 102, 105, 108, 111, 116, 121, 122, 123, 127, 131, 132, 137, 138, 140, 141, 143, 144, 148, 149, 150, 151, 154, 159, 161, 163, 165, 166, 167, 168, 184, 185, 191, 194, 199, 202, 207, 214. *See also* appearance; function; metamorphosis

France, 195, 196, 197, 198

freedom (free), 1, 20, 30, 62, 76, 98, 115, 142, 160, 204, 210. *See also* determine; necessity; ideology; communism

function, 14, 16, 17, 31, 32, 36, 75, 77, 78, 80, 81, 83, 86, 93, 100, 105, 106, 107, 108, 116, 119, 132, 133, 138, 140, 145, 150, 157, 160, 176, 185, 200, 201, 202, 203, 204, 210, 214. *See also* form; organic movement

functionalism, 34n

future, 4, 11, 13, 17, 20, 28, 66, 90, 110, 121–26, 138, 141, 145, 151, 158–69, 175, 191. *See also* potential; projection; communism

gender (patriarchy), 106, 162

general interests. *See* interests

Germany, 195, 211, 212

Gibson, Kenneth D., 112n

globalization, 6, 190

Goldmann, Lucien, 5, 35n

Gould, Carol, 91

government, 194, 195, 196, 198, 200, 202, 203, 204, 205, 208, 210, 211, 215n

Gramsci, Antonio, 121, 136, 144

Great Attractor, 156

Great Britain (England), 127, 146, 206, 210

Hampshire, Stuart, 51, 52, 53, 54, 55, 56n

Hegel, G. F. W., 3, 5, 35n, 39, 40, 41, 42, 43, 44, 45, 47, 47n, 48n, 49n, 50n, 54, 55, 59, 62, 69, 70, 102, 116, 133n, 140, 158, 159, 168, 176, 182, 183, 188

—works by: *Science of Logic,* 43; *Phenomenology of Mind,* 48n

Heraclitus, 64

Hirohito. *See* emperor

Hirsch, Max, 26

history (historical), 1, 2, 12, 13, 14, 15, 17, 19, 23, 33, 34, 34n, 35n, 37, 42, 54, 65, 66, 67, 68, 69, 72, 74, 79, 81, 84, 89, 94, 95, 98, 104, 105, 109, 110, 115–26, 131, 148, 151, 156, 161, 163, 169, 175, 185, 189, 190, 191 (*see also* past; future; relation: internal); periodization of, 78, 87, 115, 120; materialist conception (theory) of, 39, 78, 79, 95, 96, 110, 111, 115–26, 158–68. *See also* determine; necessity; economy; precondition and result; class struggle

Hook, Sidney, 35n, 38, 39, 48n

—works by: *From Hegel to Marx,* 38; *Toward an Understanding of Karl Marx,* 38; *Marx and the Marxists,* 39

Horvath, Ronald J., 112n

human (being/species/man/woman/people), 1, 12, 20, 33, 37, 38, 43, 47n, 49n, 76, 77, 79, 80, 86, 90, 91, 92, 94, 97, 98, 103, 118, 121, 123, 129, 133, 134n, 145, 167, 178; condition, 75, 88, 89, 90, 91, 92, 96, 99, 104, 123, 176, 179, 189, 190; history (society), 87, 89, 95, 118, 121, 162, 163, 167; nature, 4, 5, 76, 91, 92, 103, 104, 107; needs and powers, 87, 92, 95, 124, 133, 179, 191, 207. *See also* society; alienation; potential; communism

Hume, David, 69
Humpty Dumpty, 14, 156

Idea (Hegel), 41, 42, 50n, 151
ideal (model), 150
idealism (idealist), 40, 41, 48n, 78, 180, 184
identity: as a dialectical category, 40, 41, 42,
    49n, 53, 55, 72, 76, 77, 78, 84, 92, 111, 132, 133,
    134n, 140, 149; identity/difference, 15, 18, 40,
    41, 77, 105, 106, 131
ideology (ideologists), 13, 14, 18, 20, 62, 66, 72,
    74, 76, 78, 80, 81, 83, 85, 99, 101, 102, 103, 104,
    110, 111n, 112n, 121, 135, 138, 141, 151, 155, 164,
    178, 183, 202. *See also* abstraction; fetishism;
    alienation; common sense; political econo-
    mists; nondialectical
Ilyenkov, E. V., 111n
imperialism, 206
independence (autonomy), logical, 25, 37, 39,
    138, 146, 164. *See also* relation: internal;
    abstraction; relative: stability
individual, 17, 76, 79, 88, 91, 92, 98, 99, 103, 104,
    106, 110, 138, 145
individual interests. *See* interests
individuation, 45, 46, 49n, 51, 141. *See also*
    abstraction: of extension; conceptualiza-
    tion
inneraction. *See* interaction
inquiry (investigation, study, research), 5, 6,
    13, 14, 15, 60, 64, 75, 78, 88, 89, 97, 111, 112n,
    118, 119, 121, 122, 124, 126n, 127–30, 139, 140,
    141, 142, 144–47, 150, 157, 162, 163, 168, 173,
    174, 178, 180, 187, 190, 205. *See also* abstrac-
    tion; contradiction
intellectual reconstruction (self-clarification),
    139, 147–50, 153, 154, 157, 180, 184, 187. *See
    also* abstraction; explanation
interaction (mutual interaction, mutual de-
    pendence, inneraction, interrleations, re-
    ciprocal effect, systematic connections,
    interconnection), 1, 2, 4, 5, 12, 13, 17, 19, 27,
    34, 34n, 36, 38, 40, 41, 44, 47n, 48n, 49n, 55,
    59, 60, 63, 67, 68, 71, 74, 77, 80, 84, 97, 98,
    100, 105, 108, 116, 117, 118, 119, 125, 128, 133,
    133n, 138, 141, 146, 149, 152, 157, 158, 161, 162,
    163, 166, 175, 176, 178, 180, 181, 186, 187, 188,
    190. *See also* system; relation: internal
interdisciplinary studies, 14
interests (human/general/individual), 61, 143,
    190 (*see also* class: interests); as a form of
    value, 15, 31, 62, 68, 71, 77, 83, 105, 131, 143
    (*see also* value: surplus)
intermediator. *See* mediation

interpenetration of polar opposites, as a dia-
    lectical category, 15, 16, 18, 96, 112n, 131, 141,
    145, 157
interrelations. *See* interaction
investigation. *See* inquiry
Italy, 211, 212

James, C. L. R., 159
James, William, 47n, 59
Japan, 6, 193–215, 215n

Kamenka, Eugene, 47n
Kant, Immanuel, 40, 41, 49n
Kautsky, Karl, 23, 111
Kissinger, Henry, 137
Kodama, Yoshio, 211
Korea, 210
Korsch, Karl, 35n, 111, 136
Kosik, Karel, 5, 35n, 154n
Kugelmann, L., 48n, 49n, 129, 130

labor, 25, 28, 33, 36, 62, 65, 66, 69, 70, 77, 80, 83,
    85, 86, 90, 94, 100, 101, 102, 106, 116, 117, 119,
    122, 124, 128, 131, 132, 143, 144, 146, 153, 163,
    164, 184, 190, 191; concept of, 152; division
    of, 71, 89, 90, 92, 94, 95, 98, 110, 128, 132, 133,
    138, 166, 198, 201, 207; power (potential
    labor), 17, 32, 69, 81, 83, 109, 116; time, 29;
    wage, 34n, 66, 67, 80, 85, 88, 107, 108, 116,
    117, 122, 128, 153. *See also* alienation; value
Lafargue, Paul, 35n, 130, 151, 186
landlords (landowners, landed property), 81,
    91, 106, 128
language, 3, 5, 24, 30, 49n, 52, 53, 56n, 71, 72,
    112n, 132, 142, 153, 174, 177, 188; ordinary, 46,
    55, 179. *See also* concept; linguistic philoso-
    phy; meaning; definition
Lavoisier, Antoine-Laurent, 143
law: as a dialectical category, 19, 28, 29, 30, 97,
    109, 111, 122, 150, 163 (*see also* tendency);
    economic (bourgeois), 35n, 196; civil, 134n,
    140, 149, 155, 196
Lefebvre, Henri, 5, 35n
legitimation, 138, 194, 201, 203, 204, 205, 206,
    207, 208, 209, 211, 212, 213, 214, 215n. *See also*
    ideology; alienation; state: theory of
Leibniz, G. W., 3, 39, 40, 42, 47, 48n, 54, 70
Levy, Hyman, 50n
liberal, 149, 150
linguistic philosophy, 4, 35n
living complexity. *See* concrete
logic: formal, Aristotelian, 15, 18, 25, 27, 28, 30,
    34n, 65, 67, 69, 164 (*see also* relation: exter-

nal; nondialectical); conceptual, 182, 183, 184, 187, 189, 191, 192; dialectical, 48n, 70, 71, 72, 73, 78, 153, 183, 190. *See also* relation: philosophy of internal; dialectics: laws of

Lukács, Georg, 5, 35n, 54, 59, 63, 136, 142

Luxemburg, Rosa, 158

Lycurges, 208

MacArthur, Douglas, 206

Machiavelli, 137

man. *See* human

Mannheim, Karl, 101

Mao Tse-tung, 51, 63, 134n

Marcuse, Herbert, 5, 30, 35n, 48n, 55, 110, 159

market (trade), 73, 83, 94, 96, 102, 103, 104, 109, 110, 116, 131, 152, 190, 197, 204. *See also* exchange

Marx, Karl, works by: *Critique of Hegel's Philosophy of Right*, 48n; *Economic and Philosophical Manuscripts of 1844*, 48n, 139, 147, 148, 181, 187; *Grundrisse*, 90, 147, 148, 181, 184, 185, 187; *The Poverty of Philosophy*, 185; *Pre-Capitalist Economic Formations*, 90; "Toward the Critique of Hegel's Philosophy of Law: Introduction," 48n, 121; "Wage Labor and Capital," 185; "Wages, Price, and Profit," 185

—*Capital*, 33, 131, 139, 151, 152, 153, 190, 191, 192; vol. 1, 29, 32, 33, 43, 59, 111n, 130, 131, 138, 146, 151, 152, 181, 182, 183, 184, 185, 186, 187, 189, 192; vol. 2, 127, 152; vol. 3, 33, 82, 94, 129, 131, 152

—*A Contribution to the Critique of Political Economy*, 130, 185; preface to, 148; unpublished introduction to, 23, 86, 185, 186

—with Friedrich Engels: *German Ideology*, 34n, 147; *The Holy Family*, 28

Marxism, general descriptions only, 1, 2, 4, 6, 7, 11, 12, 19, 20, 25, 27, 30, 33, 34, 34n, 35n, 38, 47, 59, 60, 62, 63, 64, 67, 70, 77, 78, 91, 92, 93, 105, 107, 129, 131, 132, 133, 133n, 134n, 135, 136, 137, 146, 147, 148, 150, 153, 155, 158, 168, 174, 178, 181, 182, 191, 192, 193, 197, 204. *See also* science; criticism; vision; revolution

materialism (material world/existence/foundations/force), 32, 41–46, 61, 70, 78, 79, 89, 139, 180. *See also* history: materialist conception of; Critical Realism

meaning, 4, 5, 14, 19, 24, 25, 30, 31, 33, 35n, 38, 42, 43, 44, 46, 47, 54, 59, 61, 100, 127, 132, 140, 143, 144, 146, 147, 152, 153, 154, 159, 178, 179, 182, 186. *See also* language; concept; definition; relation: philosophy of internal; abstraction

mediation, as a dialectical category (mediator, intermediator), 19, 23, 112n, 150, 200

Meiji restoration (revolution), 196, 200, 206

Meikle, Scott, 63

memory, 112n

Mepham, John, 110

metamorphosis, as a dialectical category, 4, 33, 77, 82, 83, 84, 85, 90, 96, 107, 112n, 116, 131, 190, 191. *See also* organic movement; system; form; value

metaphor, 153

Miliband, Ralph, 110, 136

model, 150

moment, as a dialectical category, 20, 40, 41, 66, 68, 131, 157, 160, 161, 165, 187. *See also* process; abstraction: of extension

Mondale, Walter, 194

money, 3, 7, 24, 26, 28, 34n, 62, 65, 66, 67, 68, 69, 76, 77, 83, 85, 101, 106, 116, 122, 128, 131, 132, 145, 152, 183. *See also* value; alienation

monopoly, 128

Moore, G. E., 69

moral judgments. *See* evaluation

Mori, Yoshio, 195, 212

motion. *See* process

movement. *See* process

Murayama, Tomiichi, 195

mutual dependence. *See* interaction

mutual interaction. *See* interaction

Nakasone, Yasuhiro, 215n

naming, 31, 32, 64, 66, 133, 142. *See also* concept; conceptualization

Napoleon III, 91

nation (nationalism), 93, 106, 162, 212

nature (natural world, natural), 37, 38, 39, 40, 41, 47n, 74, 76, 78, 80, 86, 87, 89, 102, 106, 121, 129, 134n, 174, 177, 178, 188, 208. *See also* human: nature; society

necessity (necessary), 20, 25, 28, 29, 70, 115, 160, 161, 165, 166, 168, 183, 184, 191, 202, 214. *See also* determine; freedom

negation, as a dialectical category, 141. *See also* contradiction

negation of the negation, as a dialectical category, 63, 96, 112n, 157

nondialectical (undialectical), approach/method/thinkers, 14, 17, 18, 19, 20, 59, 70, 91, 96, 181, 188, 190. *See also* common sense; relation: external; ideology

Nowack, Leszek, 112n

objective/subjective, 78, 104, 105, 106, 123

observation. *See* empirical

Obuchi, Keizo, 195

Odysseus, 173

Ohno, Bamboku, 211

Ollman, Bertell, 4–7, 63, 177

—works by: *Alienation,* 4, 5, 63, 94; *Dialectical Investigations,* 6, 177

ontology (ontological), 5, 25, 71, 91, 92, 139, 141, 147, 150, 156, 157, 173, 180, 181, 187. *See also* relation: philosophy of internal; Critical Realism

oppression, 92, 93

organic movement, 17, 19, 48n, 64, 68, 71, 83, 84, 98, 104, 105, 107, 109, 116, 117, 118, 125, 145, 160, 185, 214. *See also* interaction; system

orientation, 141, 143, 144, 154n, 156. *See also* evaluation

origins, 20, 90, 104, 120, 121, 124, 138, 140, 143, 145, 160, 163, 183, 190, 191. *See also* process; past; relation: internal; history: materialist conception of

Owl of Minerva, 158

owning (owner), 93, 106

Palmerston, Lord, 91

Pannekoek, Anton, 44

Pareto, Vilfredo, 4, 5, 186

Parmenides, 39

particular, 51–56. *See* whole/part; thing; abstraction

past, 3, 6, 11, 28, 115, 118, 121, 122, 125, 138, 140, 151, 160, 164, 165, 166, 167, 168, 169, 175, 178, 191. *See also* process; history; origins; relation: internal

patriarchy. *See* gender

pattern, 3, 4, 17, 28, 55, 61, 97, 128, 149, 157, 199. *See also* revelation; intellectual reconstruction; exposition

peasants, 81, 122

people. *See* human

perception (perceive, sense impression), 13, 40, 45, 46, 52, 54, 56n, 60, 61, 65, 71, 75, 78, 89, 91, 96, 101, 112n, 134n, 141, 146, 162, 191. *See also* appearance; abstraction

personification. *See* embodiment

perspective, 16, 75, 100, 101, 102, 108, 128, 144, 151, 176, 189. *See also* abstraction: of vantage point

Plamenatz, John, 134n

political activity. *See* politics

political conditions. *See* politics

political economists (political economy, vulgar economy), 15, 18, 26, 28, 35n, 69, 76, 77, 84, 87, 88, 89, 90, 100, 104, 106, 124, 143, 146, 148, 151, 164, 182, 183, 184, 185, 186. *See also* ideology; relation: external

politics (political activity/processes/conditions), 16, 29, 34, 34n, 79, 81, 128, 137, 149, 152, 154, 154n, 167, 169, 194, 197, 198, 201, 202, 204, 206, 207, 208, 210, 211, 213

—party: general, 200; U.S. Democratic/Republican, 16, 205; French Communist, 167; Japanese Communist, 209, 210, 213; Japanese Liberal Democratic, 198, 211; Soviet Communist, 195. *See also* class: struggle; state

Popitz, Heinrich, 54

Popper, Karl, 59

population, 23, 48n

positivism (positivist), 153, 173

postmodernism, 162, 173

potential, 1, 2, 17, 28, 31, 66, 72, 74, 121, 122, 123, 125, 156, 159, 160, 165, 167, 168, 174, 183, 190, 191. *See also* future; evidence; communism; relation: philosophy of internal

Poulantzas, Nicos, 110, 136

power(s), 17, 24, 38, 90, 95, 137, 167, 194, 195, 200, 201, 202, 203, 205, 207

practice. *See* activity

praxis, 187. *See also* activity

precondition and result, as a dialectical category, 4, 29, 112n, 116–25, 161, 163, 166, 167, 169, 186. *See also* history: materialist conception of; past; future; relation: internal; abstraction; determine; necessity

prediction, 12, 17, 28, 30, 97. *See also* projection; relation: external; ideology

present, 3, 6, 20, 28, 115, 118, 121, 122, 123, 124, 125, 126n, 138, 140, 145, 151, 159, 160, 161, 163, 164, 165, 166, 167, 168, 169. *See also* moment; process; relation: internal

presentation. *See* exposition

price, 34n, 71, 80, 93, 94, 102. *See also* value: exchange; market

Priestly, Joseph, 143

private property. *See* property

process (movement, motion), 13, 14, 16, 18, 19, 27, 28, 35n, 65–67, 76, 82, 84, 100, 154, 154n, 157, 163, 187, 202. *See also* change; becoming; relation: philosophy of internal

produce. *See* production

product, 88, 89, 90, 93, 94, 132, 149, 156, 162, 175, 189, 191

production (produce, reproduce, work), 11, 15, 18, 23, 26, 27, 28, 29, 32, 33, 65, 69, 71, 75, 77, 83, 84, 86, 87, 90, 93, 95, 96, 99, 100, 104, 105, 108, 111, 111n, 112n, 116, 121, 122, 124, 128, 131, 146, 149, 152, 156, 163, 164, 186, 201; forces (powers), 17, 18, 26, 35n, 76, 78, 79, 85, 95, 106, 107, 115, 122, 124, 134n, 164, 191; means of, 1, 24, 25, 48n, 65, 67, 70, 104, 109, 122, 124,

141, 153, 166, 176, 199, 214n; relations of, 18, 29, 76, 78, 79, 95, 101, 106, 115, 128, 134n, 142, 164, 179, 191; mode of, 26, 32, 34, 38, 39, 42, 48n, 64, 79, 80, 82, 93, 100, 111, 119, 120, 154, 192, 202; mode of, double movement of capitalist, 19, 68, 76, 82, 90, 94, 97, 108, 111, 118. *See also* labor; economy; history: materialist conception of

profit, 1, 15, 62, 68, 77, 83, 84, 92, 100, 102, 104, 105, 109, 110, 131, 143, 180, 190, 201. *See also* value: surplus

projection, 15, 17, 55, 123, 124, 140, 160, 161, 162, 163, 165, 166, 168, 169. *See also* prediction; process; potential; contradiction; future; communism; evidence; relation: internal

proletariat. *See* worker

property. *See* quality

property (private), 24, 25, 35n, 75, 79, 80, 88, 94, 128, 132, 133, 134n, 153, 166, 202. *See also* alienation; value

Proudhon, Pierre-Joseph, 24

quality (attribute, property), 45, 49n, 51, 52, 60, 61, 71, 75, 78, 84, 87, 89, 90, 91, 92, 96, 98, 100, 101, l03, 105, 106, 107, 123, 128, 134n, 141, 162, 176, 188, 189

quantity/quality change, as a dialectical category, 15, 16, 17, 18, 82, 83, 84, 86, 96, 97, 107, 112n, 116, 141, 145, 157. *See also* process; change; potential; becoming

race (racism), 35n, 79, 93, 106, 162

radical, 149, 150, 178, 200, 213, 214

Ramsay, G., 102

reciprocal effect. *See* interaction

redefining. *See* definition

reflection, as a dialectical category, 70, 111, 112n, 132, 142, 146. *See also* materialism; ontology

relation: as a dialectical category, 13, 14, 15, 17, 18, 23–56, 67, 68, 69, 70, 71, 73, 82, 84, 92, 100, 106, 109, 130, 132, 140, 141, 144, 151, 152, 153, 154, 163, 176, 202; as a nondialectical category, 2, 3, 4, 5, 13, 19, 23–56, 60, 69, 72, 96, 100, 102, 110, 118, 121, 128, 134n, 138, 139, 141, 144, 154, 156, 157, 176, 183, 185, 186, 192, 201; concept of ("Verhaltnis"), 26, 34, 34n, 48n, 73, 78; internal, 1, 28, 63, 70, 71, 73, 76, 78, 79, 87, 107, 108, 116, 125, 127, 130, 132, 133, 140, 141, 142, 145, 146, 157, 158, 159, 163, 164, 177, 186, 188, 202; philosophy of internal (relational view, conception), 1, 5, 6, 7, 31, 32, 33, 34, 35n, 36–56, 61, 69–74, 78, 84, 98, 112n, 116, 121, 127, 133, 139, 140, 143, 156, 157,

174, 176, 177, 179, 180, 188; external (philosophy of), 54, 66, 69–71, 78, 99, 103, 168, 176

Relation. *See* relation: as a dialectical category

relative (general), 40, 45, 69, 142; autonomy, 66, 93, 110, 115, 138, 140, 141, 183; stability, 19, 66, 140

religion, 29, 38, 79, 93, 130, 162, 204, 206, 209

rent, 15, 62, 68, 71, 76, 77, 83, 84, 105, 131, 143, 146, 151. *See also* value: surplus

repression, 138, 201, 211, 213, 215n

reproduce. *See* production

research. *See* inquiry

revelation, 4. *See also* pattern; explanation

revolution (revolutionary), 2, 4, 16, 20, 43, 86, 122, 123, 124, 144, 165, 192, 214

Ricardo, David, 25, 33, 59, 76, 102

Robinson, Joan, 59

Rockefeller, Nelson, 199

Rubel, Maximilien, 34n, 159

Russia, 214n

Sartre, Jean-Paul, 5, 33, 35n, 54, 110

Sayers, Andrew, 112n

Sayers, Derek, 112n

Scheele, Carl, 143

Schelling, F. W. J. von, 140

Scibarra, Chris, 7n

science (scientist), 2, 47n, 64, 77, 79, 89, 129, 130, 133n, 134n, 158, 164, 173, 174, 192; concept of ("Wissenschaft"), 129, 130 (*see also* Marxism; truth); political (political scientist), 90, 135, 136, 137, 144, 148, 149, 154n, 202; social (social scientist), 3, 19, 20, 23, 27, 64, 65, 66, 91, 101, 146, 159, 174, 186. *See also* political economists; ideology

Sekine, Thomas, 182, 188

self-clarification. *See* intellectual reconstruction

sense impression. *See* perception

"Shogun," 194, 200, 206, 215n

slave, 128; owner, 165; society, 89, 90, 120

Smith, Adam, 33

Smith, Tony, 182, 192

socialism: as a potential within capitalism, Marx's vision of, 65, 123, 124, 143, 144, 158, 159, 160, 161, 162, 164, 165, 166, 168, 168n, 182, 204, 214 (*see also* potential; future; evidence; communism; projection); utopian, 125, 144, 158, 159, 166, 179

socialization, 3, 62, 71, 123, 177, 188

social movements, 90, 162

society (social reality/relations/system/whole), 11, 23, 24, 25, 31, 32, 38, 50n, 70, 71, 74, 75, 76, 77, 78, 79, 81, 87, 89, 90, 91, 94, 99,

103, 105, 106, 115, 116, 121, 122, 125, 128, 133, 137, 142, 144, 149, 153, 161, 162, 164, 165, 167, 174, 177, 178, 188, 192, 200, 201, 202. *See also* nature; relation: philosophy of internal; abstraction: of level of generality

Sohn-Rethel, Alfred, 111n

Sorel, George, 59

Soviet Union, 6, 155, 158, 195

Spinoza, Benedict de, 3, 39, 40, 42, 47, 54, 70

spiral development, 141

state, 6, 24, 30, 32, 70, 81, 100, 109, 110, 111, 112n, 131, 136, 137, 138, 144, 153, 166, 167, 193; theory of, 110, 111, 136–38, 153, 154, 154n, 201, 202, 207; Japanese, theory of, 193–214, 214n, 215n. *See also* politics; class dictatorship; community: illusory

Stewart, Jimmy, 3

Stirner, Max, 76

Strawson, Peter, 51, 52, 56n

structure (structural, structuralism, structuralists), 27, 46, 50n, 100, 110, 140, 142, 147, 150, 153, 157, 173, 174, 202; of the whole, 49n; functionalism, 20

study. *See* inquiry

subjective. *See* objective/subjective

Sweezy, Paul, 35n, 112n, 131

system (systemic), 3, 4, 15, 16, 18, 41, 48n, 68, 72, 74, 75, 77, 79, 82, 83, 85, 86, 97, 100, 107, 138, 146, 148, 150, 160, 161, 162, 182, 184, 186, 189, 190, 201, 211 (*see also* interaction; organic movement; relation: internal); theory, 20

systematic connections. *See* interaction

Systematic Dialectics, 6, 164, 182–92

systemic. *See* system

Tabb, William, 214n

Taylor, Charles, 56n

teleology, 118

tendency, 15, 29, 65, 90, 97, 109, 110, 122, 123, 124, 125, 138, 140, 145, 151, 163, 165, 166. *See also* law: as a dialectical category; process; potential

theory (general), 43, 133, 133n, 135, 136; as a material force, 32

terminology. *See* concept

thesis/antithesis/synthesis, 12

thing, as Relation, 5, 13, 18, 36, 37, 38, 39, 40, 41, 44, 45, 47, 47n, 51, 52, 53, 54, 65, 66, 67, 69, 70, 80, 82, 84, 116, 130, 140, 157, 164, 175, 176, 177. *See* relation: philosophy of internal; fetishism

totality, as a dialectical category, 4, 31, 34n, 38, 40, 63, 72, 73, 78, 139, 140, 141, 144, 145, 146,

147, 149, 150, 151, 153, 154, 154n, 157, 177. *See* whole/part; relation: philosophy of internal; truth

trade. *See* market

transformation problem, 94

truth (verification), 13, 16, 24, 30, 40, 41, 42, 44, 48n, 49n, 52, 54, 56, 56n, 91, 95, 98, 102, 103, 109, 112n, 129, 143, 146, 153, 157, 173, 174, 187. *See also* whole/part; ideology; science; totality

Tsuji, Karoku, 211

undialectical. *See* nondialectical

United States, 194, 195, 197, 198, 199, 203, 204, 205, 211, 215n

unity and separation, as a dialectical category, 112n

value, 17, 25, 29, 33, 34n, 62, 65, 66, 67, 68, 69, 70, 75, 76, 81, 83, 84, 85, 89, 90, 94, 107, 109, 110, 111, 128, 131, 132, 138, 144, 145, 152, 184, 190, 199; labor theory of, 93, 94; exchange, 23, 85, 86, 108, 164, 184; use, 85, 86, 108, 164; surplus, 15, 29, 32, 65, 77, 83, 85, 92, 105, 109, 116, 124, 128, 142, 143, 179, 199; metamorphosis of, 33, 77, 83, 84, 96, 131, 190, 191; law of, 3, 33; realization of, 201, 203, 213. *See* labor; alienation; fetishism; organic movement

Van Wolferen, Karel, 199

verification. *See* truth

Vico, 35n

vision (visionary), 2, 4, 165, 166, 192

vulgar economics. *See* political economists

wage-laborer. *See* worker

wages, 15, 83, 84, 105, 131, 146. *See* value

Wallerstein, Immanuel, 110

wealth, 80, 100, 104, 119, 124, 145, 146, 159. *See* capital; value

Weber, Max, 204

Whitehead, Alfred North, 19, 50n

whole/part, as a dialectical category, 3, 14, 15, 18, 19, 24, 27, 29, 32, 39, 40, 41, 42, 45, 46, 47n, 49n, 54, 55, 56, 60, 66, 70, 72, 74, 78, 87, 127, 139, 140, 141, 142, 150, 156, 157, 160, 161, 186, 188, 201. *See also* totality; relation: philosophy of internal; abstraction: of extension

will, 112n

wisdom, 112n

Wittgenstein, Ludwig, 140

woman. *See* human

work. *See* production

worker (working class, wage-laborer, proletariat), 15, 16, 18, 20, 24, 25, 26, 32, 66, 67, 69, 75, 78, 81, 88, 90, 91, 92, 97, 98, 101, 105, 108, 116, 119, 122, 124, 131, 142, 143, 146, 149, 159, 164, 165, 166, 168, 179, 191, 201. *See also* labor; production; alienation; class

World Systems Theory, 110
Wright, Eric Olin, 158

Yakusa, 193, 203, 209, 210, 211, 212, 213, 214
Young Hegelians, 43, 48n

BERTELL OLLMAN, a professor of politics at New York University, is the author of *Alienation: Marx's Conception of Man in Capitalist Society* (1971), *Social and Sexual Revolution* (1979), *Dialectical Investigations* (1993), *How 2 Take an Exam . . . & Remake the World* (2001), and *Ball Buster? True Confessions of a Marxist Businessman* (2002). He is the editor of *Market Socialism: The Debate among Socialists* (1998); coeditor of *Studies in Socialist Pedagogy* (1978), *The Left Academy: Marxist Scholarship on American Campuses* (3 vols., 1982–86), and *The U.S. Constitution: Two Hundred Years of Criticism* (1990); and creator of the first Marxist board game, Class Struggle (1978). In 2001 he was the first winner of the Charles McCoy Lifetime Achievement Award for Scholarship from the New Politics Section of the American Political Science Association.

The University of Illinois Press
is a founding member of the
Association of American University Presses.

University of Illinois Press
1325 South Oak Street
Champaign, IL 61820-6903
www.press.uillinois.edu

Printed by Printforce, United Kingdom